RICKIE

Frederic Flach, M.D.

BALLANTINE BOOKS • NEW YORK

Grateful acknowledgment is made to the following for permission to reprint previously published material:
ALFRED A. KNOPF, INC. AND HAROLD OBER ASSOCIATES
INCORPORATED: Excerpts from ''Dreams'' from *The Dream-
keeper and other Poems* by Langston Hughes. Copyright 1932
by Alfred A. Knopf, Inc. Copyright renewed 1960 by Langston Hughes. Reprinted by permission of Alfred A. Knopf,
Inc. and Harold Ober Associates Incorporated.
EMI MUSIC PUBLISHING: Excerpt from ''We Gotta Get Out Of
This Place'' by Barry Mann and Cynthia Weil. Copyright ©
1965 by Screen Gems-EMI Music Inc. All rights reserved. In-
ternational copyright secured. Used by permission.

Library of Congress Catalog Card Number: 89-90879

ISBN 0-345-37359-6

Manufactured in the United States of America

First Hardcover Edition: February 1990
First Mass Market Edition: September 1991

TO THE FLACH FAMILY,
with all our love

Hold fast to dreams
For if dreams die
Life is a broken winged bird
That cannot fly.

LANGSTON HUGHES

Author's Note

It was not without some trepidation that Rickie and I decided to tell our story. The public stigma that surrounds mental illness and affects everyone involved—patients, families, even psychiatrists and other mental health professionals—may have diminished somewhat, but unfortunately a good deal of it persists. We knew there would be pain in recalling those turbulent years. However, we were strongly encouraged to proceed, not only by friends and patients and their families, but also by some of my most eminent colleagues. They felt our story would offer hope to many, help open minds toward new approaches to psychiatric care, and encourage a more informed and humane attitude toward the millions afflicted with mental illness.

Our experiences are by no means intended to detract from the great contribution mental health professionals using traditional treatment methods make to the well-being of their patients, nor are they an endorsement of new, untested forms of therapy. Rather they speak to the humility and awe we all should feel, faced with so much that we do not understand. It is a wonder that neither of us bear resentment about these experiences. Suffice it to say, we do not; where forgiveness was called for, we have forgiven, and where healing was required, we have healed.

Out of consideration for the many good people involved, we have changed many names, though not all. In some instances we have also combined characters, locales, and events in the interests of clarity.

I wish to express my deep admiration for Rickie, who

courageously compiled her recollections and selected her own letters and poems for inclusion. She and I are both sincerely grateful to Kathryn Watterson, who worked so closely with Rickie to help organize, write, and edit these. Our thanks as well to Ashton Applewhite for her superb editing contributions, and to Joelle Delbourgo for making our story's publication possible, her recognition of its importance, and her unremitting encouragement and support throughout.

Frederic Flach, M.D.

Special thanks to Kathryn Watterson
for her sensitive, skillful collaboration
in the writing and editing of
Rickie's recollections

Part One

=== 1 ===

New York City, March 7, 1966

When I try to recall how it all began, I have a vivid image of myself running, frightened, breathing hard, harder than a man of thirty-nine should breathe. I am going down the stairs of our apartment house, out onto deserted, early morning Fifth Avenue, bitter cold even for March, the blocks rushing under my feet, until I reach the enormous oak door of the convent school. I stand there for a minute, my chest hurting, and in the air I hear the muffled chant of Latin sung by the nuns at sunrise mass.

Where else could Rickie have gone?

Without ringing the bell, I pushed the great door open and walked to the center of the marble hall. A tiny, ancient sister sat behind a glass enclosure, attending to an equally ancient telephone switchboard. She barely looked up.

"Did Rickie come here?" I whispered.

"I think she may be with the sisters at prayer."

Two steps at a time I ran up the wide staircase to the chapel on the second floor. No Rickie.

Her classroom, I thought. Up another two flights, pain grabbing at my rib cage.

The room was empty, the desks sitting in neat rows, waiting for the children to arrive. A series of colored photographs of Australia were pinned along the edges of the blackboard: a kangaroo and a koala bear, seascapes, the modern city of Melbourne, and the sand-blown brown desert. Rickie was supposed to have prepared an essay on Aus-

3

tralia the previous weekend, but when I'd asked to see it, she said she couldn't concentrate well enough to start it.

I was desperately wondering where to search next when I heard a muffled cry and opened the closet door. In the darkness, my thirteen-year-old was crouched in a far corner, staring into space. She looked gaunt and frail. Her dark blue emblem jacket and white blouse appeared much too big for her, and her long, dark brown hair, usually neat, was tied carelessly behind her with a rubber band.

I knelt down next to her. "Rickie. Please, come home."

No answer. Only a small tear, poised at the edge of her eye.

"What's the matter, princess?"

"I'm scared, Daddy." She stumbled over the faint words.

"Don't be scared. We love you, Rickie."

She put her arms around me and held on tightly, her head buried in my shoulder. "I'm scared because . . . I want to die."

I felt a surge of hopelessness. Why would a child of thirteen find living so unbearable? What had we done, or not done, to rob her of laughter and the joy of being young?

I began to cry, hiding it from Rickie as best I could. The two of us huddled there for minutes, holding each other, motionless. "Let's go home," I said.

When we arrived, Hillary was sitting on the wrought-iron bench in the entry hall, her eyes red, face lined with anxiousness. Rickie hugged her mother stiffly, and the two of them went into the library while I telephoned a colleague, Dr. Muriel Sanders.

She knew why. Only a week earlier, at dinner, Hillary and I had confided our concerns about Rickie's growing moodiness to this old and trusted friend, with whom I had trained in psychiatry at the Payne Whitney Clinic ten years earlier. Muriel specialized in children, and she loved Rickie as one of her own.

"It's seven-thirty," she noted. "I'll cancel my nine o'clock appointment and be right there."

While Dr. Sanders spoke with Rickie in the privacy of the library, I sat alone in the dining room, the pages of the *Times* blurring in front of my eyes. The room seemed enormous, empty despite the dark mahogany table with its two silver candelabra and four straight-back chairs on either side. Hillary busied herself seeing John and Mary off to school; they went quietly, sensing that something awful had happened but not daring to ask about it. When Hillary joined me in her usual chair at the far end of the long table, we sat in silence.

Half an hour later Dr. Sanders came in. "Is there someone who could stay with Rickie while we talk?" she asked. Hillary called the maid.

"Let's go in the living room. It's more comfortable," I suggested.

Hillary and I sat at either end of the gray sofa facing the fireplace while Muriel perched on the edge of a small French armchair, trying to hide her discomfort behind a cultivated professional stance. "What happened?" she asked.

I deferred to Hillary, who replied, "She tried to kill herself."

"We think she did," I interrupted. "We can't be sure."

"The Miltowns are gone. She must have taken them!" Hillary insisted.

"Or thrown them away," I suggested defensively.

"Try to give me more details," Muriel urged.

"I woke up around four o'clock," Hillary went on obediently. "I could hear screaming coming from Rickie's room. It's right next to ours. I tried to open her door, but it wouldn't budge. It wasn't locked, but she'd pushed a chair against it. When I got it open, it was horrible!"

"What was horrible?" Muriel asked.

"Rickie was standing there, fully dressed in her school uniform, in the middle of the room, staring into space, her arms stretched out in front of her. Her yelling had stopped. I called to her, but she wouldn't answer. She'd thrown everything around the room—crazily, I thought, until I saw that her toys and books and stuffed animals had actually been arranged in the shape of a crude cross. I kept calling her name and I went over and touched her, but she didn't move and she didn't reply.''

"I heard the commotion," I said, "so I rushed to Rickie's room. I must have gotten there a minute or so after Hillary. I shouted Rickie's name several times, then I took her by the arm. Suddenly she broke away, ran into the bathroom and grabbed a half-full bottle of Miltown—" I hesitated "—which I sometimes use to get to sleep. She ran out the other door to the elevator lobby, and I assumed she had nowhere to go but the convent. When I found her there, she still had the bottle, but it was empty."

"I doubt that she swallowed any. She doesn't seem drugged," Muriel commented. She paused, studying us both. "She's very depressed, you know," she added. "Even if she didn't try to kill herself this morning, she might easily do so, at any time."

"My God," Hillary whispered.

"But why?" I asked. "I don't understand. Sure, we've all been upset since Grandpa died last summer. He meant a lot to us, and especially to Rickie. Hillary and I have had our problems too of late, but then, everyone has problems. Why suicide?"

"This isn't just a situational reaction, Fred, you must know that. I couldn't get much out of her, but what I did was incoherent, illogical. She's very confused."

"Just what do you mean, Muriel?" Hillary pursued, trembling.

"I don't want to make a diagnosis on so little information," Muriel went on, "but I must warn you. The early morning state you've described could easily be catatonia. And that little girl in the other room is convinced that she—"

Muriel stopped, evidently wondering how much she should say. "She thinks she's a horse."

"You don't believe that, do you?" Hillary asked. "Surely she's making that up."

"I don't know."

I felt terribly frightened. I was not in the least convinced Rickie thought she was a horse. Nor was I concerned about Muriel's careless use of the term "catatonia." Catatonic patients were completely uncommunicative. They'd assume a stance or posture and maintain it for hours, even days, like a statue. Rickie certainly wasn't catatonic in my opinion. What scared me was the fundamental diagnostic implication of Muriel's statement.

"Are you suggesting she's . . . schizophrenic?" I asked.

"It is a very real possibility," Muriel admitted.

Hillary abruptly clenched her fists tightly, as if to keep herself from coming apart.

"But that's . . . hopeless," I exclaimed. "At this age . . . schizophrenia . . . I can't believe it. I won't believe it!"

"It's only a possibility," Muriel repeated.

To me "schizophrenia" wasn't just one of the bits and pieces of jargon psychiatrists tossed around to convey a semblance of scientific respectability. I had learned about young girls and boys with schizophrenia who had terrible prognoses, and I'd watched them grow old in the back wards of institutions. I was convinced they were incurable, and there was little evidence to the contrary.

"What are we going to do?" Hillary wondered desperately.

"I think she'd be better off in a hospital for a little while," Muriel replied gently. "I know a small place, upstate. It's a good place for Rickie, as comfortable as any such institution can be. I have consulting privileges, and the director is an excellent physician. Besides, I think you would prefer to have her in a sanitarium that would . . . keep it all private. After all, mental illness in the family might affect your reputation. Maybe in a month or so Rickie'll be home with no one the wiser.''

I felt utterly immobilized. How could Muriel be worrying about my professional reputation when the real issue was what was best for Rickie? Should I feel grateful? And how in one breath could she suggest Rickie might be schizophrenic and in the next that she might be home in a few weeks? I shuddered to think of how casually I had recommended hospitalization to numerous patients during the previous year, of how even a moderate degree of resistance had frustrated me.

I looked at Hillary. "What do you think we should do?" She was too distressed to answer.

"Honestly, I think that keeping her home would be too big a risk at this point," Muriel said emphatically. "Besides, a brief period of hospitalization would make possible the kind of intense evaluation necessary for a proper diagnosis. You know that Fred; you do it every day of the week.''

"I don't care what anyone thinks," Hillary snapped. "I want Rickie to have whatever she needs."

"This place is one of the best," Muriel replied reassuringly.

"I hope so," Hillary whispered.

I wanted to shout no, but I could not find my voice. It was a moment of helplessness . . . and of decision, like so many of those Hillary and I had tried to make during the past months, which we often made independently of each other. The decision to hospitalize Rickie was that kind of choice, as if, unable to think of alternatives, we happened to agree.

Dr. Sanders called the hospital and made the necessary arrangements. I reserved a car through one of the limousine services in the yellow pages, asking to be picked up in an hour. At first Hillary and I both planned to go. Then, too upset, Hillary asked me to go alone, telling Rickie that it was best that way since her father was a doctor, and promising she'd be up to see her within a day or two.

All during the long drive in the immense black car, I kept hearing Muriel's pronouncements, words charged with contradictions. Schizophrenia. Home in a month or so. Keeping anyone from finding out. Finding what out? I paid little attention to the intermittent patter of rain against the window.

Rickie slumped in the corner next to me, her face entirely blank. She spoke only once during the whole trip. "Will I be coming home soon, Daddy?"

"Soon, sweetheart." I felt betrayed by all I had learned and come to believe. By my profession. By life. By a God on whom I had come to rely so firmly.

I knew little about Falkirk other than the fact that it was a small, private place where a somewhat elegant clientele went to have their nervous breakdowns. In that sense, it seemed a good deal less "psychiatric"—more comfortably furbished and less likely to be a home for severely disturbed patients—than other hospitals we might have considered. As I sat in the small, colorfully decorated admissions office, signing the papers involved in turning the care of a child over to strangers, I felt as though I were betraying Rickie. All I could do was watch as the duty nurse escorted Rickie away, feeling her vulnerability as if it were my own.

2

It all got out of hand because of me, I think, but I didn't have any control over what was happening. But for this, I'd always been able to get myself back on an even keel.

I was so scared I couldn't feel anything. Falkirk was a hospital. I was in Falkirk, so I must be a patient. And if I'm a patient, I must be sick, very sick. Maybe that's what the feeling that there was something wrong with me was all about. I'd always felt it.

As far back as I could remember, I'd felt like I was on the other side of a glass, looking out at the world through strange, large eyes. Everything seemed far, far away. I'd reach out to people, but I couldn't get close. When I tried to hold on to anything that counted, it fell apart.

All through my childhood I used to like to crawl into closets and other dark places. It made me feel safe. Still, nighttime was scary. When I got into bed, I often felt that someone was trying to come and get me. I'd think I heard footsteps, whispering footsteps, whosh, whosh, whosh. They terrified me. They'd get louder and louder and I'd hold on to my blanket and my stuffed animals, suck my finger and clutch Howdy Doody for comfort. But when the footsteps got so loud that I couldn't bear it, I'd get up and go into my parents' room. Sometimes they'd let me get into bed with them, and sometimes they'd get mad and send me back into my room again.

I used to run to the convent and hide in the closet where

10

*it was warm and dark, where dad found me. But it wouldn't
take the pain away. Everyone thought I wanted to kill myself, but I didn't, I wanted to live. I took the pills and flushed
them down the toilet. I don't know why, maybe to scare
them, or scare myself. All I thought was it might have been
better if I'd never been born because I was so sad and lonely.
When I was eight, in the second grade, I wrote:*

> *Why
> Why? Why? Why?
> Sigh? Sigh? Sigh?
> Cry? Cry? Cry?*

*I'd been telling myself for years that eventually the pain
would go away, maybe when I grew up. Sometimes it did,
like when I was at the ocean, which was so big and full of
strength, or when I'd wake up real early and go through my
Christmas stocking and eat some of the candy Santa had
left. Or other special times, like when Daddy came home
from his office with a big white box in his arms and said he
had a surprise for me that he had bought at the hospital gift
shop. It had a big red ribbon on it. I was so excited. When
I took off the ribbon and tore open the box, it held two teddy
bears—a papa bear and a baby bear, each white and soft
and wearing red trousers.*

*Grandpa was a wonderful man. He had a big, fat belly
and, when Dad and I visited, I'd slide down it. He called
me "Rascal," and he'd tickle me and I'd laugh myself silly
and hug him and the pain would vanish. Grandpa had a
garden and I used to help him plant radishes. I remember
how, every time a grandchild was born, he planted a tree.
When he'd finished, there were four trees standing next to
each other.*

*Once when we visited him at his house in Little Silver, on
New Jersey's Shrewsbury River, he told me he had a sur-*

*prise named for me. "Go out on the dock and take a look,"
he ordered with a grin.*

*I didn't see anything until he came out and showed me.
Next to the cabin cruiser, a small gray rowboat was tied to
the dock, the name* Rascal *painted on its stern. Grandpa
made me believe the boat was mine—and it was, whenever
I went there. I'd fish, and stare at the water, and feel really
peaceful. Sometimes he'd take us to his favorite restaurant
and we'd all have lobsters. When I thought no one loved me,
I'd think how much Grandpa did.*

*Then, all of a sudden, the summer before Falkirk—he was
dead. When Mom told me, I couldn't believe it, not until I
saw Dad lying on the couch in the library and realized he'd
been crying. I felt everything sinking, collapsing around me.
If it was the end of Grandpa's life, it was the end of mine
too.*

*At his funeral I looked at him lying in the coffin, as if he
were asleep. I touched him. His skin felt smooth and cold,
like a candle that had been in the refrigerator.*

*After Grandpa died, school became harder. I had always
had to work for my grades, and I was proud of doing well.
I was in the eighth grade at the Convent of the Sacred Heart.
Very religious by the time I was thirteen, I'd go to school
with rosary beads hanging off my belt, like the nuns, and
follow them around and imitate them. I decided I wanted to
be a nun myself. At home I built an altar in my bedroom
and put flowers and candles on it. I had fantasies that I
could become a saint if I tried, and sometimes felt this to
be the real reason I felt different. I read a lot about the
saints, particularly St. Theresa of Avila. I used to wish that
I had been born in some earlier time and had lived in a
convent, when everything seemed so simple.*

*On Mondays the whole student body assembled so that
Reverend Mother could watch as the children were handed—
or not, as the case might be—their "très bien" cards. It
was terrible to lose your très bien card, worse yet to receive*

an "indifferent," accompanied by the awful reasons, read out loud. It was the worst thing you could get other than being suspended.

You'd line up with your class in a half circle around Reverend Mother. While everyone watched, you would go and get your blue très bien card with a smile and curtsey. I loved it.

But one day late that October they announced, "Rickie Flach gets an indifferent," in front of the whole school. I began to cry. I couldn't believe it. I'll never forget standing there as they read the long list. I don't remember all of it, things like my being lazy, and not getting my homework in on time, and being late for class, and looking sullen and not talking when I was spoken to. I couldn't remember having done all those things, but I knew I must have been very, very bad or this wouldn't be happening to me. I felt that I'd reached the lowest any human being could go, that I'd die, right there on the spot. Everything was reeling around in front of my eyes.

Everything went downhill after that. I wanted to be alone. At home I'd go in the library and close the door and play the Beatles for hours if I could get away with it. I barely said hello to the little kids, Mary and Matthew; I guess I thought they wouldn't even notice. John was older, though, and we used to spend a lot of time together, so sometimes I'd play checkers with him. I couldn't talk to my parents, didn't want them to touch me. My bathroom was right next to their bedroom, and I could hear them arguing with each other. The idea that they weren't getting along scared me. I didn't know what I would do. Sometimes I believed that their fighting—which had begun only recently—was my fault. To make matters worse, I started my period. I knew what it was, but I had very painful cramps, and I was embarrassed by how messy it was. I didn't want to grow up.

I started running away to the convent on weekends more often. One of the nuns tried to speak with me privately

*from time to time, but I don't think I had much to say to
her, nor to my best friend Christy either. In fact, I pushed
her out of my life, even though we'd been together for years,
playing with Ken and Barbie dolls, feeding carrots to the
horses down the lane from my family's summer house in
East Hampton, swimming, and riding bikes through the
woods.*

*Finally, I was all alone. I knew I was in trouble, but
leaving home was so sudden, and being brought to Falkirk,
where I was the only teenager, was pretty shocking.*

*They gave me a room of my own, a pretty room, with a
white wicker dresser, a wicker chair to match, and a pretty
red and blue comforter on the bed. I remember standing in
it, staring out the window. All of a sudden I felt like going
over to the window and smashing my fist through the glass
pane. Instead, I started to scream. I'd heard someone else
screaming in another room, and I thought that if I screamed
loud and long, I might get rid of the pain and the terrible
tension in my head. Then someone came and gave me a shot
of something—probably Thorazine—and I fell into a deep,
drugged sleep.*

It was nearly five in the afternoon when I returned home
from Falkirk. Hillary was sitting at a table in front of the
fireplace in the library, playing solitaire, her hands shaking
ever so slightly as she turned the cards over, three at a time.
When I put my hand on her shoulder, she shrugged it away,

never looking up, not saying a word, as if she were still alone.

"Don't you want to know how things went?" I asked.

"I'm sure you handled them well."

I walked over to the bookcase, nervously turning one of the soldiers in my collection—a Scotsman playing the pipes—to face front. The maid had obviously picked him up dusting. My copy of Marquand's *So Little Time* had been misplaced too, and I returned it to its proper spot on the top shelf. Then I went over to the bar and fixed myself a scotch on the rocks.

"Isn't it early for a drink?" she asked.

"This has got to be the worst day of my life."

"You think it's easy for me?"

"I never suggested that."

"Johnny's birthday too," she sighed.

In the frenzy, I had forgotten; March 7 was John's ninth birthday, and we'd planned a family party. Rickie had made a special card for him, which I'd spotted on her dresser, next to an envelope covered with small drawings of smiling faces. It was to have been a joyful occasion; now, instead, it would become etched in our minds as the date of Rickie's hospitalization. I slumped on the couch, the drink making my head fuzzy instead of relaxing me. A rush of memories swept through my brain. Couldn't I have noticed something sooner?

"I don't understand why we didn't notice sooner that there was something wrong," I confessed to Hillary, whose automatic search for red on black and black on red was beginning to irritate me. She seemed not to hear me.

According to Hillary, Rickie had "begun to develop," which might have accounted for her behavior. I remembered that throughout the Christmas holidays Rickie had seemed morose, spending much of her time alone in her room. I had tried to speak with her, but I couldn't find out anything. At the Christmas Eve midnight service we had sat in our usual pew. Hillary looked exceptionally beautiful, tall, thin, wearing her stark black dress with the single pearl pin, her blond hair carefully swept up and covered with a black lace mantilla. John wore his St. David's School navy-blue blazer. Mary, now six, had a sprig of holly pinned on her pink dress. Matthew, now four, sat next to me, bored, restlessly swinging his legs back and forth as we listened to the choir fill the church with celebration. When the time for communion came, Rickie slid back in her seat, forcing the rest of the family to press past her into the aisle. Knowing how sensitive Rickie was and how readily she felt guilty about little things, I felt puzzled and momentarily saddened.

In late January Hillary had organized a formal dinner party for fifty guests to celebrate my thirty-ninth birthday. She had always surrounded us with people, a gift I had unfortunately come to take for granted. I enjoyed the occasion thoroughly, but after dessert and coffee were done and we were dancing to a record on the newly acquired stereo set, I felt ominously haunted by a scene from an old film, *Heaven Can Wait,* in which a gray-haired Don Ameche dances with his wife, Gene Tierney. As the camera slowly moves farther from the couple, Ameche's voice-over tells of it being the last time they would ever dance together.

I thought of the poem Rickie had written for her mother's birthday in February. On the envelope she had printed: "For someone I love with all my heart on this special day."

A Special Poem for a Special Birthday Girl

BIRTHDAYS
Birthdays are wonderful things,
Specially when you get diamond rings!
From one to two to three to four,
And from the ocean you see the shore,
Looming before you in the morning light,
With night taking its speedy flight.

666

The shore is the growing mind,
And childhood falling far behind.

* * * * THE END * * * *

by Rickie Flach

TO MOMMY: I LOVE YOU. . . .

"You've forgotten?" Hillary finally replied, jolting me back to the present. "We did think there was something wrong, when she was eight, after she had been in the hospital for that kidney infection . . . Remember that woman analyst the pediatrician recommended? You certainly didn't think much of her."

"You didn't like her either. Besides, she seemed baffled by Rickie, and nothing positive came out of it."

"Apparently we made a mistake ending it."

"No, we didn't. There wasn't anything really wrong with Rickie then, nothing a child analyst could correct. You were always thinking there was something strange about Rickie."

"That's not true. You know as well as I do why we took her. Rickie wasn't doing well in school. She spent a lot of time alone, only had one friend. And those nightmares . . ."

"I suppose now you think Rickie's crazy?" I retorted caustically, bewildered at my inability to control my anger.

"I thought 'crazy' was a term you psychiatrists never used."

"You know what I mean."

"No, I don't. You're the expert. Why didn't you see that there was something wrong a long time ago!"

"What else do you think I'm thinking about!" I felt a dull aching, first in my neck, then moving down to the small of my back, and a painful throbbing in my calves. I sighed. "Why are we doing this to each other?"

Hillary stared at me stiffly before returning to her cards.

"How can you be so calm? Don't you realize I just took Rickie to the madhouse!"

When she said nothing, I stalked out of the room.

At dinner Hillary reassured the children, telling them Rickie was visiting a friend. But I knew she'd have to come up with a more plausible story soon. We all wore paper birthday hats, and Hillary and I made a pretense of joviality while the children reveled in John's special moment.

In bed that night I reached out for Hillary's hand, but she quickly moved it away. I couldn't sleep. I was in and out of bed every half hour, pacing the room, looking absentmindedly out the window at the night, wandering into the pantry to drink three full glasses of milk, all the while bewildered, and angered, by Hillary's sound sleep.

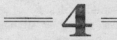

Five days after Rickie's hospitalization, we had a ten o'clock appointment at Dr. Sanders's office. She was located off the lobby of a modern, red-brick apartment building on Seventy-ninth between Lexington and Third. The decor of her consulting room contrasted sharply with her quietly old-fashioned, feminine appearance. Under a full-length white clinic coat, Muriel wore a stylish flower-print dress. But everything else in the room was contemporary; indirect Scandinavian lighting flooded lacquered white and black furniture and framed gallery and concert posters.

I knew at once that our friendship with Muriel had altered, and suspected that somehow nothing between us could ever be the same again.

"I'd like to go into things a little more in detail," Muriel requested. "I know it's not easy, but let's start at the beginning. Hillary, was there anything unusual about Rickie's birth or your pregnancy?"

"Nothing about the pregnancy, or the birth. But Rickie did seem different, even as a baby."

"In what way?" Muriel pursued.

"She wasn't responsive. She didn't seem to sense I was holding her or feeding her . . . I don't mean to say there was anything dramatic, just something I felt. And then, when she was six months old, there was the operation."

"Operation?" Muriel queried.

"She had a small tumor over her right forehead, near the upper eyelid. The pediatrician felt it should be removed. She was only in the hospital overnight, but I remember the anesthesiologist saying she was extremely resistant to sedation, that they had to give her more barbiturates than usual to get her under."

"And afterwards?"

"She seemed all right. Well, not exactly . . . Rickie never crawled or talked baby talk. One day she just got up and walked, and, out of the blue she spoke entire sentences."

"That's right," I blurted. "I remember now. I used to walk past Rickie's bedroom at night. I could hear her speaking, as if she were practicing, but if I went in she'd stop and not say another word. I do remember that. I thought it was . . . precocious."

"Everyone thought there was something different, special, about Rickie. As a matter of fact," her mother went on, remembering more, "when she started school, she had trouble adjusting. The teachers said she didn't like to play with the other children, only formed one relationship at a time. They implied she wasn't really doing very well, but when I tried to pin them down they couldn't come up with anything specific. They kept referring to Rickie as special. I honestly didn't know what they were talking about.''

"I remember once, when she was running along the pavement,'' I interjected, ''at age four maybe, she fell and had this awful bruise on her forehead.''

"Loss of consciousness?'' Muriel wondered.

"Not that I remember.'' But recollections flooded back, as if a valve had been turned and Rickie's past was pouring out in front of us. ''There was that kidney infection,'' I recalled. ''She was in the hospital for nearly two weeks, at age seven or eight, I think. Rickie was really sick that time. She had a terribly high fever. Of course, they gave her antibiotics. But then there were bruises on her arm, and the nurse said she'd been jumping up and down in her bed, and when the nurse got angry with her and told her to stop—'' I hesitated. ''—she deliberately threw herself off the bed onto the floor. It scared the staff. She could really have hurt herself.''

Muriel was carefully making notes.

"Rickie was a determined child,'' Hillary went on. ''Not defiant, really, but with a will of her own.''

"Like not wanting to go to bed at night from the time she was three,'' I said.

"Until she was past five,'' Hillary added.

"She used to keep coming to the doorway of the living room, again and again,'' I continued, ''and we'd get furious and drag her back to her bedroom and, by God, within ten minutes she'd be there again, staring at us, a funny grin on her face. Boy, that was rough on everyone. Rickie must have been terrified.''

"Of what?'' Muriel asked.

"We could never find out,'' I admitted.

"I'd ask her,'' Hillary said, '' 'Rickie, why can't you just go to bed and stay there? Are you afraid of something?' But she never had an answer.''

"We believed it was an exaggerated case of fear of the

dark,'' I explained. "I know that when I was little I wanted a light on in the hall outside my room, with the door open just a crack before I went to sleep."

"It was a lot more serious than that," Hillary remarked.

"And what did you do about this problem?" Muriel inquired.

There was a long silence, and when Hillary started to answer, I interrupted. "I thought it was a terrible idea!"

"What was?" Muriel asked.

"Locking her in her room like that, with the lights off. The poor kid was probably scared stiff."

"It wasn't my idea," Hillary retorted. "The doctor suggested it." Rickie's doctor was one of New York's eminent children's specialists. "We only did what he said, and then only for three or four nights."

Recognizing the mounting tension, Muriel cautioned, "Look, you two, no past regrets. We all make mistakes. Locking a child in her room to solve insomnia isn't an approach I'd endorse, that's for sure. But you're not the first parents to do something like that under medical advice, and you won't be the last. Besides, a single trauma like that can't account for Rickie's present condition. You're a psychiatrist, you know that."

"I know that."

Then, as if to change the subject, Muriel asked: "How old are Rickie's brothers and sisters?"

"Johnny was nine the day we hospitalized Rickie. Mary will be seven April twenty-ninth. Matthew won't be six until January," I answered.

"How are they reacting to Rickie's hospitalization?"

"We haven't told them anything. Just that Rickie's gone away for a while to a special school," Hillary replied.

"Just as well, although when they're old enough to understand, you may have to be honest with them."

A wave of panic seized me. "You sound as though Rickie may be away for a long time."

Muriel shifted uncomfortably in her chair, as if wondering why she had been chosen to be the one to tell us that the wonderful years of our lives had come to an end. "I'm going to level with you. We've already done extensive psychological testing. Although the findings are not conclusive, they look very much like autism."

"Autism?" I said, astonished. "That's a childhood diagnosis!"

"That's right."

"Autistic kids never reach Rickie's level of development."

"Some do," Muriel replied. "Besides, at this age it would be hard to distinguish between an autistic youngster at the upper range of the developmental scale and some other form of schizophrenia. You know how controversial these issues are. Maybe fragments in her testing resemble the performance of an autistic patient but really don't justify that diagnosis."

Although I had not had specific training in child psychiatry, I knew enough about what she was saying to be extremely upset and utterly confused. Unable to develop relationships with human beings, autistic children show delayed speech development and noncommunicative use of the little speech they have. That surely wasn't Rickie. I also knew that in older youngsters the distinction between schizophrenia and some form of autism was often obscure. Such children were supposed to have perceptual difficulties and some neurological motor problems as well. "Could Rickie have a neurological problem of some kind?" I asked.

"We shall surely check that out completely. But whatever her diagnosis, it's going to be a long haul at best."

"Whatever happened to your idea that she'd be home in a month?" I snapped.

"Fred, you and Hillary know how much I love Rickie. This is hard for me. I was trying to find some hope, for both of you, for myself."

Hillary put her hands over her face to conceal her fear.

"But she's only depressed," I protested. "Why can't she be given a trial on antidepressants?" Such drugs had only been introduced into psychiatry a few years earlier, and many clinicians were still skeptical or unfamiliar with their value. I had also been skeptical on first learning of them. Ronald Kuhn, a Swiss psychiatrist, first described to me the striking antidepressant effects of imipramine in 1958, just after I had begun my own research into biological aspects of mood disorders. I found it hard to believe that a drug that possessed imipramine's particular chemical structure and that required three weeks of administration to produce results could really do the job. Six months passed before I initiated imipramine treatment in a depressed patient in the Payne Whitney Clinic; in four weeks the patient, who had been depressed for nearly a year, regained his normally good spirits. More and more medical literature accumulated in support. When, in my own investigations, I found that imipramine induced a change in calcium metabolism that accompanied clinical recovery, I too became convinced of its enormous value and began to prescribe it extensively.

"Maybe with an antidepressant she'd be better in a few weeks!" I persisted.

Muriel looked at me. "One thing you're going to learn right now, Fred, is that this is one case in which you're not going to be able to direct the course of treatment." She was adamant. "You are her father, not her physician. You're going to have to leave the decisions about Rickie's care to others. I know that it won't be easy, but that's the way it has to be."

Hillary had stopped crying. "I think we should have a consultation," she said firmly.

"Of course," Muriel agreed. "If you want another opinion, that's fine. Of course, you know that in most psychiatric hospitals patients have the benefit of the input of a number of different doctors, not just one."

"Don't you think so, Fred?" Hillary asked.

"I don't know. Yes, I suppose so." I suggested the most illustrious person I could think of. "I could ask Manfred Bleuler to fly over from Switzerland." Bleuler's father had coined the term schizophrenia. "But after all, as Muriel said, in a hospital setting Rickie has the benefit of a lot of different people evaluating her. It isn't always a good idea to have some deus ex machina come in from the outside. It disrupts, could even turn the staff against a patient . . . I don't know."

"There's plenty of time to make that choice," Muriel pointed out. "A much more serious problem requires immediate attention."

"What's that?" Hillary asked, alarmed.

"We're going to have to transfer Rickie. The place she's in may be all right for mildly disturbed cases, even seriously depressed patients, but—"

Hillary gasped. "What's happened?"

"She was having a lot of trouble sleeping. She was up all night. She seemed very frightened, so the doctor on call ordered a dose of Thorazine—that's routine in schizophrenic cases, as you know—which they administered by injection since Rickie refused to take it by mouth. It didn't put her to sleep. She became quite agitated and began to scream, so the nurses had to try to calm her down, and when Rickie broke away from them, she hit one pretty hard. They feel Rickie has to be transferred to a better-equipped place where they can watch her more carefully."

"That doesn't make any sense at all!" I exclaimed. "Rickie was never violent!"

"Perhaps she was just holding herself together at home. Once she was in the hospital, her defenses collapsed and the more psychotic aspects of her behavior emerged. You know that can happen."

"I'm tired of being reminded of what I know. I don't know!" I shouted. "I only know that Rickie's in the hands of some strangers somewhere, and that she's thirteen years old and scared!''

When Hillary put her arm around me I felt comforted for a moment, and a closeness I had missed.

Muriel asked: ''Do you have a preference as to where we transfer Rickie?''

I didn't answer.

''How about the Westchester Division of thc New York Hospital?'' she suggested. ''It's probably one of the best.''

I felt stunned. ''But I'm on the staff there.''

''Not really,'' Muriel reminded me. ''You're on the staff of the New York Hospital, to be sure, but at Payne Whitney.'' She was correct, of course. The New York Hospital actually has two psychiatric hospitals, Payne Whitney in New York City, and Bloomingdale's, as it was once called, in White Plains, and each division operates autonomously. In fact, even though I had been on the New York Hospital staff for more than thirteen years, I could not have visited the Westchester Division more than a couple of times.

''I suppose so,'' I said. Obviously no one was concerned about keeping Rickie's plight a secret anymore. Things had already gone too far for that.

''We could drive out and get her and take her there,'' Hillary suggested.

''I think it would be better if you let us arrange for an ambulance. Less risk.''

By now I felt as if our whole lives were slipping through our fingers like soft, white sand. I knew Muriel was doing her best, and believed that she was correct to confront me with my inability to deal with my own child's illness. I'd sat with innumerable families myself, telling them what I intended to do for their fathers or mothers, husbands or wives, sons or daughters. I had gathered information as Muriel had, offered some seed of hope if any were possible, but always made it clear that I was the physician and that the choices about treatment were mine to make. They would sit in front of me, hanging on my every word, listening for some slip that would reveal the truth to them, a truth concealed behind my professional mask. Of course, they didn't always take my advice, but usually they did.

And, always, I saw their utter helplessness.

= 5 =

After we left Muriel's office, Hillary went to Altman's to find a present for Mary's upcoming birthday. I headed for my office, on the eighth floor of an old, sandstone apartment house on the corner of Madison and Sixty-ninth Street that had been converted to doctors' suites shortly after the war. As the elevator moved sluggishly upward, I relived our visit to Dr. Sanders. In our efforts to spell out for her the various details of Rickie's life, I felt we had failed to emphasize sufficiently the most obvious trigger for her breakdown.

My seventy-seven-year-old father had been standing alone on the beach at Sea Bright the previous July. I was sure he had gone there to watch the sea gulls hovering against the scudding clouds and to listen to the steady rush of the sea. A light rain had just stopped, and the tide was going out. An elderly woman, out for an afternoon walk, had found him lying on a stretch of sand that was empty but for a few teenagers skimming rocks some distance away. His fingers were touching the thin line distinguishing the wet sand from sand quickly drying in the sun. I had been his only son, and Rickie was Grandpa's first grandchild. He loved children, and Rickie in particular. I sometimes thought she might have found a depth of understanding in his soul, perhaps a special affinity that, for whatever reasons, she had failed to find in Hillary or myself.

I remembered that I had been reviewing a patient's chart in my office when my secretary, Bernice, came in and awkwardly told me my father's doctor was on the telephone. Grandpa—I couldn't remember when I last called him Dad—had been taken to the emergency room of the Red Bank hospital, and was dead on arrival. Trembling, fighting back tears, I called Hillary. Half an hour later she met me at the entrance to the office building and the two of us drove off silently down the Garden State Parkway, turning off at the Red Bank exit.

At the hospital we were given his few personal items—his Rolex watch, his eyeglasses, and his wallet containing forty dollars, all stuffed into an old, blue shoe box. Then we drove to the funeral parlor a few blocks away, where he had taken me nearly a year before to make the arrangements. "If you don't watch these fellows," he had warned, having just read an exposé on undertakers, "they'll bleed your relatives white when you're gone." Just as he had predicted, the mortician did try to convince me that my father should not be put into the ground in the plain coffin he himself had chosen. He even tried to engage Hillary as an ally, but in the end Grandpa prevailed.

It was a simple funeral. My mother had been in a nursing home for nearly two years, her mind gone, her few remaining memories pertaining to her own childhood. Confronted with her absence at the church, I thought how painful it must have been for my father, who had kept her home until the risk of her leaving the stove gas on became too great. He'd visited her three times a week, unsure whether or not she recognized him, and returned to a house empty except for a housekeeper who prepared tasteless meals and badgered him with astrological prophecies. Mother had become a stranger in the world she still occupied, surrounded by strangers; I knew she had no comprehension when I tried to tell her that Dad was dead.

I was too distressed to seek out many of my father's old friends; some lived in Florida, and others were too frail to attend. Thus his funeral was sparsely attended. Hillary. Myself. The children. His brother, my Uncle Joe, his wife and their two children, and my father's sister Emily. An elderly man who lived near Dad and had been his fishing companion.

During the mass I remembered the last time I had seen him alive. I'd been visiting with a friend, Bill Morris, who loved sports cars, so my father had the television turned on to the French Grand Prix when we arrived. When we left, I gave Dad a tight hug. It was a good kind of good-bye.

I thought back to how lacking in emotion Rickie seemed to be throughout the whole ceremony. At one point, at the wake, probably when she thought no one was looking, from the corner of my eye I saw her quietly approach the open coffin and kiss Grandpa on the cheek.

For months after his death I slept fitfully, often waking in the early morning hours startled by a terrifying sense of loss and despair. These feelings would pass once I had begun my day, seeing my first patient, rushing to Cornell Medical School at noon to lecture first-year medical students, distracting myself with luncheon conferences with my research staff.

Nor did I experience my grief alone. A shadow descended on our household, a silence at dinner broken by questions from the children to whom Grandpa had been so intensely devoted, questions about what would happen to his house, his boat, and Grandma, questions about life after death.

After Thanksgiving dinner I pulled out the old slide projector and flashed through the family album. Justifiably, Hillary had protested that it would cast a cloud over the holiday, since my father had only been dead about four months, but I went ahead anyway. Mary and Matthew had played in their rooms as Hillary, Rickie, John, and I sat in the darkened library, the pictures clicking in place one after another. Our cigarette smoke had curled up, casting thin shadows on the screen. There was Rickie at Grandpa's house, bundled up in her hooded winter coat, and a smiling John no more than four years old holding her by the hand. I was dressed in a velvet-collared chesterfield. Dad, standing on the ice, watched the iceboats on the Shrewsbury River.

"My God," I'd remarked. "How tiny you look Rickie." There were my mother and father in the rose garden, and then my father and Rickie beside a newly planted tree, holding hands.

"I remember!" Rickie had shouted. "He planted that tree for Matthew."

"Poplars," I had reminded her.

She asked if I had a picture of the big yellow sunflower in Grandpa's front lawn. I did. Then my father waving from the stern of his boat, and then a set of beach pictures, Hillary jumping into the ocean surf, waving, and Rickie waving from the sand castle she and I had built, and Hillary and Rickie and me holding hands, walking down the beach, and John, Mary, and Matt, each as a baby, and then Grandpa again, wearing his fisherman's hat, waving.

When I had finished the slides and turned the lights on, Rickie was sitting motionless in her chair, her fingernails digging tightly into her arms, her face without emotion. Hillary told her to read for a while before getting ready for bed, but she simply sat there. When she ignored her mother a second time, I got angry.

"Rickie," I had shouted, "get up and out of here. Go to your room or there'll be no television for the rest of the week." I was startled by my own abruptness. As soon as she was gone I felt awful, recalling how she had trembled, curled her lower lip under her teeth and bit down hard, and how I had pulled her hand away from her mouth, ordering her to her room again. Less than four months later she'd be in Falkirk.

Hillary semed to be watching me cautiously in those early days of our marriage we saw depicted in the slides. When we had been married two years, I became somewhat depressed for several months. I had just completed my internship in medicine at Bellevue Hospital, a harrowing experience, up two nights out of three, perhaps grabbing a short nap on a stretcher in some hallway, waiting for the telephone to rouse me cruelly, summoning me to the emergency room where I would face the awesome responsibility of working up a half dozen patients, each more critically ill than the last, with some semblance of guidance from the resident on call. At twenty-five years old, I was scared. The internship ended in June, but I felt dispirited and irritable for months afterwards. Hillary, only twenty-four, assumed that my distress reflected some kind of emotional instability, which frightened her. But after starting my psychiatric training at Payne Whitney the following January, I felt happy and focused again.

After my father died, Hillary was worried again. Her relationship with him had not been the best. He was an assertive person, admittedly too outspoken at times, and Hillary could not overlook this trait. But she was also fully aware of my deep attachment to him, and of his special bond with Rickie. While she did seem reassured by the external calm with which I continued to attend to the responsibilities of my life, her concern was not unfounded. An unfamiliar tension intruded itself forcibly between us; I became more sensitive, and sometimes quite irritable as I struggled with my deep sense of loss.

Curiously, of all the children, Rickie alone asked no questions. She almost never referred to my father. Only once, when I was lying on the library couch after dinner, listening to the sound track of *Doctor Zhivago*, she came in, knelt silently next to me, held my hand and confessed "I miss

Grandpa, Daddy . . . almost as much as you do . . . maybe even more.''

Now, I dialed Muriel's number. She was busy with a patient and promised to call back in a few minutes. When she did, I told her excitedly of the clear connection between Grandpa's death and Rickie's illness. ''The prognosis is always better, isn't it, when there's an obvious cause?'' I demanded, undoubtedly sounding like a rank amateur.

''Of course, Fred.'' But Muriel's dispassionate tone spoke to my own worst fears.

I was quite familiar with the layout of the Westchester Division. Even though the institution had a number of excellent facilities—a new occupational therapy building, its own beach on Long Island Sound—the dark, red Victorian buildings retained the character of an asylum.

I imagined Rickie had been heavily sedated when the ambulance arrived at the admission unit. She would have been routinely wheeled through the long underground corridors to Building A, where all new arrivals were billeted. I could envision her eyes opening, dimly making out the long row of cots, at the end of which was a glassed-in booth. Through the windowpanes she would be able to discern figures in white moving about, and she'd have heard the dim murmur of voices, more like echoes humming in a vast tunnel. She'd seen rows of beds like that before, at camp, but was probably fully aware that it was a hospital, the kind of place

where her father worked with sick people, and that she was
one of them.

Hillary and I were told that for an undefined period of
time we could not visit her. At the time, this was a common
policy with new admissions in many psychiatric hospitals.
Let the patient settle in. Study the illness. Try to protect the
family from seeing the desperate, terrifying symptoms of
insanity, and at the same time protect the patient from the
family members, who were usually presumed guilty until
proven otherwise.

*When I woke up and looked around, I knew I was some-
where else. Except for my metal bed and a high steel cabinet
attached to the gray wall, the room was completely empty.
A tightly meshed screen covered the only window. A nurse
was standing next to me gently taking my pulse. She called
me by name, said that she was Miss Henry, asked me if I
knew where I was. Of course, I knew it was a hospital. Then
I thought that maybe she meant what hospital, so I struggled
to remember. "It's not Falkirk." In a second I got it right,
but saliva was dripping from my mouth.*

*I was wearing only a thin, white gown tied in back of my
neck, which hung way down below my knees. So I got up
slowly, and with her help put on my dark blue dress and my
white blouse, the one I had worn at Christmas and again in
the big car driving with Daddy. It felt funny . . . tight, and
shorter. I thought it might have shrunk, but Miss Henry told
me that I was at an age when girls grow fast.*

*She helped me walk unsteadily down a long corridor, past
rooms exactly like mine, to a large lounge. It was painted
pale green, and vinyl-covered straight-backed chairs stood
against the walls. There were a couple of card tables with
games I recognized, and in one corner an old black and
white television set. Half a dozen elderly women sat staring
blankly at a rerun of an old film. No one was even close to
my own age. I asked Miss Henry if there were any other kids*

around, and she said "not right now." I felt really disappointed.

I sat down with the group watching television, and one woman offered me a cigarette. The first puff made me feel dizzy, but I took another and it tasted pretty good. Miss Henry said something about growing up, hadn't she?

Later that same day they gave me my "strong" dress, made of canvas too heavy to rip. Pullovers with short sleeves and an elastic waist, they came in all different pastel or light shades. I soon found out that you slept in your strong dress and simply put on a fresh one each morning.

The next day I met Dr. Phillips, who was going to be my doctor. He asked me a lot of questions, but I didn't talk much, choosing to reflect on what he was asking. For example, he asked if I knew I was sick and in what way I was sick. As I recall, I shrugged my shoulders, but I was remembering that as far back as I could remember, I liked to be sick, though of course not too sick. It got me attention. Like the time I was running down the big, wide steps from the sidewalk into our building at Peter Cooper Village. I must have missed my footing, because suddenly I fell down and hit my forehead hard on the concrete. I remember crying. A friend who was with me—it wasn't Christy—laughed, like kids do. I got up, rode upstairs on the elevator, and rang our door bell. One look at me and Mom got hysterical, and rushed by cab to the emergency room at Lenox Hill Hospital.

Another time, when I was eight, I developed a kidney infection. I woke up from a nap, ran into my mother's room and told her, "I'm seeing two of everything." My temperature was 106 degrees, so off we went to Lenox Hill again. For a few days I just lay in bed, not moving, but as I began to feel better, I got a bit rambunctious. One night I stood up in bed and started jumping up and down. I ended up falling off, right on my face, and when I came to, I was on the floor with my lip swollen and blood around my face. I'd *apparently landed on my head and been knocked out cold for quite a while. A nurse was standing next to me, telling me in a stern voice that I'd been naughty, that I deserved a bloody face, and that I was just going to have to wait for someone to clean me up. She did put me right back into bed, but no one came to clean me up for a long time. When the aide came around with ice cream later on, she too reminded me that little girls who jump on beds deserve to get hurt. I was glad to get home.*

I used to pretend to be sick and stay home from school. I suspect everyone's done that at one time or another as a child. I suppose I just didn't want to go all the time, or maybe with Johnny and the other children home—since they were a lot younger—and getting attention, I wanted to be there too. I was told that I was very jealous of John when he was born, and that I wickedly pinched his thigh in his bassinet when I thought no one was looking. I don't recall, but it does make sense. I know that by the time Mary was born, when I was seven, I was happy about it, and that I'd come to love John. When Matthew was born, I was nine. Mom and Dad asked me to be his godmother, and that made me feel very special.

After Matt's birth, however, Mom had my room (which I had previously enjoyed all to myself) divided for Mary and me to share. There were now two small beds with built-in drawers, a desk against one wall, and a closet; fortunately I had the window. Still, I didn't like the arrangement, except that it made it easy for me to pretend to catch Mary's illnesses.

Mary had an intestinal problem until she was three and couldn't eat ordinary foods, just lots of cottage cheese, and she was very susceptible to infections. Yet, I didn't seem to catch what she had. So I'd put a thermometer in hot water or on the radiator, or fill my mouth with hot water, and then present the thermometer woefully to my mother, who'd let me stay home for the day. I think I fooled her for years.

Once, when Mary had conjunctivitis, I snuck over to her

bed, *dabbed out some of the junk that had collected in her eyes while she was asleep, and rubbed it into my own. Believe it or not, my eyes were all junky the next day. Another time she had mono—infectious mononucleosis—so I went over to her bed in the middle of the night and leaned close and inhaled her germs. Well, my glands got swollen, but I had to fake the rest of it. I had no idea, of course, how dangerous mono could be.*

As Dr. Phillips and I sat there in silence, I was amazed at how many thoughts could rush through my mind in such a short period of time. The medications had numbed my pain, but my brain seemed to be rushing. I knew that he was asking me if I thought there was something wrong with my mind. But no matter what I was beginning to believe, I wasn't going to tell him, because if he thought I thought I was crazy, I might never get out of there.

As I walked back to my room through the recreation area, I could hear the juke box playing Petula Clark's "Downtown" and then starting "I Think I'm Going Out of My Head." The old woman who had given me the cigarette smiled and said that it was our song.

I kept asking myself: What choice did we really have?

Letting Rickie be hospitalized was the only sensible decision. It was consistent with my own everyday professional work; in the previous year alone, I had hospitalized nearly fifty people at the Payne Whitney Clinic, men and women I had seen in consultation and whom I felt should be in the hospital for whatever reason. Some were suicidal. Others were unable to cope with day-to-day living or trying to stay afloat in a web of hostile relatives. Some were frankly psychotic.

These efforts to justify my decision were not entirely rationalizations. In those days many of my colleagues and I sincerely believed that hospitalization offered something unique. It provided a setting for thorough evaluation and a more intensive approach to treatment. It offered safety for patients who might temporarily represent a danger to themselves. It seemed like a solid, conservative way to go, and being conservative was at that time in harmony with my whole outlook on life.

I had grown up in a small town in New Jersey, financially protected when millions stood in bread and soup lines and sold apples on street corners or worked for the WPA. We drove a Packard automobile, employed a maid and gardener, spent summers at a seaside resort on the Jersey coast, and I attended small classes in schools where little boys dressed neatly in dark blazers. Other people suffered, like Tom Jeffreys, who died of leukemia in the sixth grade. I was haunted for years by the memory of a class visit to the hospital toward the end, by the vision of his frail body and livid white skin. Kathy Ryan, whose family lost their home when the bank foreclosed during the Depression, had also suffered; I still had photos of myself with Kathy at three, sitting together on a sled in the snow. And there was Bill Tait, an upperclassman at my Jesuit prep school who'd won the role of Ben Gunn in the dramatic society's rendition of Treasure Island while I'd ended up playing one of the pirates; he was killed on D-Day in Normandy.

I was no stranger to pain and hardship, but others seemed always to bear greater burdens. Secretly, although I would never have admitted it even to myself, I must have been convinced that I and those I loved would remain magically exempt.

My life with Hillary had only seemed to prove this point. We met while I was still a medical student, in New York, at a monthly meeting of young people who came to talk with a Jesuit priest about religion and their spiritual lives. She had come from a well-to-do Irish Catholic family. Our courtship, which went on for nearly two years, made life seems so simple and exciting. There were dinners at the old Stork Club and dancing afterwards, mutual friends, daily telephone conversations about nothing at all, thoughtful presents—mostly from Hillary to me—and the special bond of our Catholicism.

We were married in a Jesuit church by one of my former teachers, a priest, coincidentally also a close friend of Hillary's family, and the reception afterwards at Sherry's remains the best party I've ever been to. Everyone was still alive then, and still dancing when we left for our wedding trip. For Hillary and me, there were no such things as empty promises.

Not that our life together had been without problems. Rickie hadn't been an easy child, but we thought we'd come to terms with that. In 1955, when Rickie was three years old, we lost a child as a result of a miscarriage, so I watched John's birth in 1957 with a special delight. The pediatrician detected a small defect in the auricle of his heart, and we lived with apprehension for months, until the doctor finally informed us it was closing on its own. Mary arrived two years later; and then Matthew, who was brought home from the Lying-In Hospital in a large, black limousine to the eight-room cooperative apartment on Seventieth Street we'd purchased in 1959. We spent our summers in a gray shingle house on Egypt Lane in East Hampton.

We could count the number of disagreements between us on the fingers of one hand, except during the months that followed my father's death, when everything seemed to be a source of irrational, and marital aggravation.

Without doubt, our shared illusion was our Achilles' heel. Together we had maintained an equilibrium of responsibility and dedication to our family. We had, one might even say, a virtuous intellectual commitment to love, moving in harmony like silent ballroom dancers but never really speaking to the soul. If we were unhappy, neither of us seemed to have been the least bit conscious of it. In some other period in history it might actually have worked quite well.

John P. Marquand had been one of my favorite authors in my teens, and sometimes I felt like one of his characters, "looking for a happy land, where everything is bright . . ." Of course, I knew that in the end all Marquand's characters had to come to terms with the emptiness in their lives, the pursuit of vain gods, but I sincerely felt that my religious faith would protect me from such folly.

As an eleven-year-old I would go out into the icy cold dawn to walk half an hour to church to serve as an altar boy, practicing Latin all the way and recalling the pastor's pronouncement that being a Christian was not an easy road. I often received communion at daily mass, moments from which I derived a sense of special strength and direction. During medical school I acquired a particular devotion to St. Jude, for reasons I never fully understood—perhaps because the chapel near the New York Hospital had a shrine to the apostle and it was convenient to drop in from time to time, to kneel for a moment before the candle-lit statue and say a brief prayer. Hillary and I gave the appearance of such urbanity, however, that few except our closest friends would have suspected how important a role faith played in our lives.

When I was struggling to decide whether or not to choose psychiatry as a specialty, I spent several days alone at a Jesuit retreat house in Poughkeepsie, taking long walks in the autumn woods, meeting with my spiritual advisor sev-

eral times a day to talk or read from the writings of Ignatius
Loyola. When it was finished, I felt that psychiatry was for
me what some people called a vocation.

Professor Oscar Diethelm, during his interview with me
when I applied for my residency at Payne Whitney, had
asked whether I saw any conflict between being a psychiatrist and my Catholicism. "No," I replied. "I really don't."
The question had struck me as irrelevant. Diethelm had been
trained by Adolf Meyer at Johns Hopkins, whose approach
to psychiatry was holistic and very much ahead of the times.
Clearly not a disciple of Freud, Diethelm was nevertheless
quite aware of Freud's unmistakably antagonistic position
toward religion, considering God to be little more than the
human being's childish attempt to deal with his own helplessness, a projection of early parental figures on the universe.

"I see no reason, Dr. Diethelm, why I can't pick and
choose, keeping those ideas I feel are sound, honest, work-
able, and rejecting those that aren't," I told him.

"It may not be as easy as you make it sound," he cautioned with a warm smile. "Becoming a psychiatrist can be
a bewildering experience for the novice. Patients' sufferings
can rub off, in unexpected ways. Carl Jung wrote of psychic
infection, speaking to the distress experienced by working
with very disturbed people. It isn't always possible to sustain the objectivity you now enjoy."

"I can certainly try," I countered firmly.

"Nor is remaining totally objective always the best way
to become an effective physician," he added.

I did try. In fact, I grew quite skilled at the art of seg-
menting my life into neat compartments. Religion remained
such a compartment, but one not directly relevant to the
profession in which I was steadily acquiring skill. My personal life was another. Day after day I involved myself in
medical practice, meticulously caring for patients, but when
the day was over, I could close the door behind me and enter

a private world. Rarely, if ever, did I speak of my work when away from it; some of our acquaintances were not sure what kind of a physician I was.

After all, vocation or not, psychiatry had not been an easy choice. My father and mother had been gently, though firmly, opposed. My father was convinced that psychiatrists were on the whole more prone to breakdowns than most other doctors, and would have preferred that I become a cardiologist or surgeon. Hillary's family wasn't entirely happy about my choice either.

Gradually, however, everyone seemed to make an adjustment. One Christmas, Hillary gave me a signed photograph of Freud as a present. One birthday she gave me a stuffed Freud doll, a popular item at Saks that year. Two years after I had completed my residency at thirty-three, my first textbook, on integrating psychotherapy with pharmacotherapy, was published, and Hillary's mother kept it in full view on her coffee table for months.

Every now and then, however, a slender crack in the fragile barrier between my personal world and that of my patients shook me. In my second year of residency I was assigned a young woman named Diane. Twenty years old, she had large sad eyes and a gentle voice. She was intelligent and poised, and her whole manner spoke of elegant breeding, made even more appealing by her vagueness and touch of helplessness. I couldn't understand why she was in the hospital, nor why my senior colleagues were so convinced she would never recover.

"Better to have a dramatic, florid kind of clinical picture than this . . . blandness," Professor Diethelm emphasized. "Bleuler pointed out that this simple kind of schizophrenia has a much poorer outlook than the patient who suddenly begins to hallucinate, hears voices and is frightened by them, or is profoundly depressed." Yet Diane seemed like so many young women I had met at dinner parties, at the club in the summer. How could she be so sick? When she was transferred to a hospital for the chronically ill, I tried to put her out of my mind.

Then there was Max Schreiben, who had built a retail empire and, at fifty, was caught in a deep depression that permeated his whole being. Max was not only convinced of his own worthlessness and that everyone knew how evil and destructive he was, but felt possessed by a devil and doomed to eternal punishment. The fact that Max had always been an agnostic did not seem to matter to him now. Yet if Max hadn't told me what was going on in his mind, I doubt I'd ever have known there was anything wrong with him. On the ward, Max would come to breakfast dressed in his gray pinstripe suit as if off to a board meeting, and with the other patients he was always charming and concerned.

By and large, however, my white coat and the logical system of diagnosis and treatment I was learning from Professor Diethelm and my other teachers reinforced the barrier between my sense of personal strength and the patients' vulnerability. And for that reason, Rickie's illness and diagnosis of schizophrenia threatened to destroy the very pillars on which I had so carefully based my immunity.

During the weeks that followed Rickie's departure I knelt beside my bed and prayed night after night. For a while in the cool April mornings I went to mass. But as my sense of futility grew, I stopped. It was hard to kneel. I would crawl into bed at night, look over at Hillary already asleep, pull up the covers, and whisper to God to please let me go on believing.

= 8 =

Dear Christy:

How are you? I'm fine. I feel better than I have felt in a
long time. I hope I can go home and go back to school in
about a month. I really miss my stuffed animals a lot. I'm
hoping that my mom and dad will come up to see me this
Saturday or soon! I miss them too.

I saw my doctor again today. Dr. Phillips smokes a pipe.
I like the smell in his office. He reminds me of Steve Allen
on television. Really, no kidding. He looked just like Steve
Allen.

The first time I met him he asked me a lot of questions
and I didn't say much. This time I felt more like talking, but
I don't think he was really listening. I told him it was all
right at the hospital and that everybody was really nice to
me. I told him maybe I expected people to be more crazy. I
told him I was hurting. When he asked me why, I started to
cry. But I stopped right away because if I kept crying I might
never get out of here.

I told him I was worried that schizophrenia might be
something you could catch from people . . . like maybe
Daddy brought it home from work. He seemed surprised,
and asked what made me think I was schizophrenic, and I
told him I had heard a couple of the nurses talking about

42

me. When I asked him if I was, he didn't say anything, just that whatever I had wasn't catching like I thought. He didn't crack a smile, so I guess that's my diagnosis all right.

I asked him when I could see Mommy and Daddy, and he said when I was ready. What if he never thinks I'm ready? Then he asked me a lot of questions about everything I could remember. He asked me about my school, and about you, and my family. When he asked me about Grandpa, I started to cry again, but he didn't seem to notice. He was already asking me about something else. He asked me if I felt my parents had failed me.

I hope you're having a good time at school. It's weird being here. I miss you. I might not mail you this letter, but I think about you anyway, and I wish we could take a walk down the lane to feed the horses. Anywhere out of here.

Love,
Rickie

"Whatever happened to that fabulous sense of direction of yours?" Hillary quipped as I stopped the car halfway down the ramp, having realized that it was the wrong exit. I gripped the wheel tightly. The wipers on the rented Chevy swished loudly, trying desperately to keep up with the torrential onslaught.

"How do you get back on? I can barely see."

"Just keep going under the overpass. There's a sign for White Plains," Hillary announced.

"I know! I know! Maybe you'd better drive."

"You know I don't drive."

"For heaven's sake, Hillary. Why are we arguing about everything these days?" I could see her fight back tears, yet something kept me from reaching out to take her hand.

Rickie had been at the Westchester Division for ten days when Miss Jeffers, a social worker assigned to Rickie's case, had called to ask us to come to the hospital the following Saturday. No, she replied to my inquiry, the doctors felt it was too soon to visit Rickie.

"I'm Miss Jeffers," she greeted us as we entered the lobby. "I'm sorry, but we don't have an office available this morning and we're going to have to meet right here, but it's pretty big. We'll have enough privacy."

I sensed Hillary's instant liking for this middle-aged woman, slightly overweight and smiling kindly, but I could barely look at her. I suppressed a shudder of discomfort at having to sit in that enormous room, filled with faded couches in various styles and colors, wooden armchairs with frayed cushions, and battered oak coffee tables bare of anything but a few dirty ceramic ashtrays. The lack of sunlight accentuated the poor lighting, wall sconces and a few standing lamps giving off a sickly yellow hue. People huddled in groups of three and four, whispering so as not to be overheard. The place reeked of guilt, I thought. There were hundreds of victims somewhere out of sight, and here in this lobby were the alleged perpetrators, presumed responsible for the awful suffering. And here was this woman, the keeper of the gates of purgatory, trying to be sympathetic. Perhaps, I considered, humiliation was the beginning of the cure.

"Dr. Phillips isn't available?" I was miffed by his absence.

"I work closely with Dr. Phillips," Miss Jeffers replied

pleasantly as she led us to a couple of black leather easy chairs near a window. Hillary sat comfortably back in hers while I, ill at ease, perched on the edge. Miss Jeffers pulled up a straight-back chair for herself.

"First, I'd like to tell you about Rickie," she began. "She's really not doing too well, but of course she's only been here a couple of weeks. It's very early."

"What do you mean, not well?" I felt alarmed.

"Dr. Phillips feels she has formed a good initial relationship with him. That's on the plus side. And she seems to have made a few friends. But she's made the incident report a number of times . . . refusing to go to activities, out of bed at night, taking food from other patients' trays. Was she difficult at home?"

"Yes," admitted Hillary, "sometimes she was."

"Surely you have the history?" I asked impatiently.

"Of course, but I need more background," Miss Jeffers explained.

I was momentarily distracted, remembering the time Rickie had asked me what it would have been like to have been born on February 29, in leap year. By the time you graduated from college, you'd only be five or six years old. And a riddle. "Who's in every house that there's a child in?" Rickie was eight at the time.

"I don't know. Who?"

"Not me."

"Not me?"

"You know, Daddy. Not me. Who ate the cookies? Not me. Who left their clothes on the floor? Not me. Whose homework is this in the living room? Not me."

I heard Miss Jeffers's voice again. "Rickie does seem to have a serious identity problem, as if she doesn't really want to be Rickie. When I first saw her, she introduced herself as Mary, and when I asked her why, she quoted the nursery rhyme 'Mary, Mary, quite contrary.' "

What was Miss Jeffers implying? Was she telling us that

Rickie didn't know who she was, or that she thought she was someone else, her little sister maybe, or that she was playing games, as kids are wont to do? I concluded that whatever her clinical experience may have been, Miss Jeffers still couldn't tell when a youngster was pulling her leg.

"I was of the opinion that most adolescents have identity problems," Hillary pointed out assuredly, voicing my very next thought.

"Of course. I'm only trying to find out how her behavior here compares with that at home."

"I think we're talking at cross purposes," Hillary said, folding her arms and assuming an unexpectedly defensive stance. "I've been married to a psychiatrist for fifteen years, Miss Jeffers. I've tried to be a good wife and do whatever I could to help Dr. Flach in his career, because I think that's what any wife should do. We don't shoptalk, but I know that psychiatrists assume emotional problems are caused by inadequate mothering. That's an idea I can assure you doesn't apply to Rickie or any of our children. Being a good mother has been the most important thing in my life."

"I never suggested—" Miss Jeffers began.

"I'm sorry," Hillary apologized. "I know you didn't. It's just that I've been around psychiatrists long enough to recognize the tendency to blame the mother when a child becomes ill."

"You know I never thought that way," I reminded Hillary firmly.

"All we want to do is help Rickie," Hillary went on. "Please, Miss Jeffers, tell us what we can do."

"Mrs. Flach," Miss Jeffers said kindly, "we don't even know what Rickie's diagnosis is yet. And even if she is schizophrenic, let me assure you I never presume parents are at the root of the problem. But I would like to talk about Rickie's relationship with the two of you."

"We love Rickie," Hillary replied firmly, "and she knows it. We haven't always done the right thing, I'm sure, but then, she was our first. And I'm sure that most parents can look back and see things they did that they wish they hadn't.''

''What about closeness?''

''I suppose you could say Rickie was a bit closer to her father than me. I'm the one who had to discipline the children. Sometimes I felt that her father was . . . too permissive.''

I thought about what she was saying. ''Perhaps,'' I conceded, shifting uncomfortably and clasping my hands together over my crossed knees, ''but I never openly disagreed with you. In fact, I really agreed, most of the time. But I suppose you could say I carried some of my professional stance over into the home, a kind of tolerance that could be misinterpreted as leniency.''

''Psychiatrists are the masters of the ulterior motive,'' Hillary pointed out, ''always concerned with why this and why that. I'm afraid that if you're going to be an effective mother, you just have to take a lot of things at face value and deal with them.''

A look of recognition showed in Miss Jeffers's eyes. ''How are angry feelings handled in your family?''

''Whose angry feelings?'' I asked.

''Between the two of you.''

''We don't have many arguments, if that's what you mean,'' Hillary answered, ''at least, not until the past year.''

A question shot across my mind that had haunted me professionally for a long time. If Mom and Dad argued with each other, there were consequences; if they didn't, there were consequences; always, there were consequences. Often I could not decide how much of the anguish of the patient in my consulting room stemmed from growing up in an atmosphere of either bitterness or unexpressed frustrations.

Miss Jeffers did not fail to grasp Hillary's statement. ''You mean that, until more recently, conflicts in the family were largely suppressed?''

"No, I don't mean that at all," Hillary responded gently shrugging. "I only mean we didn't argue much."

"At all?"

"Certainly, sometimes."

"You know, we have to consider that some of Rickie's behavior may be an indirect expression of rage. If she never learned how to express her feelings openly, she may be resorting to convoluted ways of doing so."

"Surely you're not suggesting that Rickie's illness is the result of the fact that her mother and I didn't happen to fight a lot?" I asked impatiently, tightly gripping the arms of my chair. "You know as well as I do that there are plenty of children who grow up in such families who don't end up in psychiatric hospitals."

"Please, Dr. Flach, don't jump to conclusions. I'm only trying to get an idea of Rickie's life to help us understand what's been going on. I realize it's difficult for both of you now. I'd like to know more about Rickie's relationship with her brothers and sister."

"When John was born," Hillary recalled, "she was jealous."

"How old was she?"

"Five. I guess it wasn't easy, having to adjust. Mind you, her feelings weren't that obvious . . . just that I noticed she seemed more distant from me and didn't want to have much to do with the new baby. I thought she'd have been delighted to have a little brother."

"That's one reason why we arranged for Rickie to be Matthew's godmother," I added. "It was actually Hillary's idea to give her a sense of belonging."

"A little like having two families," Hillary elaborated. "Rickie, then the others. She really didn't play with them very much, but then there was the age difference. Not that they fought. For a while she shared a room with Mary. She didn't seem to mind that. Weekends, she used to beg to visit her grandparents—her father's parents, that is—by herself, almost as though she had found another home for herself there.''

Abruptly, Miss Jeffers asked: "Have you considered seeking therapy for yourselves? It might help you deal with this situation better.''

"I respect what you have to say, Miss Jeffers,'' Hillary answered. "I know you only want to help Rickie. But I don't see the point of your suggestion.''

"We're not the patients, Miss Jeffers,'' I said, backing Hillary up. I was about to stand up, but thought better of it. "It's one thing to come here and talk with you or with Rickie's doctors and collaborate to help her get better. It's quite another to suggest her mother and I need professional treatment. Are you aware of the terrible position that puts us in? If we don't follow your advice, we're letting Rickie down. If we do, you're making us believe that we're the primary cause of her illness.''

"That's not what I intended at all. Maybe someday psychiatric care will include an integrated approach to family therapy, but right now all I can suggest is that the two of you consider talking with a psychiatrist yourselves.''

"How could that really be of any value?'' Hillary asked. "If anyone can help direct us, shouldn't it be Rickie's doctor rather than an uninvolved third party?''

"You know it's important for the patient's doctor not to have too much contact with the family,'' Miss Jeffers replied. "It could interfere with trust.''

"Confidentiality is an issue,'' I concurred in a brittle tone. "But I still think it's a bit ridiculous that Dr. Phillips didn't even see us for a few minutes today. After all, I am a physician.''

"Please, Fred,'' Hillary soothed, "take it easy.'' She reached over and put her hand on my arm. Then, after a moment of thoughtful silence, she asked: ''Has Rickie been thoroughly examined physically?''

''Every patient gets a routine checkup at the time of admission. As far as I know, there's nothing wrong with Rickie's physical health.''

''Miss Jeffers, I do agree with my husband. When do you think we'll be able to see Dr. Phillips?''

''He will be in touch with you,'' Miss Jeffers answered stiffly.

By the time we arrived home, the Saturday mail had been delivered. There was a note from Rickie, a few lines of poetry carefully printed on a torn piece of yellow, lined paper.

Dear Mommy and Daddy,

Here's some poems I wrote.

TURN ON NIGHT

Daytime
light
bright, dazzling
in my eyes
shut it off
turn on night
fixations
interesting pencil
rushing past, so fast,
trust him, love him
more, I want more
all gone.

BLOWN MIND

The drums,
The hollow drums,

Beat.
The purple onions,
Cluttered in the bag,
Sit.
The merry-go-round
Swirls and sings
People pass by and stare
Check again
What they see
Figures block my mind
Dragons breathe fire
Turn on the gas
Look and see
Fires everywhere
A yellow bike with no rider.

=== 10 ===

Making an exception to the usual rule that resident physicians took on new patients more or less at random, the chief of the inpatient service had undoubtedly considered the nature and complexity of Rickie's problems and the fact that she was the daughter of a fellow staff member in choosing Dr. Norton Phillips, because he was one of the brighter, more promising residents. It is still common practice for all patients in psychiatric teaching hospitals to be directly under the care of residents in training, who in turn are supervised by more experienced clinicians. It's a trade-off. The patient, protected to some degree by the involvement of a

senior staff member, is nonetheless being treated by a novice. But in psychiatry that isn't necessarily a bad thing, since
the fledgling might bring an enthusiasm and optimism
sometimes lacking in older doctors, and an absence of the
theoretical biases that so often interfere with therapists'
open-mindedness and imagination. I assumed Phillips would
be carefully supervised—much as I had been when I was in
training. The role I subsequently assumed at Payne Whitney—providing the experience and clinical acumen the resident lacked, making rounds, seeing each patient a few
minutes each week, highlighting topics to explore in psychotherapy, and being ultimately responsible for major
treatment choices—was in Rickie's case taken by Dr. Arnold
Stuart, a specialist in the then-new field of adolescent psychiatry. It was a discipline born of the profession's recognition that teenage patients had special needs, different from
those of children or adults. Although it had always been
known that certain types of schizophrenia usually emerged
in adolescence, psychiatrists were starting to encounter more
and more cases of depression, as well as substance abuse,
in this age group. They were responding to what some correctly predicted could become epidemic. At the time of
Rickie's hospitalization, however, there were still few adolescents in hospitals, and the system was not really geared
for them. I considered Stuart's involvement fortunate.

Even though Phillips had chosen not to see us, I did not
understand Stuart's absence, unless both Phillips and his
supervisor thought they were avoiding the complications of
"special handling." We all knew about patients who because of fame, wealth, position—or just because the family
of fellow doctors was involved— fared poorly because doctors were lured into treating them in a different way. On the
other hand, it seemed to me that even a few minutes with
us would have helped assuage our unspoken guilt, and that
we at least deserved a chance to hear about Rickie from her
own physician.

The following Monday, however, Dr. Stuart did telephone my office. "Frankly," he admitted, "I wasn't sure what procedure to follow, and as it happened, I had to be in Detroit for a conference."

"That's perfectly all right." I saw no point in being openly critical.

"I've had a chance to talk with Miss Jeffers this morning. I'm afraid she took your being a psychiatrist a little too seriously. I explained that it's one thing to be a psychiatrist and quite another to be the patient's father. In the end, the gut response you're going to get is that of the father, not the doctor."

"I appreciate your saying that."

His voice sounded warm, reassuring. "That lobby's also no place to meet anybody, and I plan to speak with the clinical director about it this week. But let's get to the subject of Rickie, shall we? I want to check a few points that Miss Jeffers obtained in her history, if you don't mind. Rickie's mother's father died when her mother was still a child, is that correct?"

"Yes."

"And Mrs. Flach's mother remarried a man who died some years ago, and proved a rather problematic stepfather."

"To say the least."

"I gather her mother is something of a mainstay in the family?"

"She's a remarkable woman, gracious, intelligent, someone who we all love and respect a lot."

"And your own mental health?" He sounded at first hesitant, then almost jocular. "At least Miss Jeffers was discreet enough not to ask you about that."

"It's okay. Oh, I had a rough time for a few months toward the end of my internship at Bellevue, and recently, right after my father's death. And of course now, with Rickie, but I'm not sure I'd call that unhealthy."

"Sounds appropriate to me," Stuart commented.

"Have you been able to discover any clue . . . ?"

"To Rickie's situation? A few. We can't be sure yet."

"We've all been under a lot of stress this year."

"True."

"Maybe it's chemical," I suggested.

"Maybe. That is your bias, isn't it?"

"Not really. I do quite a bit of psychotherapy, but I try to consider all the variables in my understanding of patients."

"I do too, let me assure you. I'm a bit reluctant to use drugs in teenagers, though, tranquilizers especially. But I've had to let Dr. Phillips give Rickie Thorazine from time to time, although I'm not sure she tolerates the phenothiazines very well. Personally, I don't think she's assaultive, but the staff can get panicky, as you know, and their disquiet can bring out the worst in a patient."

"Has she . . . struck anyone?" I asked.

"No. She's been difficult, though. Yesterday she refused to go to occupational therapy and went to her room, where we found her banging her head on the mattress. When the nurses tried to stop her, she fought back. Then, last night, she was up and wandering around for hours. When we tried to get her back to bed, she just stood there, back against the corridor wall, resisting any efforts to move her."

Before I could ask him why he was describing Rickie's disturbed behavior in such detail, he explained. "I'm being extremely frank with you, partly because you are a doctor and partly because I think you should have some idea of what we're trying to deal with here."

"Did Rickie know we visited Miss Jeffers Saturday?"

"Dr. Phillips didn't tell her, nor did Miss Jeffers. But the walls have ears here. I wouldn't be the least bit surprised if she knows. And of course if she asks, I'll tell her."

"Could that have accounted for her behavior?"

"That's a possibility."

"What do you think her diagnosis is, Dr. Stuart?"

"I can't be sure. Maybe schizophrenia, but then again maybe not. Could be a very atypical depression."

The word depression aroused my first spark of hope since the nightmare had begun. "Depression!"

"Please," he said quickly, "don't set your expectations too high just yet. You and I both know the odds against this being a simple depression."

The relief vanished.

"Look here," he went on, "this isn't the first time I've treated the child of a physician, but it is my first time for a psychiatrist's child, much less a colleague on the same staff. I can easily imagine what you must feel. You know, people used to criticize the fact that there was so little contact between the staff here and those at Payne Whitney, but now, maybe it's just as well. You can be assured we will treat this entire situation with the utmost discretion."

"I appreciate your saying that," I said, "but frankly, at this point that's the least of my concerns. When do you think her mother and I can see Rickie?"

"I'll let you know. Soon, I hope."

"Do you have children yourself, Dr. Stuart?"

"I have one daughter, seventeen."

After our conversation ended, I felt reassured that Rickie seemed to be in caring hands. I could only hope they were competent ones as well.

=11=

I used to think my memories of Westchester were sparse because of all I went through there. But it seems that many friends my age also possess a kaleidoscope of bits and pieces of their past. It's funny, though, how certain memories never go away, like black and white tile floors, and green lawns, and odors especially. The hospital smelled like Falkirk, the odor of cleaning fluid used in old hospitals and old schools. You could smell the metal screens on all the closed windows too.

And certain people. I'd been there nearly six weeks, was going to be fourteen on May first, but there were still no young people at the hospital, at least not on my ward. I remember talking to a lot of old people, many of whom had been there for years. One older woman—maybe forty or forty-five, but of course she seemed old to me—took a special interest in me. She was an opera singer, a large, tall woman, with dark hair that she'd wear either hanging down or up in a bun. What a beautiful voice she had! She took me on as a pupil, playing the piano and getting me to sing. I remember she had me practicing "Love Is a Many Splendored Thing." I was no singer, but she'd clap her hands anyway and say "Wonderful! Wonderful!"

They had activities in the gym. I especially loved the arts and crafts in occupational therapy, maybe because I was good at them, and because the activities people were especially nice to me. We made wooden bowls and bread bas-

kets. Mom loved some of the bowls I made for her, and Dad still uses the cutting board I gave him. They were nice things, and I was proud of having made them. I learned to play backgammon there too.

There wasn't any school on the premises, I guess because there were so few young people. Dr. Phillips told me that if and when I was in shape to attend classes, they would arrange for me to go to a public school nearby. That made me shudder. The way he said "when" made me feel I might be there for the rest of my life.

Leona, Macy, and Violet, black aides on the day staff, were good to me, and so was the nurse on the unit, Miss Henry. She was a very special person. Another nurse, Miss Robling, was different, a tough cookie, and we didn't like each other much. She made me feel like I was nothing (not that I didn't already feel a lot like nothing), so I was always fighting her. For a while she always won, until I learned a few tricks from some of the other patients that gave me more power. In April, I wrote a letter.

Dear Mommy,

Please excuse my awful handwriting, but I guess the medicine they give me makes me shake. It makes my mouth real dry too, and my tongue feels heavy. Sometimes it gets stuck against my lower lip and I have to use my fingers to move it away. Right now I'm not feeling too good. I miss Falkirk. It was smaller and cozier. There's one good thing about this place, though. My doctor is good. I think I can talk to him easily now, even though he doesn't say much and always keeps a straight face.

I hope you're feeling good. I miss you and everyone. Have to stop now. They're going to take us for a walk in the garden.

Rickie XXOO

When Hillary passed the letter to me, I could imagine the garden, a place where patients from the more disturbed units could briefly touch the real world. In my mind's eye, fifteen or so women walked in a circle no more than forty feet in diameter, some looking as if they were on an errand, others as if they were going nowhere. Some would wear the white-and-blue-striped bathrobes the hospital provided, others might be in gray, canvas dresses. A middle-aged woman might have her hair pasted down with too much spray and walk with her chin high in the air. Some would stumble on uncoordinated legs, nearly falling but seldom doing so, as others brushed by in hurried indifference. Rickie would be told to walk the circle like all the rest.

Walk the circle, Rickie. Follow the yellow brick road, Rickie, with the lion and the scarecrow and the tin woodsman. But there isn't any Oz, Rickie, just a circle, going around and around, nowhere, and no one there but "not-me."

12

The only person I then felt free enough to confide in about Rickie and all that had happened was Bill Morris, probably my closest friend. We had met in medical school and had done our psychiatric residency training together at the Payne Whitney Clinic.

Once every other week or so, usually on a Tuesday, Bill and I would have lunch alone together at the Cornell faculty club, a small but elegantly furnished lounge and dining room situated between the main entrance to the New York Hospital and its administrative offices. Even though the food was prepared by the same kitchens that served the basement cafeteria directly below the club, somehow even the sandwiches seemed tastier, perhaps because of the gracious surroundings.

Because Bill was invariably ten or fifteen minutes late, I usually found myself sitting comfortably in the paneled lounge area, surrounded by portraits of some of the hospital's late great physicians, idly reading and nodding hello to colleagues on their way in and out. Then Bill would arrive, looking a bit rattled and always apologetic, and we would go in to the table I'd reserved.

Rickie had already been hospitalized for nearly two months when, at one such lunch, I was able to muster the courage to tell him. Bill was visibly shaken. "I don't know how to react," he murmured. "You know how much I love Rickie. She's like my own daughter. Thirteen years old. It breaks my heart to think of her . . ."

"Fourteen last week. May the first."

"She spent her birthday there?" He looked appalled. "I hate to say this, but you know what I think of hospitals. They're certainly not set up to meet any of the basic needs of teenagers, except maybe sports—if they can find people in good enough shape to make up a team," he said sarcastically. "I'd have kept her home."

"How could we, Bill?"

"You know you're only trading off one set of risks for another, and possibly a worse set at that. Who's taking care of her?"

"A resident named Phillips."

"Green behind the ears," he grumbled. "What can I say?" He reached across the table to put his hand on my arm. "She'll be all right. Rickie will be out of there in no time. Most of our patients get better, don't they? Whatever better is . . . Maybe the Rickies are the only ones who make sense, dropping out, giving up the ridiculous struggle against stupidity and indifference. Who is mad, really, the patients over in the psych building, or the brilliant minds who think of atomic war as a problem-solving option and brought us Vietnam as an appetizer? Maybe, in her own way, she's a lot more clear-headed than all the rest of us put together.''

I appreciated his reassurances, but they did little good.

"What scares me a little is what happens when they put a diagnosis on her,'' Bill went on.

"What do you mean?''

"Diagnosis, my friend, is destiny. Shaking loose of the label, useful or not, can be a tough job. It's a little like not doing too well when you start school, and being pegged as a loser forever. Only in our business, the consequences can be a lot more serious.''

Bill had been antiestablishment in his medical thinking as long as I had known him. And while I felt uncomfortable with what he had said, his words still did not strike me as relevant to Rickie or to most of the patients I encountered.

"How are you holding up?'' he asked.

"It's hard to concentrate, as you might guess.'' That was indeed an understatement. For weeks now, a patient would occasionally stop talking, look at me, and ask whether I had heard what he'd been saying. I'd straighten up sharply, reassure him, and with a strong effort of will listen carefully to see if I could pick up by deduction the thread that I had missed. Sometimes I would find myself fighting back tears.

One patient, a successful writer in her sixties, caught me doing so. "Are you all right, doctor?'' she inquired.

"Fine, fine. Why do you ask?''

"You just don't seem yourself.''

What do I do now? I wondered. Lie? Make her feel that her own perceptions are askew? Tell her the truth and violate the age-old rule that therapists should never reveal themselves to their patients? I opted for the truth.

"As a matter of fact . . .'' I choked on the words. "One of my children isn't too well.''

She leaned forward in her chair, as I had at moments

when she had revealed particular sadness. "Is there anything I can do?" she asked compassionately.

The previous week I'd chaired a meeting at the Academy of Medicine, introducing the various speakers. I literally couldn't see the program in front of my eyes. A fellow psychiatrist sitting next to me on the podium must have figured something was wrong, so before each new speaker he'd whisper the name and the title of the paper in my ear. I was convinced that the entire audience could see that I was falling apart.

Bill Morris had been there. "I didn't notice anything was wrong, Fred. You have a lot of presence."

"You're telling me the truth?"

"About that? Yes. But frankly, you've obviously lost some weight. You look tired, exhausted, in fact. How do you do it?"

"What do you mean?"

"Go on working, seeing patients, making rounds?"

The painful tension to which I had nearly grown accustomed instantly welled up. I wanted to avoid his question, turn the conversation to movies, books, people, travel, but instead I answered him with a faint effort at humor. "You know the old joke about psychiatrists? Who listens?"

"Funny . . . and not funny."

"How do you think I function?" I asked. "On my way out in the morning I look in Rickie's room and see her stuffed animals and her dolls and her school uniforms hanging in her closet, and I choke up and wonder what God's doing with our lives. Then I walk to the office, and if Bernice is there, I say good morning, and I go in my room and I perspire and shake and wish that everyone would cancel their appointments for that day and maybe forever. But nine o'clock comes sooner or later, and they start talking about how unhappy they are or describing how they feel compelled to go around the house turning the lights on and off, again and again, and a kind of numbness sets in. I lose myself in what they're saying, and then the hour's up and it all begins again, and when lunchtime comes, it's as if a great weight is lifted from my back. Hour after hour I see Rickie, sitting there in front of me, saying, 'Help me, Daddy, help me. What's wrong, Daddy?' I want to say nothing's wrong, let's go to the beach and build a sand castle and let the waves wash over it and then we'll build another one, and when evening comes we'll cook a steak outside and your mother and the kids will watch old movies.

"You know, Bill, I was sitting up at two in the morning the other night and *Gigi* was on. I could barely look at it; I cried on and off for over an hour. The hardest thing for me to do is to go to the hospital and make afternoon rounds. My patients are mostly over thirty, depressed, no schizophrenics. I can take that, really. But when I have to go through the wards and see those young girls, some of them stuporous, some suicidal, some begging to go home, I think I'll go out of my mind."

"How's Hillary taking it?"

"Quiet. Distant. We don't talk much about it. Somehow I feel she blames me or thinks I blame her, I can't say. She doesn't cry, at least not in front of me, not since the night Rickie was transferred to Westchester. Every time I try to bring it up, she avoids me. Oh, she goes about her business, sees girlfriends, goes to the school parents' meetings as if Rickie were still there. She spends a lot of time with her mother. Last week she took Christy, Rickie's closest friend, to lunch and the movies, something she used to do with the two of them. In some ways, it's as if nothing's changed. I know she's just trying to keep herself in one piece, but I can't bear the way she's pulled away from me."

Bill looked apprehensive. "You'd better watch things, Fred. You know as well as I do that family crises like this—children getting sick, even dying—can blow two people apart more often than bring them closer together."

"I know that, Bill. But it's as if everything is spinning out of control."

"Well, get it back under control, old friend."

13

As the weeks grew into months and summer approached, Hillary and I tried to get used to the idea that Rickie was ill. However, it was impossible to overcome the fear that it might take years for her to recover, or that she might always remain a cripple, or never recover at all. From time to time we pressed Dr. Stuart for permission to visit, but each time he said no, reassuring us that Rickie understood that our absence was not of our choosing.

I still tremble when I read one of Rickie's poems from this time.

> *Have I been forgotten?*
> *Please let this not be.*
> *Will they all remember*
> *Memories of me?*
> *The sky looks dark, yet bright*
> *The sun feels cold, yet warm.*
> *Will I ever see the light?*
> *As tender as a mother,*
> *As beautiful as the sky,*
> *I love her, oh I love her*
> *Until the day I die.*

Not knowing was awful. When a child needs surgery, the parents are there at the bedside day after day, and the doctors explain their treatments in detail. But in those days the psychiatric patient's situation and the physician's thoughts were blanketed in secrecy. Families were left to the torture of their own imaginations.

More than once I would arrive home after work and find Hillary painting in the living room, her easel set up in front of one of the large windows that overlooked Seventy-ninth Street and the row of town houses that gave the neighborhood a decidely European feeling. I would sit near her, watching the faces on her portraits take shape, or pick up one of the finished canvases to take a closer look at the bright colors and particularly the penetrating eyes, all the time wanting to talk.

But she wouldn't look up, not even to say hello. Then, after five minutes or so, she would suddenly tell me to get out and leave her alone. I'd get furious and yell, "How can we work anything out without talking?" Maintaining she was too upset to talk, she would tell me that my persistence was only making things worse. I began to think better of Miss Jeffers's suggestion that we seek counseling for ourselves, but Hillary would have none of it. "If you want to talk things out, you go," she suggested, "but I prefer to think them out alone. When I'm done, then maybe I'll be ready to talk to someone."

Gradually inquiries from the few friends who knew about Rickie stopped. Mary and Matt were easily quieted by our comments to the effect that their sister would be coming home soon. I had no doubt that Johnny knew what had really happened, however. One evening after dinner he joined me in the library, looking especially pensive. "Is something bothering you, Johnny?" I asked.

"Rickie," he replied frankly.

"What about Rickie?"

"She's sick, isn't she? She's gone to a hospital. Has something gone wrong in her mind?"

"Come over here." He curled up on the couch beside me. "Yes, John, Rickie's sick. And she is in a hospital. She may be there for a long time, but she is going to get better, and one day she'll be home with us again. There's nothing wrong with her mind."

"Does it have something to do with what you do, Daddy? Psychiatry?"

"Yes."

"You don't think we'll get sick too, do you, Daddy?"

"No, Johnny, I'm sure we won't."

"I feel sad for Rickie. I miss her. Maybe, when I grow up I'll become a doctor too and help people like Rickie get better."

"That's a nice thought Johnny." I put my arm around his shoulder and hugged him tightly.

There were times when it all assumed an unreal quality. I would find myself wondering if Rickie had ever existed at all, or if she had only been a very special figment of my dreams, an actress in our home movies, dancing around and around in a red velvet dress, laughing with joy. When I glanced through an album of old snapshots, I was actually startled to see her there with the rest of us, then reassured. But we were slowly becoming a family with only three children, and the thought grieved me terribly.

Hillary and I also grew accustomed to long silences between us. She would read for an hour or so in bed, and whether she turned the light off before I came in the room or simply rolled over and went to sleep while I was still reading, it was without the usual "I love you" or even "good night."

My pain over what was happening to us and to Rickie refused to go away. I could only guess what her pain must have been, since she never spoke of it to me.

I decided to visit my old analyst, Dr. Leo Kobin, who

had just returned from a six-month tour through Europe and the Middle East. Then in his seventies, Kobin saw very few patients, spending most of his time writing, lecturing, and traveling. Born in Boston and educated at Johns Hopkins, he had known Sigmund Freud personally, and in the beginning had been one of his most ardent disciples. Over the years, however, Leo Kobin had become a maverick. His points of view won him both admirers and enemies, but he seemed to possess a unique insensitivity to both. Married and divorced three times, Kobin's weak point was women, but for years now he had lived alone in an East Side brownstone, absorbed in his work.

When my analysis had been completed years before, Kobin had warned me not to presume that I was some kind of superman, that all that had to be solved had been solved. He was genuinely saddened by my reason for consulting him again.

"I'm so sorry to hear about Rickie," Kobin said compassionately. I'd used the term schizophrenia, but I knew that Kobin thought in pre-Bleulerian language: dementia praecox, the insanity of the young. He ushered me into his consulting room.

"Please, Frederic. Sit down. No need for the couch now," he said, smiling. The room was just as I remembered it, with a large marble fireplace, the heavy stuffed furniture, the black couch with the white tissue on which the patient rested his head, the walls lined with leatherbound books. Kobin knew me as well as anyone alive, but now I was beginning to feel that no one could really understand, and that my recollections of this room and of this man were part of a world that was fast disintegrating around me.

I moved hesitantly about, almost sitting in one chair beside the leather couch, but then hastily choosing another on the other side of the room.

"Much has happened in eight years, Frederic," Kobin remarked casually. "From time to time I read your papers on calcium changes and thyroid function in depressed patients. Interesting work. Are you still running the metabolic research unit at Payne Whitney?''

"Yes. I've been lucky, the work's gone well."

"And you still have your practice? How many hours a week do you see patients?"

"Twenty-five or so."

"Quite a schedule . . . But obviously that is not what we are here to talk about. How is Rickie?"

"I don't know. I haven't seen her in months. Not well," I admitted nervously.

"I'm sure it hasn't been easy."

"That's an understatement. It's affected everything."

"Everything?" Kobin asked gravely.

"My work, my spirits, my marriage . . . Frankly, I feel like I'm falling apart. I don't know how long I can go on working. Maybe if I were a banker or lawyer, anything but a psychiatrist, I could lose myself in my work, but being faced every day with Rickies . . . "

"So you feel . . . desperate?" Kobin lit his old meerschaum pipe and leaned back in his chair.

"Sometimes I want to quit psychiatry altogether. Get out of it, never see another patient, never listen to another problem . . . "

"Nonsense," Kobin retorted briskly. "What you are going through can only make you a much better therapist. Anyone who says they can practice psychiatry and do a good job of it without having suffered is a liar or a fool."

"But everything seems to be . . . out of control. I've stopped going to church . . . "

"Freud would call that progress! Jung, on the other hand . . . " Then, in a more serious tone, Kobin went on, "I know how terrible that must be for you. Your faith was so much a part of your life. To lose it . . . "

"I haven't lost it. I feel I've lost touch with it."

He muttered something.

"What did you say?"

"Guilt!" he thundered.

"I don't think I feel guilty anymore, not really."

"How could you not feel guilty? Faced with Rickie's suffering, how could you not ask yourself where you failed, or perhaps, what you are being punished for?"

"Rickie's the one who's suffering!"

"Oh? She is the sacrifice?"

"If I were guilty, I'd spend all day praying, trying to make amends," I replied angrily.

"That's not the way guilt works, Frederic, and you know it!" Kobin sat forward in his chair. "It has, more often than not, the very opposite effect. It can destroy the very ethic that it has been designed to protect. You're a student of literature, and you're also a psychiatrist. You know the ravages of guilt."

"All right. I do feel guilty, but I've done nothing to warrant it."

"Does that matter? You also know enough about human nature to know that's completely irrelevant. If you really didn't have any guilt, then I might think you really were responsible for this tragedy, but I know you too well. And what would you do with this guilt? Throw away your profession? Throw away your life? Do you think that destroying yourself would bring Rickie back?"

I recognized the absurdity of my denial.

"The paradox of religion," Kobin went on, "is that, at the very moment when you need it most—when you feel desperate, remorseful, needy—it can be the hardest lifeline to get hold of. You must have more faith . . . in your God, in yourself!"

"That's a strange thing for you, a nonbeliever, to say."

"How do you know what I believe, Frederic? But that is not what is important. What counts is that you believe."

"In what? In a God that strikes down an innocent child like Rickie?"

"Now you are being self-centered! You have always known that disease and suffering and even evil are part of the fabric of life. You simply never thought it would reach out and touch yours. What is happening is that the wonderful sense of being special—oh, I remember it in our work together years ago, fortune's darling, I called it—has been shattered. That's where you hurt, my friend, and that's what you must come to terms with. Do you really think your God has singled you out for punishment? Don't be ridiculous. If anything, if there is a God, perhaps He has decided it's time to teach you some humility."

"And Hillary?"

"What about Hillary?"

"Why does she deserve—"

"Deserve! There's no such thing as deserve. And what about Hillary?"

"Our relationship is falling apart. We don't talk to each other, except about trivia, and not much of that. She avoids me as if I had the plague. We can hardly be together without a tension that I find unbearable."

Reaching up with his fingers to stroke the deep furrows on his forehead, Kobin appeared saddened. "I have never met Hillary. I have only your description of her. During your analysis there seemed nothing problematic in your marriage." He was obviously struggling to remember. "You were both very young when you married, perhaps too young. Rickie came along right away, and I recall she was difficult at times. You were still an intern and resident, dependent on your families for financial help, working long hours. A brief episode of depression, as I recall, but that is not unusual. You had friends. You had a good life together, affection . . . "

"Well, it's all become a nightmare. I can't figure it out. I don't understand her at all, and all she seems to want is for me to leave her alone."

"And do you?"

"What do you mean?"

"Leave her alone? Let her work things out her own way, let her deal with her own grief?"

"Nothing gets solved if it doesn't get talked out."

"In the right way, at the right time."

"You make it sound as though it's my fault."

"Guilt again. The issue of fault is not our concern, Frederic. How you handle the problem is. Hillary has her way, you have yours. And, apparently, they are diametrically opposed."

"But how can she sleep at night and seem so collected when—"

"Oh, we are all supposed to react to terrible stresses in the same way? You know better than that. As a matter of fact, before you began your own analysis you were a rather private person yourself, if I recall. In many ways you still are, I am sure. But between your analysis and your work with patients, talking has obviously become a channel, an outlet for you in a way it never has for her. Incidentally, was she analyzed herself?"

"We agreed it wasn't necessary."

"It doesn't matter. I'm sure you know there are plenty of instances of husbands and wives both going through analysis; they change, and the marriage doesn't work out anyway." Perhaps Kobin was thinking of himself.

"Are you telling me," I pressed nervously, "that our marriage is in serious jeopardy?"

Kobin was quick to answer. "That frightens you? It should. Life is full of danger. You have always looked for certainty, but there is none. People think that a serious illness in a child—even a child's death—should bring families closer together. Nothing could be further from the truth."

Bill Morris had told me the same thing.

He paused, then quietly, seriously, asked, "Are you by any chance embarrassed about Rickie's illness?"

I flushed slightly. "Embarrassed? I hadn't thought about that . . . Maybe."

"You know what people say about psychiatrists and their families. If you're as concerned as you once were about what others think, that could also be a problem, but certainly not the central one. I can easily imagine how you must feel, being a doctor yourself. I also assume that Rickie's illness must involve more than losing a daughter. Like losing part of yourself. You were very close to her, weren't you?"

"Very." I began to feel tears coming.

"On one level you may feel compelled to share Rickie's suffering with her. On another, being the perfectionist you are, you undoubtedly feel the need to go on, always in command. You may try to shut out feelings that are quite natural."

"How should I behave? What am I supposed to feel?"

Kobin shook his head. "There is no 'supposed to.' You know that. Sooner or later this may shatter you completely. But it could also be the most important experience of your life, a turning point, and a costly one, but a road to strength, if you survive it."

"I came here for—"

"Reassurance. And I can give you little. If I were a magician I could wave my wand and make everything right again, and believe me, if I could, I would. But there are no such things as magicians, Frederic. The situation you are in will test every fiber in you and your marriage, in a way they have never been tested before. This much I can tell you: I have great faith that somehow you will survive, and be better for it."

He stood up to show that our time together was over. "Believe me, Frederic, I speak to you not as a doctor, but as a friend, and from the perspective of what seems to me a series of lifetimes."

=== 14 ===

Sometime around the middle of June I did something that gave me some power—or so I thought—over Miss Robling and some of the others who wouldn't give me space. I had been transferred to a more open unit, where you could actually go outside if there was someone to go with you. I wasn't there long when I experienced this overpowering urge to hurt myself.

As I stood there in the patient lounge, the feeling welled up in me, like a compulsion, and the more I tried to get rid of the idea, the more intense it became. Suddenly I walked over and punched my fist through one of the windows, tearing my flesh in the broken glass. There was blood over everything. I was terrified, and so was the staff.

A surgeon sewed up the wound, repairing a severed tendon in my hand. I remember waking up with a big cast around my hand and arm. I was instantly sent back downstairs to the closed ward again, via the seclusion cell, where I stayed for a couple of days.

After that I kept getting that urge to hurt myself from time to time. It wasn't like a voice telling me to do it. It was just a thought that intruded into my consciousness and wouldn't go away, like when you have the urge to have a cigarette and you try to put it off and it keeps building up. Then, after you've smoked one, you relax, and because the urge has been released, for a while you're free of it.

When I got the urge, all I knew was that I felt numb all

over, and at the same time this enormous tension was build-
ing. Sometimes I'd be smoking a cigarette and I'd think of
putting the lit end against my arm. When the urge wasn't
too strong, I could get rid of it. Otherwise I'd work myself
up, as though hypnotizing myself, and then I'd do it. When
it hurt, I'd breathe faster so that I could hold it there just a
little longer, until it hurt enough so that I'd have to stop.
Then I'd go put ointment on it and a bandage, and then
they'd give me a shot of Thorazine or something and put me
on "constant watch," meaning that someone was assigned
to be with me all the time. Or, if they were shorthanded, I'd
end up in seclusion—without my cigarettes, of course.

I guess I was trying to feel something. A lot of times, when
Dr. Phillips asked me what I was feeling, I'd say "nothing,"
and gradually it became true. In that place it seemed pref-
erable. Also, provoking an incident was a reliable way to
get noticed, and it stirred everyone up in a way that not
much else would have. In a strange way, it almost made me
feel in control of them, instead of the other way around.

Seclusion was the place they put patients when they were
bad, or when the staff felt they had no other way to control
them. I wasn't really that bad. I never attacked anyone, like
some did. Only myself. Sometimes, even in seclusion, I could
get to them by banging my head on the floor, or by lying on
the floor and banging my feet against the door in protest. It
would drive them crazy. I liked that! They'd have to have
someone stay with me until medication put me out. I don't
know what they gave me, but it would put me into oblivion,
and I liked that too.

Unfortunately, sometimes my behavior backfired and I
would be put in a cold pack instead. Sometimes called a
wet pack, that's when they wrap you like a mummy in cold,
wet sheets for two hours. The only thing sticking out is your
head. After two hours the sheets start to get warm, so they
put you in another set of cold, wet sheets or you get out. I
spent a lot of time in those sheets. They knew I hated it, and

*maybe they wanted to remind me who had the upper hand.
Let me tell you, when they tried to hold me down for the
cold pack, I'd fight like a banshee.*

*The other treatment was a big tub of water with canvas
stretched across it up to your neck. They called it therapy,
and they used it to calm you down. They knew I liked the
tub treatment better because the water was warm, which is
probably why I usually got the cold pack.*

*This whole scenario—hurting myself and being punished
for it—vanished for a while when a girl my own age named
Carlie was admitted in early July. At last I didn't feel all
alone, and I wasn't so awfully bored. We had so much fun
pulling antics together and laughing ourselves silly. Of
course, the staff hated it. Once Carlie and I hid ourselves
in the bathroom near the rec room with the jukebox in it.
We were backed up to the toilet with the door closed and
our feet on the toilet bowl. They couldn't see us at all, and
they went berserk looking for us. The only reason they found
us was because Carlie farted and we laughed. They tried to
push the door in while we held fast. When they finally got
to us, we made a big scene, kicking and screaming as they
carted us off. I don't have to tell you where they put us.*

=15=

In July, Dr. Stuart finally called to make the long-awaited
appointment, the prelude to our first visit with Rickie.
Nearly four months had gone by, during which he and I had
spoken weekly on the telephone. Frustrated by his contin-

ued refusal to let us visit and the sparseness of his communications, I nonetheless accepted his explanation that it was a sound, intelligent strategy specifically designed to reassure adolescent patients that their physicians were really their confidants, not pawns of their parents. It was consistent with what I had been taught throughout my medical career. Confidentiality between doctor and patient has both ethical and legal ramifications. It is a particularly delicate issue when the patient is a minor, and learning how to protect the privacy of the patient's communication while still sharing responsibilities with a parent or guardian is an exacting task. The experience of having someone other than a peer who keeps what he is told a secret is a new and unfamiliar one to most adolescents, one that he can only grow to trust over time.

As a resident-in-training at Payne Whitney, I was once assigned to take care of a fifteen-year-old depressed girl. After she had been hospitalized for several months, my supervisor included me in a meeting with my patient's father. The two of them were already together in his office when I arrived, and in response to several benign questions from my supervisor and her father, I was completely mute. Finally, with amused exasperation, my supervisor said: "I do understand your dedication to protecting your patient's confidentiality, Fred, but you're acting as though you'd never heard of her. After all, her father does know that she's a patient in the hospital and that you're her psychiatrist. There are some things we have to discuss to get on with plans for her treatment."

I used to consider this a humorous anecdote, but now the incident no longer struck me as the least bit funny. I felt a new compassion for my patient's father and struggled against the urge to demand more details from Stuart. Even had he obliged, I realized that every bit would be speculated upon by the doctor in me, even as the part of me that was Rickie's dad would be profoundly distressed.

When Hillary occasionally expressed her own impatience, I tried to reassure her. Once I pointed out, as I had sometimes done with patients and families, that while those of us on the outside have schedules to meet and dates to keep, in the sanatorium, there is no calendar. Months could go by barely noticed. I did not mention that those months might consist of completing a painting or two, several hundred starchy meals, seventy psychotherapy sessions, a thousand hours of television watching and other forms of idleness, all devoid of boundary or definition.

Dr. Stuart met us in the lobby, firmly shaking our hands. He was a tall, Lincolnesque man, slightly stooped, with tousled gray hair, meticulously dressed in a brown plaid suit, his white clinic coat unbuttoned to reveal a Phi Beta Kappa key hanging from a gold chain across his vest. His smile was quick but friendly. He ushered us to his office, a room furnished in typical hospital style, with two overstuffed leather chairs, a leather couch, and a dark wooden desk behind which he took a seat. Only a few pictures on the wall, and photographs on the desk of a woman and a teenage girl who must have been his daughter, spoke to the fact that this office belonged to Dr. Stuart and not any one of the other staff psychiatrists.

"Is Dr. Phillips joining us?" I asked.

"No."

"Don't you think it's about time we met Rickie's doctor?" Hillary pursued.

"Not now. I'm afraid things haven't been going well," he said bluntly. "For a few days at a time Rickie seems better. Then, without any obvious trigger, she relapses. We tried to get her interested in doing some schoolwork—we have an arrangement with a local school—and she went for a couple of days; then, on the third, she created a storm on the unit, screaming and crying. She had the accident I spoke with you about on the phone, injuring her hand and wrist. And she burned her forearm several times with a cigarette.

I'm afraid you'll see the scars. We'd like to give her more freedom, but we don't dare. Right now is actually one of her better periods. That's why I thought it would be a good time to visit. I don't want her to feel . . . deserted.''

"Is she on any medication?" I asked.

"One of the major tranquilizers from time to time, usually Thorazine. She can have a rough reaction, but they do control her.''

"Thorazine's a drug for schizophrenics, isn't it?" Hillary was dismayed.

"Not necessarily," I explained. I had done a good deal of research with the major tranquilizers when they were introduced in the mid-1950s. "The phenothiazines cut into a lot of emotions, like fear and agitation, regardless of diagnosis. But I'm more concerned about antidepressants, Dr. Stuart. Have they been tried?"

"They're not really indicated.''

"How can you be sure? If nothing else is working . . . "

"We'll give it due consideration, Dr. Flach.'' He seemed sincere, and I wanted very much to trust him. I'd made a number of inquiries, and without exception, colleagues rated him an excellent psychiatrist. But my apprehension persisted; even the best can make mistakes.

"Do you think we should have a consultation?" Hillary asked.

"That's an understandable question, Mrs. Flach," he replied, "but I think it's too early. Maybe, if we don't make any real progress over the next few months . . . "

Hillary and I walked slightly behind Dr. Stuart as he escorted us to Rickie's ward. I felt myself trembling, but I could not discern what Hillary, head erect and looking straight ahead, was feeling. He led us across a wide lawn, along a fieldstone pathway lined with bright flowers, until we came to a large, nineteenth-century red-brick building where patients were housed. Once inside, he drew a large bunch of keys from his coat pocket, unlocked the heavy gray door to Rickie's unit, and stood aside to let us enter first. Hillary hesitated. "You go first, Fred," she whispered.

Dr. Stuart instantly caught the attention of a nurse. "Rickie's parents," he explained as she approached. "She'll take you to Rickie. I'll see you afterwards."

Hillary was obviously dismayed by what she saw. Several middle-aged women in plain dresses and wearing no makeup wandered aimlessly around a drab lounge area furnished with a few metal tables and chairs. We stood there silently as Miss Henry went to get Rickie from her room at the far end of the unit.

As Rickie slowly walked toward us, the sight of her filled us with a despair we struggled to conceal. She had grown two inches to five feet seven or eight, and the thin creature we knew had become a heavyset, overweight young woman. The paleness of her cheeks was accentuated by dark brown hair that had been cut very short, and her lips were erratically smeared with purplish lipstick. Her dress, too small, ended slightly above the knees and pinched at the waist, and she wore tennis socks and sneakers. Her hands and arms shook with a fine insistent tremor.

"Daddy," she cried. "Mommy!" Running awkwardly, she pulled us together in a single hug and held on tightly. I noticed the scars on her right arm.

"I miss you so," she said plaintively, in a tone that sent a chill through me. "Please. Take me home."

Hillary squeezed her tightly and fought back tears.

"We miss you too, sweetheart," I said, nearly choking on my words.

"Is there someplace we can visit alone?" Hillary asked.

"Only here in the lounge," Rickie replied apologetically.

Several more patients had come in from their rooms to sit in front of a television set. We found three straight chairs in a corner as far away as possible, Hillary and I on either side of Rickie. Each of us leaned forward as if to create a wall of privacy between us and everyone else on the unit.

"Tell me, darling," Hillary began clumsily, "how have you been?"

"Okay, I guess," Rickie answered, clasping her hands together in her lap to keep from shaking. "I have friends. I like to swim in the pool, when they let me. The head of rec is neat. I'm going to try out for the badminton team. It's all right here, I guess . . . but I want to go home."

"We'll talk about that later, dear," Hillary replied. "Did you get the things we sent you, the toys and things?"

"Yes," Rickie answered, smiling absentmindedly. "They let me keep Raggedy Ann in my room if I'm good. Of course, if I'm not, they take them away."

"I'm sure you're good, Rickie."

"Not always, Mom. Sometimes I do bad things. Something inside my head tells me to do things, and I do them."

"We don't have to talk about that."

"What kinds of things?" I pursued.

"Like this." She held out her arm. "I burned myself with a cigarette."

"You don't have to talk about it if you don't want to, Rickie," Hillary insisted.

"But I want to. Marilyn did that, once, when I first got here. She was a patient here then."

I looked at the scars on her wrist and felt afraid of the terrible things she must be learning here.

"They transferred her . . . to a state hospital," Rickie went on. "Is that where I'm going to be sent, Daddy?"

"No, sweetheart."

"You sure?"

"I'm sure."

"Do you treat schizophrenics?"

"Most of my patients are not schizophrenic, Rickie."

"That's good. Maybe I'm more like your patients, Daddy."

"I'm sure you are."

She looked at her mother. "How's John, Mary, and Matt . . . ?"

"Fine. They miss you, Rickie. We all miss you."

She was a stranger, I thought. It's Rickie, but it's not Rickie. An insane idea flashed across my mind: Rickie's dead and they've brought out another patient who looks a little like her, and they're trying to pass her off on us as our daughter.

"When can I go home?" she repeated.

"When the doctors feel you're ready," Hillary assured her.

"Can we ask them now?"

"We'll see Dr. Stuart again as soon as our visit's over and we'll ask him, Rickie, I promise." I was embarrassed, knowing the gesture to be meaningless.

"Do you always do what the doctors tell you, Daddy?"

"The doctors really know best," I reassured her gently.

"I wish I could offer you something to drink, a Coke or something," Rickie said, "but the machine's broken. Oh, hey, there's Judy. You want to meet her?"

"Not now," I said.

"Of course we want to meet Judy," Hillary said, annoying me by encouraging a stranger to intrude on our precious time with Rickie. But as Judy approached, we both greeted her cordially.

Judy was a singularly unattractive, heavyset woman, probably in her early thirties but looking ten years older, her curly blond hair dirty and unkempt, and wearing no makeup. "Hi." Judy assumed a nonchalant pose, hands on hips. "So you're Rick's parents. Glad to meet you. Rick's a good kid, really." Without a further word, she walked on.

"She's an alcoholic . . . and suicidal," Rickie murmured in a low voice. "Just came off constant."

"Constant?" Hillary asked.

"Having someone follow you around all the time," Rickie

explained rather impatiently, as if she expected her mother
to know.

Dr. Stuart had asked us to limit our visit to half an hour,
but as we stood up to leave, Rickie begged us to stay longer.
Her mother saw no harm, but I'd given enough doctor's orders to believe they served a purpose, even when, as now,
we were on the receiving end of them and I could not honestly say that I understood Dr. Stuart's purpose.

We walked to the unit door together. As Miss Henry unlocked it, Hillary hugged Rickie, and I fought back tears as
I put my arm around her. We stood, waving, as the door
slowly shut. We could hear Rickie's voice from the other
side, calling out, "Don't forget, I want to come home."
The lock engaged with a loud click.

Back in Stuart's office, he asked us: "How did you find
her?"

"I don't know how to answer that question. As you described, I suppose." I felt confused. Rickie had seemed as
she always had, yet totally different. My memory of her was
that of a willowy, winsome, little girl. The person we'd been
with a few minutes before was a lost, tired, not terribly
attractive young woman. Maybe when children grow up in
front of your eyes, I thought, the change is so subtle that
parents hardly notice, but even a short separation has effects
that can be startling. In Rickie's case, they were heartbreak-
ing.

"She's gained so much weight," Hillary observed glumly.

"Rickie does eat a lot," Stuart explained. "Not unusual,
in teenage girls, especially in hospital, but I'm afraid the
food is rich and the energy isn't burned off as quickly as it
should be. How did you find her emotionally?"

I assumed he was asking me that doctor to doctor. "A bit
flat, depressed. But her thinking was clear. You can't miss
the side effects of the Thorazine, the trembling. Is there
something wrong with her eyes? While we were talking, I
thought that they were . . . moving around in a funny way,

as if she weren't looking at us sometimes. Did you notice that Hillary?''

"Now that you mention it," she said, puzzled.

"Rickie's been thoroughly examined," Dr. Stuart reassured us. "What you saw is probably another effect of the medication."

"She wants to come home." I knew the answer I would get.

"I'm sure you realize that's out of the question, Dr. Flach. Today's one of her better days. There's no way we could permit you to take such a risk."

"How much longer—"

Dr. Stuart did not let Hillary finish. "I can't honestly say. Several months, perhaps. These things take time. You have to be prepared for the long haul."

"Will she get better?" Hillary could not hide her fear.

"I have a great deal of confidence in Rickie. You should too," Stuart replied.

Hillary seemed slightly reassured, but I had spoken similar words to families so often that his token of hope hardly touched me. I did admire the way he phrased it. Nothing about illness or treatment. Confidence . . . in Rickie.

"When can we visit again?"

"Let's see how this visit went before we decide that. You'll be in your office Monday?"

I nodded.

"I'll call you, about eleven."

"Half an hour with Rickie seemed so little," Hillary remarked on the drive home. "I wanted to take her in my arms and hold her, but somehow, there, in that place, I felt so . . . restrained, and Rickie seemed almost . . . grotesque."

"Pathetic would be more like it."

"I don't think I was attractive at that age. Awkward. Overweight . . . Look out! You nearly cut that car off!"

"I can drive!" I snapped. "I didn't cut him off. He was over the white line!"

"Well, I don't want to have an accident. You shouldn't drive when you're upset. I've told you that before."

I had been doing sixty. I lifted my foot from the accelerator and reduced my speed to thirty-five.

"There. That better?"

Hillary said nothing.

As I turned into the Hertz rental-car garage and down the curving ramp, I felt a jolt as the edge of the right fender scraped against a concrete pillar. I muttered under my breath. Reaching the bottom, I slammed on the brakes hard and turned off the ignition. There were no attendants in sight. Neither of us moved to open a door. I was shaking slightly, my hands still tightly gripping the steering wheel, Hillary staring ahead.

"What do you really think?" she asked.

"About what?"

"About Rickie. You're a doctor. You must think something."

I took her hand. "I nearly didn't recognize her," I confessed. "Maybe, if Stuart hadn't told me it was Rickie, I wouldn't have known. I know that sounds ridiculous. I think it's awful! I suppose I didn't really want to see her grow up. Nobody likes to see their children grow up. Certainly not like that!"

"I meant medically. What do you think medically?"

"I'm trying not to look at Rickie medically. Don't you realize that? If I look at her medically, I get totally confused. I have to believe that they'll find a way to get her better somehow. What was it Stuart said? Oh. Yes. We have to have confidence in Rickie."

She drew her hand away and reached for the door.

Monday morning, on schedule, Dr. Stuart called. "I'm afraid things didn't work out too well. Rickie was very upset

Saturday evening after you left, she grabbed a bunch of pills off the nurse's tray at medication time. She was a bit sick, that's all, but it could have been serious. I think we'd better put off another visit until we make a little more progress.''

Monday evening, after dinner, Hillary told me that she'd had several visits with a doctor to talk about Rickie, herself, and our situation. I asked her his name.

"Dr. Rumsey. He's very well thought of, Fred. I just didn't want to speak with anyone we already knew. I got his name from a friend. He wants to see you.''

Elated, I thought, now, at least there's a chance to improve things between the two of us.

16

I remember Dr. Rumsey vividly. In his late sixties, he was no more than five feet seven, balding, stocky, and he wore a tight, wrinkled cashmere sports jacket and shiny patent-leather shoes. We could not have spent more than half an hour together, during which Rumsey paced back and forth across his consulting room as I sat in an uncomfortable, straight-back chair, too stunned to speak. His cheeks grew scarlet as he lectured venomously, calling me an incompetent human being, harping on the theme that I was too young to be complaining so much about fatigue, as Hillary must have described me. When I tried to say something, he consistently interrupted, telling me that nothing I had to say mattered to him.

I left his office dazed and frightened, and that evening,

when Hillary asked me how the appointment had gone, I didn't know how to reply. "He seemed . . . strange, to tell the truth."

She was immediately on the defensive. "Because I chose him without consulting you?"

"Not that. But all he did was rant and rave and carry on like a lunatic, telling me I had no right to be tired and upset."

"I spoke to him on the phone this afternoon," Hillary said. "He told me he liked you very much."

I felt totally mystified.

Sounding intensely rational, Hillary proceeded to tell me that Rumsey had helped her come to realize that we were basically incompatible and would be better off living apart, at least until Rickie was well again. "You pull me down, Fred. Some little thing doesn't go right and you lose your temper. You're always wanting to talk about things, first Rickie, then us . . . and I don't have anything to say."

I knew that the stress of Rickie's illness was undoing both of us, and I said so.

"That's part of it," Hillary readily conceded. "Sickness and psychiatry fill every room in this house; I just can't stand it anymore. But that's not all there is to it. In the past weeks I've had a chance to think about us, and it's just no good. I was only twenty-two when I married you, Fred. I didn't know what life was all about. I need time now to be alone."

Agitated, I launched into a litany of memories, evidence of how good our marriage had been. When I saw that she had begun to cry, I stopped. But when she failed to respond to my pleas, I went on: "We can't get divorced, Hillary. We're Catholics."

"I'm not talking about divorce, just a separation. But Catholics do get divorced, just like everyone else," she pointed out tearfully. "Please, Fred, respect me enough to leave, while there's still time, before we do any more damage to each other.''

Utterly baffled, I could not understand how everything had come so completely apart.

═══ **17** ═══

I slept on the library couch that night, and the next afternoon moved into the Morris's spare bedroom. Bill's wife Celia pan fried a steak for dinner and Bill opened a bottle of rare Bordeaux, but I could barely eat and ignored the wine. They both tried to assure me that every marriage went through tribulations and that Hillary and I would be back together in no time at all. Bill, who had looked Rumsey up in the directory of physicians and found that he had no hospital affiliations, kept urging me to report him to the ethics committee of the county medical society.

''The guy's a Queeg,'' Bill argued. ''He's taken an already precarious situation and blown it to kingdom come. I can't blame Hillary. She's completely vulnerable right now. But God knows what the consequences will be for Rickie, the kids, everybody. Rumsey should be put in jail and the key thrown away.''

I couldn't muster the energy to share his rage.

I took a sleeping tablet around nine o'clock, but at two in the morning I was still awake. Groggy, I stared at the strange wallpaper and unfamiliar shadows. I floated away on visions of people and places, fragments of the past, in color, real, immediate, sometimes so tangible I felt if I reached out my heavy hand I could grab on and hold them tightly. In the last moments of life all the memories are supposed to flash in front of your eyes. A flood of incoherent images rushed through mine now.

My earliest memory? How often I had asked patients to recall theirs. Jung said it held a vital clue to one's whole adaptation to life. The crib. The day my parents bought me a new, big boy's bed. I missed the crib and wanted to get back into it. Yet at the same time I was enormously drawn to the prospect of growing up.

I was obsessed with visions of houses, the white colonial clapboard house I had grown up in, and the brown-shingle beach house, and the apartment that until that morning had been my home.

Once, during my analysis with Dr. Kobin, I had recalled lying ill with measles or some other common childhood malady in the king-size bed in the guest room facing the garden. I heard my parents' voices faintly outside the closed door, my mother asking: "What will we do if he dies?" My father answered: "Don't worry. We can always get another." I remembered the awful sense of terror and abandonment. Kobin and I reconsidered it, acknowledging that it must have been an illusion and that my parents had most likely been talking not of me but of the willow tree that had been blown onto its side in the hurricane.

I could see myself saying good-bye to my father at the train station when I was just short of eighteen, on my way to basic training in the Navy during the Second World War. Finding it hard to bear the thought of my leaving, my mother had stayed home. I had been out celebrating the night before with a few college friends, my train had been late, and I had run home two miles in the snow to be with Mother and Dad. On my first leave home, ten weeks later, I was saddened by how much older they looked to me.

My father moved with vigorous, impatient strides, always communicating a purpose, always going somewhere, to Edmonton, Winnipeg, Tacoma, Seattle, Minneapolis, and Chicago. Once, when my mother and I went to the railroad station to see his train pass through, my father stood on the platform of the observation car and threw a tennis ball for me to catch. I was ten years old and felt an incredible sense of excitement as I saw him there waving above the roar of the train rushing past. When the doctors told him to cut down on his sailing and business activities at seventy-four, Dad asked, "What for?" But he began to walk more slowly, stopping every now and then, breathing hard, to let the pain in his chest subside.

Once a year he spent several days in prayer at a Jesuit retreat house; the year before his death, I had accompanied him. I could see him standing with a group of men, myself among them, leading them solemnly in the rosary. He believed in God even when my mother began to be forgetful, wandering around the house at night, looking for things she had lost, and he must have realized that after nearly fifty years together, they would soon have to part.

What would he have done about Rickie? He certainly wouldn't have sat back and let things take their course.

I sat upright in bed.

All there is is now, I thought. Now, here, this room, this time. I got out of bed slowly, inched my way across the room, stubbing my toe on an unfriendly chair leg hidden in the unfamiliar darkness, and stood at the window looking down on the deserted street.

Bill had encouraged me to call home after dinner. Now I desperately wished I had. Just like a play, I thought. Life has no more reality than a play. I clasped my hands tightly together, held them out in front of me and lowered my head. But I could not find the heart to pray.

═══ **18** ═══

"When Rickie learned of your and Mrs. Flach's separation," Dr. Stuart told me on the phone, "at first she didn't seem to show much feeling at all. Like all kids her age, of course she was worried about what would happen to her, where she'd go when she left the hospital, whether she'd see you again. One of her friends here has divorced parents and never sees her father, but I tried to reassure Rickie that that wouldn't happen. I don't have to tell you that she felt that somewhow she was the cause for your breakup. All children do. It was a good chance for me to emphasize that she wasn't responsible for what happened in her parents' lives."

"Did she seem to understand?"

"At one level. But the nurses reported an episode of hysteria a few hours later, followed by lying on her bed, not talking. She seems to be a bit better now."

"This will really complicate things for her, won't it?"

"It'll complicate things for all of you," he pointed out. I thought I detected a compassion made all the more genuine by the fact that I could connect a face to this now familiar voice. "Rickie's no exception. But learning to accept reality is a necessary part of her adjustment, isn't it?"

I closed my eyes, unable to continue the conversation. I thanked him for his kindness and hung up.

Several days later I received a letter.

Dear Daddy,

I am sorry about you and Mommy. I'm sorry if I had anything to do with it. I hope it's not my fault. I talked to Dr. Phillips about it, but he never says anything to me. He only asks me how I feel.

I feel like a rope being tugged at each end, someday to be broken in half, or snapped at the end, or else to be dropped in the middle, left lying on the grass.

Where will I live when I get out? With Mommy? With you? Maybe not with either of you. I plan to finish school and go on to nursing school someday. When I get out of here, I'm not going to come back here ever. I'm going to make a life of my own, working for what I want. I am going to try to live for myself, giving as much as I am able to the people who need *and* want *help! I've got lots of people who want me to make it, including you and Mommy. And when I do make it, I will stay out and live.*

Well, I guess I've said all I can say, so I better say good-bye for now. I love you.

Rickie

I had been in the habit of writing Rickie a note or sending her a card once a week with a ''thinking about you, missing you'' message. This time I wrote more carefully, tearing up several versions before this one.

Dear Rickie:

Mom and I do miss you so. Please don't feel badly about what is happening with us. We really do love each other. It's just that sometimes people have to part for a while, to straighten out their lives.

And please, don't feel an ounce of guilt. Mommy and I are big people and we can take care of ourselves.

Believe me, you have nothing to feel guilty about.

When you get out, you can live with both of us. Now
your job is to get better, and I know that will be soon.

A big hug from Dad.

I signed an earlier draft "Daddy," but I decided that it
was time for me to just sign it "Dad."

Raggedy Ann had been a special present for Rickie's sixth
birthday; she had slept with it every night, and it was one
of the few things she had wanted to have in the hospital.
Much later I found out that after she learned of our separation, she had taken Raggedy Ann into the bathroom and
twisted the cloth doll until she had pulled the arms and legs
completely off.

=== 19 ===

Celia had spoken with Hillary several times, but Hillary
remained steadfast in her conviction that separation was the
only answer to our dilemma. At first Hillary seemed content
with an informal arrangement, but then, urged by several
friends, she consulted an attorney. She was in East Hampton, the last August that she and the children were to spend
there for many years to come. I was still staying with Bill
and Celia when the usual dispassionate lawyer's letter arrived at my office by certified mail, changing forever, as
such letters have a way of doing, the dimensions between
us.

Sydney Schwartz had been my attorney for several years.
His office was in an old building downtown, on Broad Street,

near the Stock Exchange. He practiced alone, a secretary in
her late fifties sitting outside the frosted-glass door that led
to his own room. He had furnished it with a large, rolltop
desk, a swivel chair into which his slight body had a way
of nearly vanishing—he could not have been more than five
feet four—and two small leather chairs for conferences with
clients.

He and I had just finished reviewing the financial details
of the separation agreement, which seemed quite straight-
forward, when he peered over his spectacles and started to
rap his fingers on the arm of his chair. "As soon as the
separation agreement is signed, Hillary apparently wants to
fly down to Mexico and get a divorce."

I was taken entirely off guard. The idea of divorce struck
me as terribly final. "That wasn't what I had in mind,
Sydney!"

"I know, I know. I figured it would be upsetting to you.
You still want to work it out. Okay, but let her have her
divorce. Sure, the two of you may change your minds and
get married again. You might want to get married yourself
a couple of years from now, to someone else, you never
know. And if you're not divorced and Hillary wants back in
or just feels in an obstinate mood, she might not be so
cooperative. People change."

I felt utterly defeated.

"Have you lost weight, Fred? You don't look too well."

"I'm not feeling too well."

"Now, about Mexico."

"I'll go."

"No way," Sydney said firmly. "She goes. Then, if
there's ever a question in the future, she can't contest it."

How could we sit there, I thought, cutting our life into
little pieces like butchers? I was trembling so much inside
that I could hardly follow Sydney's determined logic. "It
doesn't make any difference who goes to Mexico, Sydney.
I'm a Catholic. I can't marry again."

"I wouldn't count on it," Sydney replied. "I've got plenty of Catholic friends, and clients, who've married twice. I've been married twice myself," he chuckled, "and I'll tell you it's a lot cheaper to make the right decision the first time around. Knowing you, I can't see you spending the rest of your life alone. You're a good-looking guy, a doctor, a prospective mother-in-law's dream. You'll be in plenty of demand, if you make a little effort. Enjoy yourself! Have a good time. Just don't jump into anything too quickly."

With the best of intentions, he was only making me feel more despairing. "I'm obsolete, Sydney. The world's changed since Hillary and I were dating."

"What are you? Thirty-eight?"

"Thirty-nine, forty next January. Can you see me hanging around the singles bars on First Avenue saying 'Hi there, my name's Fred, what's yours, toots? How about a quick trip to Nassau for the weekend?' "

"What's wrong with Nassau for the weekend?"

"Everyone has their own set of values," I replied.

"All right, all right! Have it your way! You'll just have to do whatever suits you."

"What about the children?"

"You'll have the usual visitation rights—every other weekend, a month in the summer, and vacations."

"And Rickie?"

"Hillary has agreed to give you custody of Rickie. She figures that you being a psychiatrist, you'd know what to do more than she."

"I'll have to find a place to live. I can't stay with the Morrises indefinitely. Somewhere with two bedrooms, so I can set one aside for Rickie, put her things there, give her the feeling there is a place for her when . . ." I couldn't finish my thought.

"You sure you're all right?" Sydney scratched into his graying, curly hair. "You sound really depressed."

"Wouldn't you be?"

"You've got to have more confidence in circumstance, in yourself. In spite of romantic notions to the contrary, marriages aren't made in heaven. It's two people signing a contract, doing their best to stick to it, but if it doesn't work, it doesn't work. And as for Rickie, she's only been in the hospital for six months. That's nothing. A client of mine's nephew was hospitalized for over two years. He got better. I've known plenty that do."

"I don't even know where to begin making a life of my own."

"You do what every other divorced guy does, Fred. Take the kids on outings, get yourself convertible couches for when they visit, and learn to fix a few meals so you don't go broke eating in restaurants. Take them to McDonald's and for drives in the country, maybe rent a place for the summer, find some baby-sitters, help them with their homework, make sure their visits aren't boring or unpleasant, and hope they want to keep on spending time with you, which they won't when they get into their teens anyway." Sydney was obviously a veteran.

"I know whereof I speak. You'll devote the next ten years to them and they'll grow up and leave you. You can't center your whole life around them, so you're going to have to make some new friends. Mind you, I'm not suggesting you fall for the first female that comes along. Matter of fact, if you're even the slightest bit interested, give me a ring and I'll put handcuffs on you for a week until the impulse wears off. You're more vulnerable than you realize. And being a doctor, you know that married people are healthier, live longer. I can spot the domestic type when I see it. Why, I'll bet you a hundred, right now, that you'll be married again in less than five years."

I didn't take the bet.

On the way back uptown I found myself shaking as if the temperature were well below zero. On the subway I closed my eyes for a few minutes. As the train jerked its way into

the next station, I was shocked to see a platform sign that
read Atlantic Avenue. Where was Atlantic Avenue? I suddenly realized that in my confusion I had taken the wrong
train and was already deep into Brooklyn.

=== 20 ===

At the end of the same week, I received a poem from
Rickie. She said she had written it one afternoon looking
out the rec room window.

> ### YELLOW BALLOONS
>
> *Yellow balloons dot the pink skies*
> *The clouds above cry rain*
> *A hand reaches out and plucks the sun*
> *From the sky*
> *The sky bleeds*
> *God is angry*
> *The sky blackens*
> *All is like night*
> *But yet it is day*
> *The wind whips through the trees*
> *A beetle on the rock*
> *Is crushed by a falling branch*
> *The world is in terror*
> *People run*
> *Ants scamper into their holes*
> *Zap!*

Everything stops
Nothing is moving
But, yet, all lives
Only God is in motion
God must fix his sky
The sun shines again
Zap!
Motion
Life is the same again
Almost
But the branch still lies on top of the
Dead beetle upon the rock
Once again
Yellow balloons dot the pink skies.

=== 21 ===

No matter how hard I tried, I couldn't shake off the terrible sense of gloom consuming my spirit, finding it harder and harder to make decisions or be on time for appointments. I suspected that my absence from staff meetings at Payne Whitney might be conspicuous, but I often could not bring myself to leave my office until I had to go back to my consulting rooms to see patients at around five.

During the nearly twenty years I had spent at the New York Hospital, the last twelve as a member of the Payne Whitney psychiatric staff, I had formed a strong attachment to the center, especially the eight-story white Gothic building that stood separate from the main building, perched above the East River, its paneled lobby speaking to a passing age of elegance when even nervous breakdowns could be experienced with a measure of style. In a few short months the clinic had lost much of its special aura, quickly becoming one more impersonal institution for the care of the mentally ill.

My own office was located on the fifth floor, overlooking the river, accessible via a slow, clunky elevator and three locked doors. One afternoon as I sat at my desk, stacked high with unread reports, watching a coal barge churning past, Dick Kohl, then clinical director of the hospital, knocked on the partly open door. Dick was a good friend. We lunched together once a week; he'd come to our home as an extra man at dinner parties, and at least once a summer he spent a weekend with us in the Hamptons. There was also a distance between us; he was dedicated to permanent bachelorhood and a café-society life-style that had prevented him from fulfilling his intellectual promise.

Never in the years that I had known Dick had he come to my office unexpectedly. When he asked if everything was all right—he must have known of Rickie's illness and of my separation from Hillary, but he made no reference to either—I roused myself, sat upright, picked up several papers, smiled faintly, and reassured him that I was indeed fine. Dick sat down, swung one leg across the other and began to describe his weekend at the Westport estate of one of his many wealthy acquaintances: who was there, what had been served for dinner, who was dating whom, and other various intrigues, delicious gossip like that in a Somerset Maugham novel. I found his prattle diverting. As he left, about ten minutes later, he asked once more if I was all right. I nodded my head. Had he noticed how slowly I moved, how I couldn't think of anything to say?

The next morning I called Dr. Kobin. His secretary told me he had gone to Los Angeles to give a lecture and wouldn't be back for several days. I immediately phoned

Bill Morris, who had half an hour free between patients and asked me to come over to his office. I once joked with Bill that the only objects in his consulting room less than a hundred years old were a framed photo of himself in a BMW racing car, and his telephone. He once retorted that his furnishings were his Keogh plan.

I described Dick Kohl's visit. "He must have known something was wrong, not that I really care in Dick's case," I told him. "But I don't think I can keep up this pretense much longer."

"Neither do I."

"And I can't go on living with you and Celia indefinitely."

"You're welcome as long as you want."

"Thanks," I said, shaking my head. "I'm supposed to go to Europe for a week right after Labor Day, for the World Congress of Psychiatry in Madrid . . . if I can make it."

"You'll make it. But a week's not enough."

"What do you mean?"

"Look, they're obviously not going to let you visit Rickie for a while. I can cover your practice, and certainly the clinic can do without you. Take a month. Take six weeks. You've never been abroad before. It could be just the medicine you need. Come back with a clearer head. Do it for your family, for your patients, if not for yourself. You're no good to anyone the way you're going now. Of course, if you prefer, you could stay here and talk with a psychiatrist three times a week . . ."

He did make me laugh quietly. "You've got a point, Bill. I'll see what I can work out," I agreed halfheartedly. Then I said: "Level with me, Bill. How bad do you think I am? Would you give me a . . . diagnosis?"

"You want a diagnosis, I'll give you a diagnosis, if that makes you any happier. Shell shock. I saw plenty of it in France. Battle fatigue. What you do is take them out of the front lines, get them to pour their guts out to you, send them for some rest and recreation, and then off to face the enemy again as soon as possible."

Bill's diagnosis was certainly one I could live with.

Except for reading my own paper on calcium metabolism in depression, I scarcely attended the sessions of the congress. Instead I went shopping and in a little shop a few blocks from the Ritz bought a charm bracelet and a small gold trinket, a cross, which I intended to save for Rickie when she was well. Then I traveled to Avila, where I thought of St. Theresa and of how Rickie had once spoken of wanting to become a nun.

From Spain I flew to Copenhagen, spending a week in Denmark. In the Bing and Grundahl shop I found four statues of children standing each next to the other on the shelf; as if they had been made to special order, they resembled my own four children. There was Rickie, crouching nimbly and holding a white bird; Mary, curly-headed, face uplifted, laughing; Johnny, standing tall, gripping a fishnet; and Matthew, complete with Prince Valiant haircut, a mischievous sparkle in his eyes and a white sailboat in his hand. I bought them at once. A short distance down the avenue I found a jewelry shop, Rasmussen's—it seemed that every jeweler in Copenhagen must have been named Rasmussen—and there I purchased my second gold trophy for the charm bracelet, a ballet dancer.

In Baden-Baden I stayed at Brennar-Park and spent one

evening at the casino, winning all of forty dollars at rou-
lette. A handsome blond woman in her early thirties watched
me play from the far side of the table, and when I was done
playing, she walked around the table toward me. "You must
be American," she said.

I nodded, flattered by her attention. Also an American,
she quickly had me talking.

"I don't think I've met a man in years who devotes most
of his conversation to his children," she commented, after
I'd described each at great length. I'd referred to Rickie as
if she were at Noroton, a Sacred Heart convent boarding
school where Hillary and I had once thought of sending her,
and felt a jab of the pain that I had almost come to shed.

"I assume you're divorced."

"Yes, I mean, just about to be."

"Then why are you still wearing your wedding ring?"

During the first few weeks after we had separated, I could
not bring myself to remove the ring, and by this time I'd
forgotten I still had it on. I twisted it nervously. "Habit, I
guess."

"Everyone's doing it these days," she said, "getting divorced, I mean. Pretty soon it'll be more the rule than the
exception."

I felt embarrassed.

"Oh, here he comes." She referred to a slightly balding
young man in a tuxedo approaching us with drink in hand.
"I'd like you to meet my husband, Peter." The three of us
spent the rest of the evening together, and before parting
we agreed to meet for dinner in London a few weeks hence.

My second night in Rome I was awakened by the telephone ringing.

"Fred. It's Bill. How are you doing?" Fred, I wondered,
in my half-conscious state, who's Fred? I'd been away from
New York for nearly four weeks and I was starting to feel
like someone else altogether.

Bill, covering for me, needed some information about one

of my patients. "Celia dropped by Hillary's new apartment a couple of days ago," he went on. "Hillary is fine. So are the children. Hillary especially asked her to have me tell you that she went out to visit Rickie once, thought it went pretty well. In fact, they're talking about a visit out for Rickie."

I couldn't believe what I was hearing.

"I'm afraid I don't have any other details," Bill said, anticipating my questions. "So how's your love life?"

I told him of my encounter in Baden-Baden, adding that she was married. "Actually, this afternoon I was walking across a square near Trevi Fountain," I recalled, "and there was a girl coming toward me, carrying books. Sandy-brown hair blowing about, probably American, and I thought, now there's someone I'd like to meet."

"And did you?"

"Of course not."

Bill sighed. "You're going to have to learn to make more of the moment, my friend."

The day before I flew home from London, I found yet another trinket for the bracelet, this time a replica of the English crown. I was starting to believe that what I had left behind only five weeks earlier was a terrible nightmare from which I was only now awakening. My energy had begun to return. I can surely live on my own, I thought. I have friends, and my children. Rickie has been in treatment for less than eight months, and as psychiatric treatment goes, that's not long at all.

For a week after my return I wandered the Upper East Side streets, talking with doormen until I finally located a two-bedroom sublet at Sixty-fifth and Third, on the fourteenth floor of a new building with a package desk that made it particularly convenient for a man living alone.

Our apartment on Seventy-ninth Street had been sold while I was in Europe, and with her usual efficiency, Hillary had moved to Ninetieth between Fifth and Madison, a neighborhood crowded with families because of its proximity to private schools. We hadn't spoken with each other in nearly two months. I had to arrange to pick up my belongings, but had put off phoning her for several days. When I finally did, I felt awkward, unsure of myself, torn between the need to tell her how much I missed her and the children and the desire to sound self-assured and in command of my new life. Our conversation was brief and pointed. I agreed to come by when she was out.

Hillary was pleased that I intended to see John, Mary, and Matthew every weekend, and, as soon as I was organized, to keep them overnight. When she also told me about her visit to Rickie and that she had been informed that if Rickie continued to do well, we could expect to have her home with us for a day in the near future, maybe for Thanksgiving, my sadness abated.

When I came by to pick up my things, Hillary had left signs meticulously identifying every piece of furniture that had belonged to my family, and she thoughtfully added some basic chairs and a couch. She had also earmarked Rickie's possessions. Alone, I sat down on the living room couch for a few minutes and looked about nostalgically, wanting to remain among so many familiar things. Then I abruptly pulled myself up and, after some searching, found a telephone on top of a packing carton and arranged for the movers to come.

Celia Morris helped me pick out more items at Altman's. She was amused when I dragged her to a toy store where I purchased two sets of Märklin electric trains, arranging to have the tracks nailed onto an enormous sheet of plywood so they wouldn't have to be reassembled each time.

"What kind of a bachelor apartment are you planning to have?" she chided. "What'll you do with these when you give your first dinner party?"

"Lean them against the wall, I suppose."

Celia sighed.

I felt immediately comfortable in my new, crisply modern, white-walled apartment. I bought handsome soft green drapes from the former tenant and had a wall built to separate the entry hall from the living room. It reminded me of the apartment in which we had lived during the happiest years of our marriage, but its freshness also spoke to me of a new beginning. Not long after I was ensconced there, I took off my wedding ring and, together with the charms, placed it in my safe-deposit box at the bank. The Bing and Grundahl statues found a special place in my bookcase.

23

Dr. Stuart confirmed Hillary's impressions. Rickie was doing better and was about to be moved to a less restrictive unit, where, as he reminded me, living conditions were a good deal more comfortable. I assured him that even though I had legal custody, Hillary and I would continue to act jointly in any significant decisions. When I asked about visiting, he told me to wait until after her trip home, adding that he had scheduled only one more visit for Hillary, who wanted to bring John along. John did accompany his mother, but since he was too young to be permitted on the floor, Rickie was escorted by an aide in order to spend a few minutes with him in the vast waiting room where Hillary and I had spoken with Miss Jeffers months before.

Hillary sent me a copy of a letter she received shortly afterwards.

Dearest Mommy,

It was so great to see you and John on Saturday. I could see, though, that you were a little bit tense during the visit. Well, so was I, and I'm sure John felt that way too. You must realize we three haven't been together for ages, so naturally we were a little bit nervous. We would be pretty strange people if we didn't have feelings toward each other.

The visits we have are important, but they can't be all good. If we thought that every visit was going to be great, we would be out of touch with reality. What I am really trying to say to you is be yourself, don't hide things from me. If you feel some way, tell me. You will find that things will come much easier and many questions will be answered, just by talking!

I have given it quite a lot of thought and talked it over with Dr. Phillips and think it is time for me to start visiting home. Before you start thinking, what if this or that will happen, try and understand that if I were not strong enough to visit home, I would not even think of mentioning it. I am very sure of myself now. I can take a lot more than ever before. The main question here is, do you feel you could handle the situation? If you feel not ready for this yet, please tell me. I can always wait . . . (anxiously, though!) . . . I am looking forward to seeing home again, your new home, I mean.

I am a very lonely person, even though I have many good friends. When you visit me, I really feel like a whole person, knowing that my mother is sitting right beside me, as we share together our happiness, sadness, laughter, and tears. I am a lucky person to have you as my mother. Someone I can count on, knowing that if I ever felt down or anything, I could talk to you. I love you, Mommy.
All my love.

Rickie xxxooo

24

On Halloween I began a ritual that was to continue for years to come. I picked up the children at three-thirty and we drove to Madison, New Jersey, an affluent suburb near Morristown. Johnny dressed as a pirate, Mary as a ballet dancer, and Matt as a cowboy. There was no fear of razor blades in apples or drugs in candy in those days. I felt that, out of the city, they would have more fun going from door to door and being greeted with delighted laughter and things to fill their shopping bags, as I had as a child.

Owning my own car was a luxury, to be sure, but one that I rationalized as part of my rehabilitation effort. I'd driven a Mercedes in Europe, but in the States in those days the price was still little more than that of a first-class American automobile. I'd bought a four-door maroon sedan which the salesman assured me would last better than a decade.

The first weekend in November we all drove past Morristown to Mendham, a quaint eighteenth-century town not far from where my mother's family had owned a farm before the Second World War. Her own parents had died in Montana when she was a little girl, and Mother, an orphan, was brought east and grew up here. She often took me to the farm to see relatives when I was a small child. Now, as we went along the same narrow country roads, I could smell the moist farmland and the familiar crisp aroma of burning leaves, and I felt a sense of home.

Small wonder that as we passed the Old Mill at Ralston,

a stone building erected in 1730 that had provided flour for Washington's troops during his winter campaign in Morristown, I felt the For Sale sign posted near the gate was more than coincidence. I called a realtor and purchased the property. In the 1930s the mill had been renovated as a residence, and it would serve as our second home for the next five years, a place where I could bring the children weekends and summers, to swim in its pool, trade tales about its hauntings, and walk along the rippling stream whose sound reminded me of Spanish fountains.

On Election Day I had my first date. I felt slightly foolish as I climbed the five flights of stairs in the remodeled brownstone that led to Marion's apartment. A casual friend of Celia Morris's, Marion worked as a copywriter for a large advertising firm. She was in her late twenties, originally from North Carolina, with soft, light brown hair, large hazel eyes, and a round, pretty face. Marion loved to cook. After finishing her graduate work in English literature, she had taken a year off to go to Paris to study at the Cordon Bleu. Although I had asked her out, she had insisted on preparing a gourmet dinner, and I had readily confessed I was getting tired of eating in restaurants. We were seated on the couch in her living room, surrounded by a sea of bright-colored flowered chintz and walls crowded with prints of exquisitely drawn vegetables and fruits. As we were waiting for her surprise dinner to find its way to perfection, she gently asked me about my divorce.

"I've been separated for four months," I said. "Hillary and I have been officially divorced for about three weeks."

"Celia said that your breakup was really quite a surprise. The two of you were always thought of as the perfect couple."

I laughed. "Well . . . that only shows you."

She went back to check her dinner. "Maybe you and Hillary will still get together again," she called out.

I wanted to say "maybe." Instead I said: "I doubt it."

"You never know. Would you, if she wanted, go back to her?"

"That's a funny kind of question."

"Didn't you know? All single girls get around to asking that of divorced men sooner or later. Just protection against getting involved with a man who's still hung up on his ex-wife."

"And if I said yes, I'd go back?"

"Then I'd hope you enjoyed dinner and I'd like to be friends, but nothing more."

Over dinner, the most delicious veal piccata, Marion asked about my children. "You have three or four?"

"Four."

"How old are they? Boys? Girls?"

"Girl fourteen, Rickie. John, nine; Mary, seven; Matthew, five."

"They're living with their mother? In New York? In school?"

"Yes." Then I added, "All except Rickie, that is."

"Oh. Where is she? Boarding school?"

"No. Not exactly." Bill and Celia had kept my confidence. "Rickie is . . . ill. She's in a psychiatric hospital." To this day I don't know why I chose that moment to break my silence.

Marion could not hide her shock. Choking slightly, she reached for some wine. "That's awful," she said. "I mean, that must be terrible for her, for you, and her mother."

"It has been."

"How long?"

"Nearly eight months."

"Is she getting better?"

"It's too soon to say."

We sat there in silence for a few minutes. Then timidly, I asked: "Would you . . . would someone like you . . . ever marry a man my age, with four children and one of them mentally ill?"

"What kind of a question is that, Doctor?"

"I mean . . . I mean . . . I don't know what I mean."

"If you love someone," she replied thoughtfully, "why not?"

"Love? What is love?"

"Don't get cynical on me. I think you're a very attractive and interesting man, and you're hardly old, even if you probably sit around listening to Frank Sinatra sing about being in the autumn of his years, which I doubt you do."

"As a matter of fact—"

"The fact your daughter is ill, well, that and alimony, which I assume you have to pay, and child support and whatever, are enough to give a sensible girl pause. But if she loved you enough, of course she'd marry you."

I couldn't be sure whether I was being offered empty reassurance from a very kind young woman or an honest reply that was very hard to believe. I chose the latter. "Well," I sighed, "no matter what, I couldn't ask anyone to share my life now, the way it is. Besides . . . I'm Catholic."

"My God!" Marion shouted, feigning horror, "you should have told me sooner! Our wonderful romance has just come to an end! I don't ordinarily date Catholics!" She laughed. "I've heard all about the gold and jewels buried under the floors of the Vatican, waiting for the Pope's take-over of the world." She stood up, smiling. "Help me with the dishes and we'll have some coffee."

Later she told me she was planning to move to California, to work for an agency in Los Angeles.

"When?"

"Next month. The job doesn't start until after the first of the year, but that will give me time to locate a place to live and get used to it."

"I'm sorry. I . . . I really wanted to see you again."

"All it takes is an airline ticket and a couple of days."

As it happened, I did see Marion again, a few years later, but only once. She was still working in L.A.; she had mar-

ried and had one child. Her husband was a Catholic and it
was his second marriage. I remember Marion clearly to this
day because she was the first stranger to whom I spoke of
Rickie. She also made me begin to believe that someday I
might marry again.

=== 25 ===

I put my gloveless hands into the pockets of my sheepskin
coat, shivering a little, deeply inhaling the clear, brisk cold
air. As I strode toward Hillary's, I found myself playing the
child's game of walking along the pavement without step-
ping on a crack. It was a rare day, Thanksgiving. And Rickie
was coming home! Only for a few hours, but for the first
time in over eight months.

I felt awkward ringing the bell. Hillary answered, non-
chalantly kissing me on the cheek, and showed me to the
living room. So many familiar things: framed photographs,
the antique card table, the pair of Oriental lamps we had
picked out years before in Boston. Hillary alone had begun
to look curiously unfamiliar. John sat in the far corner of
the room, busily struggling to play his newly acquired sax-
ophone. Mary was in her room reading. Matt ran up and
down the long hall shouting, first pretending he was a policeman, then a space invader, then a soldier, then a policeman again.

Rickie ran out from the kitchen and hugged me tightly
before I'd really had a chance to look at her. I held her for
a moment, my hands on her shoulders, pleased by what I

saw. Except for a bit of lipstick, she wore no makeup. Her navy-blue blouse and plaid skirt fit perfectly; Hillary's doing, no doubt. She'd lost much of the weight that had made her look so bloated in the hospital and her hair was growing long again.

Hillary had rented a car and driver and picked her up at the hospital. "How long have you been here?" I asked.

"Oh, maybe half an hour."

"Welcome home," I said, the words invested with new meaning.

"It's nice to be here. . . ." It seemed she would say "home," but the word vanished before she could express it.

"I wanted to come see you at the hospital after I got back from London," I told her, "but Dr. Stuart thought it better for me to wait until today. I guess he had his reasons." I didn't want to divulge Dr. Stuart's concern over an emerging pattern in which Rickie became more disturbed after hospital visits; if at all possible, he did not want anything to interfere with her planned excursion home.

"Why don't we all sit down in the living room," Hillary suggested, taking Rickie by the arm.

John had stopped playing. He stood up and walked over to stand in front of Rickie. "Hi."

"Hi again," Rickie said, smiling, as she ran her hand through his curly brown hair. John smiled back.

"I saw Christy and her mother last week," Hillary said. "We went shopping. She's staying on at the convent for high school. Has she written you? She said she would."

"I got a card last month. It was cute, one of those funny get-well things with a picture of someone in bed with a bandaged leg, up in a sling."

"Heard from any of the other girls?"

"No."

Most of the girls at school were aware of Rickie's illness, but maybe they didn't know what to say. Or maybe their parents had suggested they just leave Rickie be and let her get better on her own. What do you write to a mental patient? Hope you're not hearing voices anymore? We hope you get better, even though no one ever really does?

"Graduation was lovely," Hillary said. That had been six months earlier.

"You already told me about graduation, Mom."

"Oh, did I? I'm sorry."

I hadn't seen Rickie or Hillary for months, and even though I'd been with the other children practically every weekend, I felt uneasy sitting there listening to their conversation about school and friends and things that had once been part of our everyday life, like some nineteenth-century Nantucket ship captain returning after a two-year voyage to find that his family has established a pattern of living without him. He remains the father, but with regard to daily comings and goings, challenges and triumphs, he has become extraneous.

"Tell us about your friends at the hospital," I suggested.

"Well, you know, there's this girl Mary who was admitted for using drugs, heroin or something like that," Rickie began eagerly, "who comes from this really rich family and her arms are all marked up. The first day she was there she had convulsions. Drugs must be terrible. I certainly wouldn't use them. And then there's Sarah. She's about twenty and she had an abortion and got really depressed. She tried to shoot herself with her father's gun but it was empty. Her parents got her into the hospital and the doctors gave her shock and she can't remember anything."

Hillary was horrified. "Please, Rickie, I don't think we want to hear about all that in such grisly detail. I realize you're seeing a great deal of sad, sordid things, but it isn't a good idea to talk about them here, now."

"What else do I have to talk about?" Rickie asked innocently.

"Well," I interjected briskly, "what kind of things do

you do to keep busy all day? Did you finish that scarf you were knitting?''

"A long time ago, Daddy. Right now I help Sarah get back on her feet, sometimes. And we go to gym. They have this funny old yellow school bus, and in the summer they put all the patients allowed out in it and we went to the beach. It was fun. We ate hot dogs and potato salad and played volleyball. Of course, I only went twice because I was on the closed unit most of the summer.''

Hillary, no doubt thinking she didn't want John and Mary to hear too many more details of hospital life, suggested, "Why don't you go to your rooms and straighten them out until dinner.''

"I don't want to, Mom," John protested. "I want to stay with Rickie.''

"Do as your mother says," I ordered.

Matthew ran, panting, into the living room. "Bang. Bang. Bang. You're dead, Mom. You too, Rickie.''

"Please, Matthew," his mother said. "To your room until I call you." Hillary excused herself and went into the kitchen, which gave me a few minutes alone with Rickie.

"I wish you could stay overnight," I said.

"I do too. But Dr. Phillips said I couldn't, not the first time.''

"He's probably right," I admitted halfheartedly. "How's the food?''

"Horrible! For a while I stopped eating altogether, but they got worried and started to tube feed me.''

I shuddered.

"So I started again. But it's worse than anything at camp. Potatoes, spaghetti, meat loaf, although we don't think there's much meat in it, S.O.S.''

"S.O.S.?''

"You were in the Navy during the war, weren't you Daddy?''

The scar on Rickie's wrist caught my eye. "That seems to be healing nicely," I commented, hiding my distress.

"The doctors took care of it," she said flatly. "Of course, that got me another bath."

"A bath?" Suddenly I realized what she was talking about, visualizing the enormous rooms where long rows of empty tubs stretch forever along bland tile walls.

"I had to sit there for I don't know how long. I kept staring at the large clock on the wall. It had black hands and a red sweeping second hand moving around and around. I felt . . . hypnotized. While I was there they brought in this old lady and put her in another tub. She reminded me of Grandma. It was relaxing. I liked the pine smell . . . but then I had to go to the bathroom. It hurt, but they wouldn't let me. They wouldn't let me smoke either."

"Smoke?"

"I have a cigarette every now and then. It helps pass the time."

"I don't think that's too good an idea, Rickie."

"Everybody smokes!" she protested. Rickie fell suddenly silent, staring into space. "I thought of something when I was in the tub."

"Oh?"

"Did I kill Grandpa?"

"What?" Her question startled me.

"Did I kill Grandpa?" she repeated.

"That's ridiculous, Rickie! Where did you ever get such an idea?"

"Remember? The time he gave me *Rascal*?" That was the name of the little dinghy my father had given Rickie in the summer of 1964. "Remember? I loved *Rascal*. You warned me, you and Grandpa, but I took it out too far into the river and I got caught in the current. You looked so small, standing on the dock. I tried to row back but the water was too strong. I was so frightened. Then you came out in the motorboat and saved me. You were so mad! I cried and you told me it was all right. It was one of those things you learn to grow up. But when we got back to the dock, I could see Grandpa standing there, holding his hand to his chest, breathing so hard. His face was so white! Did I kill him?''

"Of course not, Rickie. Grandpa loved you and you loved him. You didn't hurt him. Besides, he didn't die for over a year after that.''

"But he was sick. Everyone was worried.''

"Grandpa was in his late seventies, Rickie. An old man just goes to sleep one night or stands on a beach, and God takes him. Grandpa died peacefully,'' I reassured her.

"I started to tell Dr. Phillips about it, but he didn't seem too interested. I don't know what he wants to know. He's so serious. I asked him why we never laugh, and he said there was an important article in the psychoanalytic journal that showed how important it was for analysts not to engage their patients in humor. He's got a thing about me trying to punish myself, and he keeps bringing it up, over and over again. I don't really want to punish myself, but he keeps talking about it so much I think maybe he's right . . . and then I start thinking about how to do it.'' Rickie squeezed her fists tightly.

"Dr. Phillips wanted to know if I was angry with you for putting me in the hospital. Everybody there knows you're a psychiatrist. They say the children of psychiatrists are always crazy, but they don't understand why you just put me there and left me there.''

I was taken completely off guard. "I . . . don't know what to say. Are you angry?''

"Only at myself.''

"You mustn't be, Rickie.''

Hillary had come back into the room, and I was thankful she had not heard our conversation.

"Can I wash up before we have dinner?'' Rickie asked.

"Of course. Use the bathroom in Mary's room. I fixed it up with fresh towels for you."

After she was gone, Hillary turned to me nervously. "Is it safe to let her be alone?"

Not wanting to make her any more apprehensive, I replied: "You don't think they'd let her out if they thought she was a risk, do you?"

"Those things she was talking about, they're really terrible."

If she only knew the whole of it, I thought.

"I'm afraid that in a place like that Rickie's going to see lots of things no child her age normally would. I don't like it," she said, worried.

"I'm worried about something else," I admitted.

"What?" Hillary asked anxiously.

"What if all she's exposed to in the hospital is making her worse, not better?"

"Are you saying that to upset me?" Hillary asked accusingly.

"Of course not. Never mind. Actually, I've begun to feel more optimistic. Maybe today is a real turn for the better."

I instantly regretted sharing my concern with Hillary. That day, I didn't want to think about Rickie from a doctor's viewpoint, but I couldn't help thinking of the many patients who get better, then relapse for no discernible reason. Just the excitement of coming home could have put Rickie in a particularly good frame of mind. Dr. Stuart had told me she was off all medications, which struck me as good, but if she were suffering with some form of depression, I also knew she had no protection against black moods engulfing her again. Though I had often confidently hospitalized patients, I was beginning to appreciate firsthand the demoralizing influence of hospital environments, especially on youngsters.

Rickie ate three helpings of turkey, stuffing, cranberry

sauce, and potatoes, devouring them like a refugee from a concentration camp.

"We have mince and pumpkin pie. Have your choice, or both," Hillary urged. Rickie took a piece of both.

"How are things at school, Mary?" Rickie asked. Her tone was pleasant but detached, as if she were referring to people and places that were a part of Mary's life, never her own.

"Fine," Mary replied somewhat self-consciously, smiling, pleased by Rickie's interest.

"Mother Sebastian still there?"

"I think so."

"She's asked about you a number of times, Rickie." Hillary spoke up, trying to recapture some of the casual intimacy that Rickie and the rest of the family had once been able to take for granted.

"I liked Mother Sebastian, and I always thought she liked me too," Rickie replied. "But I remember once, not long before I went to the hospital, she found me in the washroom. I'd missed a class. I was afraid to go, I guess, I don't know why. And she said my behavior was hurting my parents and myself. She told me that if I didn't change I'd be putting another thorn in Jesus' crown. I felt horrible. I didn't want to hurt you . . . or Jesus."

I was furious.

"Of course, that wasn't as bad as the time they called me up in front of the whole school at assembly and took away my très bien card and gave me an indifferent. I was so embarrassed . . . I thought I'd die." There were tears in Rickie's eyes.

"I didn't know about that 'thorn in Christ's crown' thing!" I exclaimed. "Did you, Hillary?"

"Rickie did mention it at the time."

"That woman ought to be thrown out of the order!" I muttered.

"She was only trying to be helpful," Hillary pointed out.

She'd always had a way of defending practically anyone I criticized, even when she agreed with my opinion.

"Helpful! Telling a kid she's adding to Jesus' suffering when she's upset, and embarrassing her in front of the whole school? I'd hardly call that helpful."

"The teachers couldn't have known what Rickie was going through!"

"They should have." I noticed a vague look cross Rickie's face. "Let's drop it. I just think it's outrageous, that's all."

"Why don't we have coffee in the living room," Hillary suggested.

"Can I have some coffee?" Rickie asked.

"Since when did you start drinking coffee?" her mother inquired.

"At the hospital everyone drinks coffee. It wakes you up in the morning, and it sure helps pass the time."

We returned to the living room and sat pretty much as we had before dinner. Matt had brought a few soldiers from his room and was playing with them, while Mary lay on the floor absorbed in a book and John slouched on the sofa, half asleep.

"Do you go to mass at the hospital?" Hillary asked.

"I went once," Rickie answered. "They have a very nice chaplain there, a Father Vickers. Everyone thinks he drinks, but I don't think so. He comes to see me from time to time and we talk. He does funny things. Like every time he says good-bye, or hello, he says "God bless you," like someone sneezed. Once he walked along the corridor from the unit to the recreation area, making the sign of the cross at everyone he passed. Sarah thinks he's sweet."

Thinking I'd caught a look of sadness cross Rickie's face, I asked if something was wrong.

"There are patients at the hospital who have been there for years. Some say it's like home to them, and they can hardly remember what their lives were like before."

"Well, that's something you don't have to worry about, Rickie," I assured her. "I have a room at my place especially for you. And you know you can stay with your mother anytime you want."

"I thought maybe I'd go to boarding school."

"That's an idea," I said encouragingly, knowing it would be a much better arrangement for her than living with a single father.

"If they'll take me."

"Of course they'll take you."

"I don't know about that. There's this one girl who's been in the hospital for two years, on and off, and she says that when she was ready to leave the last time, she couldn't get into any good school because she was crazy."

"Nonsense," I retorted. "I've known plenty of patients who've left hospitals for perfectly fine schools."

"Except that I can't read a lot of the time."

"What do you mean, you can't read?" Hillary was startled.

"I mean that when I try to read, the letters disappear right in front of me, or break up into little pieces, and the harder I stare, the harder it is to see anything. Dr. Phillips says it isn't unusual for a person's ability to concentrate to disappear when they're sick like me, and he says it's going to come back, but I don't see any signs."

"It will," I reassured her.

"I hope so," Rickie sighed. Then, quite unexpectedly, she asked: "Have you been to visit Grandpa's grave?"

"What an odd question, Rickie," Hillary mused. "Why do you ask?"

"I was just wondering. I thought people visited people's graves. If I died, you'd visit mine, wouldn't you?"

"Please, Rickie, don't talk about things like that," her mother cautioned. "You're not going to die."

"But everyone dies, Mama."

Silence.

"I mean, I miss Grandpa. He used to make me feel so . . . alive."

As I drove Rickie back to the hospital, she seemed quite cheerful, and we chatted about my trip to Europe and the Bing and Grundhal statuettes. She couldn't wait to see them, and told me how much she loved the Mercedes, especially since it didn't make her feel motion-sick, as so many automobiles had before. I noticed none of the nervousness or dismay I assumed she might show upon returning, and began to feel genuinely encouraged. Maybe she would hold her improvement, maybe this visit would be the precursor of more visits, and she might even be able to stay with us for a while over the coming Christmas holidays.

However, Dr. Stuart called the following Wednesday to report that Rickie had suffered a serious relapse. "The visit seemed to go well," he assured me. "It's as if she's afraid to get well, as if she doesn't believe she can cope with the challenges of growing up." I knew that recovery from psychiatric illnesses seldom took place in a straight line upward. More often it occurs as a series of improvements interspersed with what seem like relapses in a two-steps-forward, one-step-back pattern. His words were all too familiar—I'd offered similar opinions regarding my own patients, and I had even anticipated them. When he told me that even hospital visits would have to be postponed for a while, my old frustration and despair surged up, but I kept these feelings to myself. I informed Hillary, who now would have to pack up Rickie's presents in brown boxes, mail them at the post office, and hope they reached her in time.

We both knew that this Christmas would be as no other had ever been. We would do our best to make it as happy an occasion as possible for the children, who, as most children of divorced parents, would join reluctantly in two celebrations instead of one. They would undoubtedly notice Rickie's stocking absent from the mantelpiece; Hillary would have sent it, filled with presents, to the hospital. We

could only hope to bear in mind what Christmas was really
all about.

== 26 ==

Rickie wrote to Hillary the week after Christmas.

Dear Mommy,
  *I just wanted to drop you a note and say thank you
for the lovely gifts. Daddy sent me some great ones too.
I'm sorry they won't let you visit right now, but maybe
soon, and let's hope there's no snow to stop you from
coming. Do me a favor. Don't send me anything to eat.
I'm watching my weight. There is one thing I would
like—some more cough drops. The pierced earrings are
perfectly lovely, and the holder is wonderful too. You
know what was really cute, the stuffed snail. I feel the
same way you do, this next year is going to be a great
year for all of us! I made the best I could of Christmas
and I found I really could enjoy it. I am sorry we were
not together for it, but there's always next year. Thanks
for calling me on Saturday. I was surprised they let me
speak on the phone. It made me feel much better.
Thanks again. I love you. See you soon !!!*

                              Much love,
                              Rickie xxoo

=27=

Dr. Stuart called me in early January to inform me that he and Dr. Phillips would be presenting Rickie's case at the medical staff conference the following week. Several outside consultants would be there to evaluate her progress and possibly contribute ideas. "Frankly, I've postponed doing this for a while," he explained. "As you know, patients are usually presented within two or three months. Inasmuch as Rickie is your daughter, I had hoped to get around it, but I'm afraid I can't any longer. I don't know what they'll come up with. You know what these discussions are like. In any event, I'd like to talk with you about it afterwards."

The following week I drove to Westchester. Dr. Stuart led me to his office, gestured for me to sit down, and offered me a cup of coffee, which I refused. He got right down to business. "Dr. Michael Hendricks was at the conference. I believe you know him."

"I've met him a couple of times." I could visualize the white-haired Hendricks, an elderly man so thin and fragile that a gust of wind might push him over. He was considered one of the world's experts on schizophrenia.

"He has, of course, an organic bias," Stuart said.

"I know." While Hendricks did not reject psychological theories and psychotherapy out of hand, he did believe that most serious psychiatric disorders were biochemical in origin and that their treatment required appropriate medications and even electric shock treatments.

121

"Hendricks feels that even though Rickie's not obviously psychotic, at times her illness so overwhelms her ego structure that she should be viewed as episodically psychotic. He wondered about periodicity, but could honestly find none. I must be frank with you. Hendricks would have been happier if the picture were more florid, with sudden acute hallucinations and severe panic. As it is, dating to childhood, developing insidiously, never quite schizophrenic, never quite not, he regarded Rickie's primary diagnosis as a simple, undifferentiated form of schizophrenia, with a poor outlook unless somatic treatments are used effectively. And even then—"

"What treatments?"

"Electric shock. Hendricks recommended a course of fifteen, perhaps twenty, given at a rate of twice a week." Before I could say anything, Stuart went on. "Elliot Goldman, of course, disagreed vigorously."

"Goldman? The borderline man? I've never understood what he's been driving at—a 'neither-nor syndrome'—in between. Bordering what from what?"

"Come now," he replied impatiently. "The term isn't all we'd like it to be, but it isn't the term that's important. Poor ego structure, real problems with dependency and separation, great difficulty leaving home to go away to school, not wanting to grow up, self-absorbed, narcissistic—"

"Please spare me the lecture. I'm perfectly aware of the fact that the borderline syndrome's been carved out of the wilderness between schizophrenia, mood disorders, and characterologic disabilities. I can't tell you why the classification seems contrived to me, but it does. I presume Goldman felt Rickie fitted his category." Some portion of my intensity was rooted in the fear that Rickie might fulfill the criteria for a borderline diagnosis, and the realization that my colleagues considered such patients among the most difficult to treat successfully. I was also afraid my own estimate of Rickie's condition as a form of depression would be further discounted.

Stuart smiled slightly. "Naturally," he replied. "And if Rickie is borderline, Goldman felt the worst thing would be to subject her to shock. He recommended intensive psychotherapy. One therapist, three or four sessions a week, relying heavily on the doctor-patient relationship and transference as the treatment of choice. That could go on for—"

"Several years," I glumly finished his sentence.

"He considered medications contraindicated," Stuart added.

"Including antidepressants?"

"Well, not entirely, although he believes antidepressants may stimulate distress and disorganization as often as help in such patients."

"What about lithium?"

"There's no periodicity, no mood swings in Rickie's case."

Schizophrenia. Borderline. Depression. Categories that I had used so assuredly in the past buzzed crazily through my mind like so many space particles, fast losing their meaning, though none of their power to dictate treatment. Yet still I yearned for her doctors to seize on one of them, to end uncertainty with their pronouncement. "What do you now think Rickie's diagnosis is, Dr. Stuart?"

"Frankly, I still don't know. You know how very difficult it can be to arrive at a diagnosis in an adolescent. I've even considered hysteria. Rickie's a young woman, with disturbing life situations she can't handle, onset of menses, an erratic course of illness, symptoms that change their appearance like a chameleon and some that don't make sense, like her numbness and her complaints of poor vision at times, or sudden, seemingly unprovoked outbursts of rage which vanish as quickly as they come. From a psychological point of view, she has a very close attachment with you, her father, who, I need not remind you is a psychiatrist. Maybe we're dealing with hysteria or a hysterical character disorder.''

If Rickie's condition could be explained on the basis of hysteria, I knew her ultimate prognosis should be excellent. ''You mentioned that at the conference?''

''They accused my countertransference of showing,'' he said, implying that his favorable attitude toward Rickie might have invested his diagnosis with a favorable outlook. I recognized that he was trying hard, but unsuccessfully, to lighten our conversation. ''Goldman and Hendricks both thought I was struggling to deal with my own fondness toward her. She's a charming, warm, intelligent person, and it's hard to be completely objective.''

''And the final decision?''

''Mine to make. I think she should have a long trial of active psychotherapy.''

''How long?'' I asked.

''A year. Maybe two.''

Being confronted so bluntly with what seemed like an eternity, I couldn't hide a look of profound dismay, although in those days it was still not unusual for patients to spend several years in sanitarialike the fashionable Austin Riggs in Stockbridge, Massachusetts, or Chestnut Lodge in Maryland, engaged in probing psychoanalysis. In contrast to today's quick in-and-out practice, these prolonged stays were not only considered a far more effective form of treatment, but they were regarded as a special prerogative of the rich, the famous, the talented, the select and favored few.

''Look,'' he admitted, ''it isn't easy to know what to do. I've tried to handle things as objectively as I could. I have a daughter of my own, and it's easy for me to put myself in your place. The fact that you're a psychiatrist and on the staff colors this whole situation. It's even occurred to me that Rickie's illness might be a bid for your attention.''

"Dr. Stuart, you sound like you're reaching pretty far. I don't think the question now is so much why Rickie became ill, but why she can't get, isn't getting, better! Do you have an answer to that question?"

"No, Doctor. Do you?"

Part Two

== 28 ==

The battle to cure Rickie continued at Westchester throughout 1967, 1968, and into the winter of 1969. Rickie's fifteenth birthday had come and gone, and her sixteenth; she was fast approaching seventeen.

I suppose I could sum it up in four words—more of the same—although that seems an ironic description of two and a half years of my life. But that's what it was. I had sessions with Dr. Phillips and saw Dr. Stuart on rounds once a week. I made more pottery and wrote more poems. I watched the Vietnam War on the evening news, soap operas in the daytime, and The Fugitive *with David Janssen. It was the story of this doctor falsely accused of having murdered his wife. Week after week he would have a new adventure, running away from a policeman who was intent on recapturing him and putting him in prison. As I watched the film clips of Robert Kennedy's assassination, I thought that maybe I wasn't so bad off after all. At least it wasn't me or one of my parents, even though it was terribly upsetting.*

Patients came and went, except for some of the old regulars. Winters and summers passed, and we had an occasional trip to the hospital's beach on the Sound. I didn't have much school. Every time I tried to take a class—I still hadn't finished the eighth grade—I'd only last a few days. When I knew I couldn't learn anything—it was as if I just couldn't get the information into my head, much less keep

129

it there—I'd get upset and create a scene or hurt myself in
some way, and the usual results would ensue.

I thought of suicide, sure. Who wouldn't under those cir-
cumstances? But I'd pray, and dream about a future, fuzzy
dreams, telling myself to hang on and try again.

I now realize that the fact that neither Hillary nor I moved
to have Rickie transferred elsewhere for reevaluation and
perhaps a different approach was a vivid example of Pavlov-
ian conditioning.

Pavlov demonstrated a principle called intermittent stimulation. In one of his famous experiments he showed that if
you ring a bell and consistently offer the caged laboratory
animal food, the rabbit or guinea pig will rush to the feeding box whenever the bell is rung. If, with equal consis-
tency, there is never any food in the box when the bell
sounds, the animal will quickly learn not to respond to it.
However, if when the bell rings there's sometimes food and
sometimes not, the animal will eventually be confused and
immobilized by the complete lack of predictability.

We were immobilized by Rickie's unpredictable episodes
of improvement and relapse, our anxieties ameliorated by
the promise that lasting recovery would eventually result
from "long-term dynamic psychotherapy," "milieu therapy"—a term used to describe everything else that takes
place in the hospital from nursing care and interactions with
other patients to playing baseball, making pottery, and taking part in dramatic skits, all hopefully designed to restore
patients' morale and teach them corrective things about
themselves and others that they somehow failed to learn
outside—and "efforts to relieve her distress by various psy-
choactive drugs." I do think she was given lithium for a
while—a salt compound used in the treatment of manic-
depressive patients—because I was told that she had been
seen by an expert consultant in the use of lithium who had
recommended it. But I never obtained a coherent, detailed

accounting of the particular medicines that Rickie received. I have always assumed that this lack of communication was partly attributable to an unspoken policy aimed at reducing the likelihood of Rickie's psychiatrist father's intrusion in her various regimens. In those days, moreover, physicians felt less compelled to inform families of such specifics, and the "right to know" had not yet been as legally clarified. Of course, I could have insisted, but I was honestly afraid of interfering in any way that might jeopardize her care.

Separately now, Hillary or I would drive up to the hospital every few months when Rickie appeared to be better, and take her to White Plains for shopping and an ice cream soda; almost invariably, Dr. Stuart would inform us within a few days that something—our visits perhaps, or an undisclosed event on the ward, or a push to have her start school—had triggered a recurrence of her painful emotional state or agitated behavior, and that once again the no-visiting policy would have to be put into effect. Stuart's bimonthly telephone reports began to sound so similar that they might have been prerecorded and delivered on a cassette player.

"She did have a very nice birthday party that the nurses and patients arranged for her," he told me. "Yes, she did get your present and her mother's. No, the fact that you haven't heard from her doesn't mean anything. She's having difficulty writing. But she knows we talk and she always asks me to remember her to you and her mother and the other children. No, she's not asking to go home. I'm not at liberty to pass on to you anything she tells me. Confidentiality is particularly important to teenagers. Rebellious? Suicidal? No. Not now. No, there really aren't any new drugs. Trying to help her resolve a lot of guilt. Want her to take more responsibility for herself. You might call it weaning. We did try to get her back in school again, but it just didn't work out. I haven't altered my thinking. I speak with Rickie's mother once a week. Incidentally, Mrs. Flach has been asking about orthomolecular therapy—you know, that vitamin stuff. I told her that the Canadian Psychiatric Association has a study going on that just about disproves that theory. Would you mind helping clear her mind about that? Thank you. I'll speak to you next week.''

He did once mention that he had tried the antidepressants, but had stopped them after two months because, in his opinion, they seemed to be having little real effect. When I tried to inquire as to which of the antidepressants had been used and whether Rickie had been given a sufficient dosage for an adequate period, he said he didn't recall offhand and would have to check the chart. I brought the question up again some weeks later only to be reminded gently but firmly that my medical opinions were not welcome when it came to Rickie's care. Although her own information about nutritional therapy was sparse, Hillary urged me several times to press for it; however, knowing that it would never be implemented at Westchester, and having learned from colleagues familiar with it that orthomolecular therapy was held in general disrepute, verging on charlatanism, I did not.

It was as if Rickie had been sucked into a black hole somewhere in the middle of distant stars and vanished.

During those years, I often reminded myself that the only reality is the one we know, a premise that guided me in carrying out psychotherapy. I tried to help patients see another reality, beyond and better than the one to which they had grown accustomed. I couldn't help worrying about the fact that Rickie, being so very young, had so few frames of reference from the past against which to measure and interpret her passage through adolescence, especially given the decidedly unnatural context of a psychiatric hospital.

My own reality consisted of work, which filled up my hours and gave me a feeling of continuity, a sense that past and future were still somehow connected. Each week I lectured first-year medical students in language relevant to everyone's life and with such enthusiasm that the number of graduates who chose psychiatry as a specialty nearly doubled. I continued to direct the activities on the metabolic research unit at Payne Whitney, where biochemist Farouk Faragella and I made use of new procedures such as labeled isotopes. We discovered that calcium loss manifested by depressed patients not only reversed itself with recovery, but that the calcium actually returned to bone where it belonged. I also began to dabble with new ideas, extensively reading about the nature of creativity, spending an occasional weekend at one conference center or another, perhaps an encounter group with Sherman Kingsbury or a meditation experience with Alan Watts, intentionally trying to allow more originality to creep into my own thinking. I was also rapidly regaining my expertise at separating my professional career, which once again appeared to be moving forward, from my personal life, which was also slowly emerging from its shambles.

My children helped. Whether I was showing John how to outline a history textbook, so he could more efficiently review at test time, or taking Matthew for a drive into the country in the middle of a thunderstorm to reassure him there was nothing to be afraid of when lightning splintered the evening darkness, or sitting with Mary at a Walt Disney revival of *Snow White*, her hand holding tightly onto mine, the children were bearers of life, energy, love. Sensing how much I needed them, they gave of themselves without restraint or ambivalence, with the freedom and innocence of which children alone are capable. On weekends they stayed with me; if I had to go out, on return I could hear them scrambling to reach the door, shouting with delight. They were my children, and they were fast becoming my friends.

I wasn't made to live alone, and Catholic or not, I gradually came to the conclusion that I would remarry should the opportunity arise. The radical changes taking place in those days in the cultural fabric of the country, and within the Church itself, helped put my conscience to rest on this matter.

However, I was becoming slightly discouraged about my prospects, until, in the fall of 1968, Celia Morris informed me that a mutual friend of ours had moved back from Washington with her two children and was living only a few blocks from me. Recently divorced, she had taken a job as a social worker. Remembering Joyce as a vivacious, somewhat temperamental, highly intelligent young woman, I telephoned her without hesitation.

An only child, Joyce had attended a small private school for girls in Brooklyn and had been elected to Phi Beta Kappa at Mount Holyoke College, where she had majored in religion. She too had been brought up Catholic, but that was no more a deterrent to ending her marriage than her reluctance to disrupt her children's life and to hurt her husband, whom she nonetheless respected while feeling they were seriously unsuited to each other.

Although she was in her late twenties, I felt no age difference. And I was sure she knew about Rickie, having undoubtedly kept abreast of events in my life through the grapevine of mutual acquaintances. She offered an important quality of the familiar, and I felt comfortable with her. Joyce was also a singularly attractive woman; tall, though not as tall as Hillary, lithe, athletic, dark-haired, with a remarkably enchanting smile.

The first few times we saw each other, however, I saw little of her smile. Reminding me of myself two years earlier, she had lost weight and looked tired, for the past months had been a painful ordeal. Understandably, she seemed much more interested in patience than in romance, and in me she found someone who had indeed grown long in patience.

We began to see each other several times a week. In the beginning I divided my time between Joyce, Joyce and her two daughters—Lisa, then five, and Laura, three—and my own children. Gradually we did more things all together, spending weekends in the country at the mill, trick-or-

treating, hanging birthday balloons, eating ice cream sun-
daes, going to movies, and all the other adventures that
divorced parents come to rely on.

When she found herself again, we occasionally spoke of
marriage. I understood her own uncertainties, and although
Joyce had seemed most understanding of and unruffled by
my ongoing responsibilities to Rickie, I nonetheless felt unable to embark wholeheartedly upon a new life until Rickie
had finally recovered. And I had no sense left of when that
might be.

One evening during the 1968 Christmas holidays, Joyce
had taken her children to visit her parents and I was alone
in my apartment. I took out my copy of my old wedding
album. There were the black and white photographs of
Hillary leaving her apartment on the way to the church, the
doorman holding an umbrella to protect her against the light
rain; the reception line full of faces I had not seen in years;
my father and mother dancing with each other; and Hillary
and myself, looking so young in the backseat of the limousine, driving away. I glanced through letters I saved from
our courtship and early on in our marriage, the clever card
she'd made and sent to me the summer I was studying trop-
ical medicine in Cuba. I reread the brief note that had accompanied the statue of St. Luke the Physician, her gift on
my thirtieth birthday, in which she told me how happy she
was with our life together and how much she loved me. I
reread the letters to reassure myself that all that had happened had, in fact, happened. In the end, convinced that I
had no choice but to begin again, free of lingering attach-
ments, I carefully put away a few of the more cherished
ones and threw the rest down the incinerator.

I knew it was little more than a gesture, that the events of
the past were deeply embedded in my mind forever and that
I could, if I wanted, call them back at will. I had more than
forty years behind me to help orient myself in time and space.

Rickie did not. I asked myself: What if Rickie could not

hold on to memories of home, of childhood, of family and school? What if they slipped away, ever so quietly, so that the hospital and the patients and the universe of illness became her only reality?

A few days before my forty-second birthday, I received a poem from Rickie in the mail along with a handmade birthday card.

MY WORLD

My world, my world alone
Upon which no man has traveled
Ideas, fantasies, delusions, imagination
Is my world
In my world
The air speaks to me softly as it
Whispers through the trees
The clouds are cotton balls
Stretching across the sky.

I stand at the cornerstone of my world
Looking around, up, down, across
And beyond there's a fire over the hill
Burning out useless ideas
Bad thoughts all turn to ashes.

In my world, the sun shines always
It never sets
Nothing ever ends.
My world is filled with past, present, and future.
My world is so large it would
Take me 'til eternity to explore it all
Yet it is so small a man could hold it
In his bare hands.

In my world, there is everything imaginable.
But still something is missing.

Maybe someday I shall find this something.
Then I can rule my world forever
In peace.

The only reality, I reflected sadly, as I had that night at Bill and Celia's, is the one we know.

29

It was Valentine's Day, 1969. I had trudged through a heavy February snowstorm and had just brushed off my coat and hung it up when Bernice buzzed me on the intercom.

"There's a young woman on the phone for you. She says her name is Donna. Won't tell me what it's about. Shall I tell her you're in session with a patient?"

"Yes. No, wait a minute. That name sounds vaguely familiar . . . I'll take it."

"Is this Rickie's father?" She spoke so softly and in such a hoarse voice I could hardly make out what she was saying. "I'm a friend of hers."

"Of Rickie's?" I was bewildered.

"At the hospital. I'm calling you from a pay phone . . . I only have a minute, because I don't have permission to make calls. So please, listen. It's about Rickie. She's being kept in isolation. She's been there for nearly two weeks. If you don't do something, I think she'll die!"

"Please, Donna. I appreciate your calling, but . . . are you sure?"

"Believe me, I'm telling you the truth. Oh, Miss Henry's coming. 'Bye."

I dialed Dr. Stuart's number as soon as Donna had hung up. His secretary told me that he had gone abroad to a medical meeting and wouldn't return until the following Monday. It was two o'clock. I canceled my late afternoon appointments and was at the hospital by three.

The nurse at the visitors' information desk was firm. "I'm sorry. You should know better. Rickie isn't permitted any visitors. You should have called Dr. Stuart."

"He's away. Look here, I've just learned that Rickie's been in isolation for two weeks. That's outrageous! I drove all the way from the city and I want to see her. Now!"

"Parents are requested to telephone first. That's the rule."

"Didn't you hear what I said? Right now!"

"You'll have to speak with the doctor."

"Which doctor?"

"I'll have to find out."

"How about Dr. Phillips?"

Ignoring me, she pushed several keys on the switchboard. I tried to hear her conversation, but she unabashedly turned away and whispered into the mouthpiece.

"Dr. Phillips feels it best for you to speak with Dr. Wheelock," she informed me, looking up again.

"Who's Dr. Wheelock?" I asked impatiently.

"He is covering in Dr. Stuart's absence." She directed me to a makeshift office, empty but for a gray metal desk and a couple of straight chairs, where I waited for ten minutes.

"Well, Dr. Flach, I don't believe we've met before." Wheelock was a tall, blond-haired man, with large, craggy features and a heavy chin. He used carefully measured phrases, speaking in a deep raspy voice and coughing several times as he took a seat behind the desk. "As a matter of fact, I was just reviewing Rickie's case this afternoon. I have her file here. Would you care to look at it?"

I was startled that he seemed about to treat me as a consultant on the case instead of a father. Quickly recognizing his faux pas, he opened a drawer and shoved the folder inside.

"I'd rather see my daughter!"

"I'm not so sure that would be wise . . . for Rickie's sake, you understand." He bit his lower lip nervously, as if to contain annoyance.

"Two weeks in isolation, for anyone, is positively inhuman," I said grimly. "Who made this decision? Phillips? Stuart?"

"As a matter of fact, I did." His arrogance irked me. "The first lesson we try to teach our patients is the consequence of unacceptable behavior. That's a lesson Rickie's had a hard time learning." Then, almost as an afterthought, he asked: "How did you learn of her most recent development?"

"I'd rather not say."

"I can put two and two together," Wheelock insinuated. "I suppose someone here at the hospital keeps you informed . . . a staff member perhaps . . ."

"Keeps me informed! What kind of a statement is that for a doctor to make to a patient's father?"

"Don't misunderstand me. I don't know Rickie very well, though I gather she is a sweet child in many ways. But it's our job to make her understand that certain kinds of behavior are simply . . . out of the question."

"What kind of behavior?"

"Sneaking cigarettes in the bathroom. Breaking things. Screaming at nurses. Refusing to take medication. Not eating. You've seen this a hundred times yourself, I'm sure, in schizophrenic patients."

"Dr. Stuart hasn't been so sure of that diagnosis!"

"Dr. Stuart is entitled to his point of view. So am I. I believe she is schizophrenic . . . and that she may or may not be curable. You and her mother must be prepared for that possibility.''

"There are some people, Dr. Wheelock, who feel that schizophrenia is nothing more than a wastebasket—a category for people whom we doctors don't understand.''

"Come, come. Surely you know how easy it is for parents to deny their own youngster's pathology.''

"Don't be condescending!''

"I'm trying not to. But you seem to forget that you're a physician. I should think a man in your position would know that we're attempting to create a community of patients here—''

"By putting them in isolation? What kind of a community is that? What impact do you think a hospital environment has on a suggestible child? How often have you done this to Rickie before?'' I was trembling with rage.

"Isolation is a discipline that works.''

"I asked how often Rickie has been treated this way, without my permission!''

"Surely you know, Doctor, that we do not have to defer to you in such matters as isolation, cold wet packs, or any other routine procedure designed to control patients.''

"What are you running, a hospital or a prison?''

"A damned good hospital!'' he shouted. "You ought to know. You're part of it.''

"I am not a part of it! I would never consider treating anyone the way you're treating Rickie!''

"Are you always such a difficult man?''

"I've learned to be.''

"You know as well as I that we didn't make your daughter ill. Children don't become what they are in an emotional vacuum. Childhood, home, parents all contribute.''

"Damn you, Wheelock. I'm very familiar with all the theories. I don't see why I should sit here and listen to someone I've never seen before, who isn't even Rickie's doctor, go on about her this way. I don't know how much you even know about the case. I want to see my daughter!''

"Let me remind you that when you admitted Rickie, you signed papers agreeing to abide by our rules. Controlling visitation rights is one of them.''

"Are you telling me I can't see her?''

"It wouldn't be good for either of you.''

"Let me be the judge of that! What happens if I refuse to go along with what you're saying?''

"Well, you're her father. You can always take her out,'' he said, half smiling. "Rickie hasn't been our easiest patient.''

"What are you saying?''

"Either you follow our regimen or remove her.''

"Why, you . . .'' I found myself struggling with an intense urge to punch the man.

"I think we'd better end this discussion, Dr. Flach, before one of us says something he'll regret. Dr. Stuart will be back next week. You can review this whole matter with him then.''

I felt utterly powerless and dreadfully negligent. How could I have put my faith . . . ? I felt like seizing his keys, letting myself onto Rickie's unit, and taking her out of there once and for all. Only the fact that no alternatives were apparent and that Stuart would be back in a couple of days kept me from insisting on her immediate release. On the way out I stopped by his office and made an appointment to see Stuart the day he returned.

=== 30 ===

Hillary accompanied me to the meeting.

"Winter's my favorite season." Stuart gazed immediately out at the snow-filled gardens, calling our attention to a snowman some patients had built, carrot nose and all, about ten feet away.

"You know why we're here?" I could not hide my anger, but I felt confident that Stuart knew it was not directed at him.

"I do."

"How could you do such a thing?" Hillary asked plaintively.

"It wasn't my idea. In fact, if I had been here, it would never have happened. When I found out, I was as angry as you are."

"How could Dr. Wheelock have dared permit something like that to be done to another doctor's patient?" Hillary demanded.

"As the supervisor in my absence, that was his prerogative. I'd like you to know that Dr. Phillips wasn't happy about it either, but as a resident, he didn't have the authority to countermand Wheelock's orders. Wheelock and I often don't see eye to eye on things. I'm sure your husband will tell you that can be the case among professionals working in the same institution."

"Still," she sighed.

"And you have to realize that his action was partly taken out of desperation."

142

"Desperation?" I was frankly disbelieving. "The man's a poor excuse for a human being!"

The look on Stuart's face betrayed his full agreement. "Rickie's been here a long time, nearly three years," he commented. "What's more significant is that she's obviously not progressing the way any of us would wish. In the last month she's been quite regressed."

"What does that mean?" Hillary asked apprehensively.

"Loosely—not being able to cope with ordinary responsibilities, self-destructive, disorganized. I see a real risk of her becoming chronically disabled."

"What are you getting at?" I asked pointedly.

"I went directly to see Rickie this morning. She was still in isolation. When Miss Henry and I tried to help her up off the floor, she took a few steps, lost her balance, and fell down again. She struck her head and broke her nose. It's really not a serious injury, but she is in the infirmary. I told her that her father had been here the other day and that you were both very upset by what happened. She just didn't seem to care . . . about anything."

Hillary gasped.

"I've always tried to level with you, and I won't make an exception today. After I left Rickie, I called in Dr. Hendricks again. He feels, as he always has, that Rickie should receive electric shock treatments."

"We'll take her out before we permit that!" Hillary stated categorically.

"She's much too ill for you to even think of that," Stuart said. "Believe me."

"Shock treatments to a girl of sixteen?" I was surprised.

"It's done, and not infrequently, as a matter of fact."

"How many treatments?" I asked.

"Fifteen. Maybe twenty."

"Twenty!" Hillary exclaimed.

"That's standard in regressed schizophrenia."

"I just don't know," I said tiredly.

"Just what are these treatments like?" Hillary asked sternly.

"They're not as awful as people make them out to be," Stuart replied. "Your husband can describe them."

"I'd rather you," I said.

"The patient is given intravenous medication to put her to sleep, along with muscular relaxants so there's no actual physical convulsion, even though they're called convulsive treatments. The treatment is administered by means of two electrodes placed over the temples. It's all over in seconds. When Rickie wakes up, she won't even remember having had it."

Hillary shifted uneasily in her chair.

"There's another matter I have to bring up with you," Stuart went on. "Dr. Wheelock conveyed the details of his encounter with you to some of our colleagues. I'm afraid some of them expressed the opinion that if you aren't happy with what the hospital has done for Rickie, you should remove her."

"By whom was this opinion expressed?" I was infuriated.

"I'd rather not say, Dr. Flach, particularly since you are officially a staff member yourself, and because personally, I think they've taken an outrageous position."

"Do you really think we'd leave her here after this?" Hillary said determinedly.

"I guess someone just doesn't want to be reminded of the fact she isn't any better," I added caustically.

"Look here," said Stuart, trying to soothe us, "shock just might bring her to a better level of functioning. If she responds, perhaps she could even go to a halfway house, where at least she might be less of a problem and suffer less."

I stood up and began to pace the room. "Between her

mother and myself, we've spent a great deal of money on Rickie's care. Even if she stayed here, and even with the courtesy the hospital has extended, we couldn't afford to go on indefinitely.''

"She could be transferred to a state facility," Stuart pointed out.

"Oh, no!" Hillary gasped.

"That's not the worst thing in the world," he insisted. "Some of them are well run. I've seen patients who've done poorly in private settings improve rather dramatically in other kinds of hospitals. Exhausting family resources is not an uncommon problem in this sort of disease. I personally think it's important not to get to that point, to keep something in reserve to help the patient once she's discharged."

"So it boils down to shock or a state institution?" I asked, bitterness mingling with resignation.

"Pretty much so."

"What would you do if Rickie were your daughter, Dr. Stuart?" My question was sincere.

"Rickie's not my daughter . . . although I've come to love her dearly. You have to make this decision yourselves, the two of you."

"I'm so scared," Hillary confessed miserably. "Do you really think it might help Rickie?"

"I honestly can't say," Stuart replied frankly. "When I was studying in London some years ago, shock was quite widely used. The results were uneven. Some did well, others didn't. Frankly, I never cared for it. But I must acknowledge never seeing any serious physical complications result."

"I thought there was a terrible memory loss and brain damage," Hillary said.

"The memory loss is usually temporary, and there's never been any real evidence of brain damage. I think the worst part of the whole procedure can be the way it convinces patients—and families—that what is being treated is a form of insanity. It has a demoralizing influence, particularly for those patients who don't respond favorably.''

I concurred. ''I won't agree to anything like this without another opinion.''

''Of course.''

''Does Rickie know about this?'' Hillary wanted to know.

''I've discussed it with her.''

''And what does she think?''

''Rickie said she'd do anything to get better.''

Rickie had endured hours, weeks, years of anguish, I reflected. If she refused to give up hope, who were we to let ourselves do so?

=== 31 ===

Dr. Phillips told me they were going to give me shock treatments and that my parents had agreed.

At first I didn't mind them. You knew when you were scheduled—like Monday, Wednesday, and Friday—and you'd go to the shock room and lie down on a stretcher. You were in your strong dress or some cotton pajamas, and covered with a sheet. You'd put out your arm so they could give you an IV with Sodium Pentothal. It induces sleep, and it was always a great sleep.

In Westchester they had the jukebox in the shock room, since it was also our rec room. It had beds in it along one wall, and on the assigned days they folded up the Ping-Pong table and pulled out the beds. After a shock session was over, they'd push the beds over and open up the Ping-Pong tables again. We spent a lot of time there, one way or another!

Through it all, I was listening to the music I loved. I went along with the Beatles and Simon and Garfunkel. In all of the songs, a lot of us would find personal meaning. There was this one song, "The End of the World," where the words seemed to be speaking right to me:

> *It's the end of the world*
> *Why does my heart go on singing,*
> *Why do these eyes of mine cry;*
> *Don't they know it's the end of the world*
> *It ended when you said good-bye.*

Most of the time I wanted to get better. That's why I looked ahead to shock. I believed it would help me.

Eventually they ran out of veins in my arms and they had to find one in my neck. Toward the end of the regimen they put me in a criblike bed because giving me Sodium Pentothal in the neck was so painful; I might jerk and fall out of a regular bed.

Once, I woke up after a treatment and couldn't breathe. Apparently they had given me too much muscle relaxant. I was terrified. Fortunately someone noticed my plight and got me breathing again in a hurry. I didn't look ahead to treatments after that. I was just afraid.

I was afraid the treatments would work too, since getting better was a very frightening prospect. After three years in Westchester, I was afraid I didn't have the skills I'd need to make it outside. If I improved, I'd have to move to an open unit, eventually out of the hospital altogether, and I didn't cope too well with change. I'd get close to a staff nurse and then they'd transfer her to another ward or she'd go on to a different job, and often I'd have what they called a relapse. When I heard that song, I would think of a nurse leaving or my being moved again, or of my grandfather dying.

There was another song we all had a lot of fun with, "They're Coming to Take Us Away Again, ho ho, hee hee . . . " We had a ball with that one.

Another one of my favorites went:

> *We gotta get out of this place*
> *If it's the last thing we ever do*
> *We gotta get out of this place*
> *Girl, there's a better life for me and you!*

My urge to run away got stronger. I had always had it. In the hospital I'd take every chance I had to be alone or to get away from people. Even on short walks on the grounds, I'd take off. They'd catch me right away, though. Often I'd lay in bed at night and try to figure out how I could escape and never have to come back. In my dreams I'd run and run, all night long. But in the morning I was still right there.

32

By the time Rickie's course of eighteen shock treatments had been completed, it was nearly the end of July. She later told me of her fear of them, and of her amazement that afterwards she could recall so little of the experience. As usual, the hospital grapevine had been replete with horror stories of patients claiming to remember every detail, the electricity surging through the brain, thrashing around on the table, biting off pieces of their tongues, helplessly aware of Frankenstein's assistants laughing as they pressed the button again and again. Not for the first time, I was struck by her genuine courage.

Hillary and I met again with Dr. Stuart, and to our surprise, Dr. Phillips was there too. In his late twenties, he did indeed resemble Steve Allen. Unlike Allen, however, he seemed tense and reserved and spoke little.

"You're going to see Rickie in a few minutes," Stuart told us, "and I think you'll be surprised. I am, a bit. She seems like a new person. If her improvement holds over the next few weeks, we can start talking about discharging her."

It seemed so simple.

"You're not thinking of having her come home?" Hillary blurted. "I mean, I'm so thrilled she's better, I can't find the words to express it. But . . . I couldn't handle her. I have three other children to take care of. I wouldn't know what to do with Rickie . . . unless you can guarantee me she's out of this for good."

"She can live with me," I offered eagerly. "That's really been the plan all along. I'll have to get a housekeeper, and Rickie would have to be able to adjust to a school program—"

"Not back to the convent," her mother added.

"We're in complete agreement there, Hillary."

"I think Rickie will need a special school," Stuart suggested. "She's been away from studies for a long time. Have you considered a boarding school, one with some psychiatric input?"

"Such as?" Hillary inquired.

"There are several. If you can afford it, you might consider Cherry Lawn, in Connecticut. It's one of the better programs. I've sent a number of youngsters there after discharge, and they've generally done well. Of course," Stuart went on, "you'll have to visit the school first, and so will Rickie. I can arrange for that. But first things first. Let's go see your daughter!"

We hadn't seen Rickie since the treatments, and as so

often in the past, the information in our possession was secondhand. We had no idea what to expect. What would she remember? How would she react to us? Would she be angry at us for agreeing to the treatments? Would she really be better, or was the word only a euphemism to reassure the doctors that she had responded well to shock?

I felt awkward, self-conscious, uncertain as we entered the unit. At my first glimpse of Rickie I could not help but be startled by how womanly she looked in a rose-colored dress that Hillary had sent for her birthday, her eyes sparkling, a bit pudgy, but on the whole a very pretty young woman. When she'd been feeling well in the past, she'd always run like a child to greet us, but this time she walked briskly toward us, her high heels tapping on the tile floor. She embraced first Hillary, then me.

"How are you, sweetheart?" I asked.

"I really feel great!"

Hillary hugged her again. "You look so grown-up."

"I am, Mom. Of course, my memory's not too great. In fact, I don't remember much of anything. Except for a headache every now and then, the treatments didn't hurt at all. But I must have been awful."

"What do you mean, Rickie?" her mother asked.

"I mean . . . well, Miss Henry tells me I used to behave badly and that they had to put me in isolation for a long time. Was I awful?"

"No," Dr. Stuart spoke up. "You were very sick, Rickie, and now you're better."

"Sometimes I feel really . . . normal."

"You are." I seconded Stuart's observation.

"Can I go home now? Today?" She looked straight at Stuart and Phillips. Phillips said nothing. "Not today, Rickie, but soon," Stuart replied.

"How soon?"

"Oh, maybe a visit next week, and then, if everything goes well, a couple more, and then good-bye to this place."

"Forever," Hillary cried enthusiastically.

Rickie swung around like a ballet dancer, raised her arms and shouted: "Good-bye Ward B! Good-bye! Good-bye! Good-bye!" her mood was contagious, and I thought that both Stuart and Phillips were about to applaud.

An old woman sitting at a bridge table writing a letter was the only other patient on the floor. "Hey, Rickie," she called out, "don't make us all feel so bad. Some of us have to stay on here forever. Besides, you'll be back! You'll see. How can we get along without you?"

"I will not!" Rickie yelled. "I hate this place! I'll never come back here!" She turned to Dr. Phillips. "Wait here. I want to get something."

She was back in less than a minute, holding a dilapidated, roughly resewn Raggedy Ann in her arms like a newborn baby. "This is for you, Dr. Phillips."

Phillips took the doll from her and stood there awkwardly holding it.

"Why, Rickie . . . no. Raggedy Ann is your favorite thing," Dr. Stuart said.

"Raggedy Ann belonged to the Rickie who came here a long time ago. He's been my dearest friend. I want Dr. Phillips and you to have him. He doesn't belong where I'm going."

Rickie's brief visit to New York went well. She spent one night in my apartment, in the extra bedroom filled with her old toys and mementos. Once during the night I thought I heard Rickie moving about in the little room, but when I got up to check, she seemed sound asleep, the covers pulled tightly over her head. I looked around the room and smiled. Evidently she had been playing with her dolls, as she had so many years before.

I was amazed how quickly everyone, including myself, began to distance ourselves from the nightmare of the past years. Talk of school and friends replaced words like "treat-

ment'' and ''progress.'' Hillary, Rickie, and I visited
Cherry Lawn and agreed that it was the place for her. On
the way back, I dropped two very happy women at Altman's
to shop for an appropriate wardrobe for a young lady about
to reenter school. How quickly we forget. I noticed a subtle
but very significant change in Hillary's attitude toward me—
greater warmth, at times a genuinely affectionate tone in her
voice.

Rickie seemed determined to succeed in her new life.

''What if I am two years older than my classmates? What
if I have spent the last three years in a mental institution?
I've got enough energy for . . . ten kids! When I get down,
I think of Grandpa and how brave he was and how much I
want to be like him . . . and you and Mommy, and how
much we all love each other.''

I wondered at the spark in Rickie's soul that had enabled
her to prevail. She had survived all that had happened to
her at the hospital. Perhaps that was what her teachers meant
when they used to say there was something special, different, about Rickie. Whatever it was, I felt humbled in its
presence.

For the first several weeks at Cherry Lawn, Rickie seemed
to be adjusting very well. Then, one morning, she was late
for her first class. She said it had taken her longer to eat her
cereal, drink her coffee, get dressed. She felt in the grip of
a kind of lethargy she hadn't felt since Westchester.

* * *

I remember walking across the green grass to the class-room building. My new friend Marge was with me, and Alan, this quiet boy with terrible acne who would always shake when he talked.

Miss Johnson, our teacher, snapped at us for being late. She was always telling us: "Pay attention, now! Pay attention!" I liked her. I remember once she asked our ages. When it was my turn, I said I was sixteen but that I hadn't even finished the eighth grade. She said: "Age doesn't mean a thing. Only effort counts." That made me feel so good!

That morning she put some arithmetic on the blackboard. I couldn't make any sense out of the numbers, though I stared at them until I began to feel nauseous. I tried to get my mind off how I felt by concentrating hard on Miss Johnson's piece of chalk. When I looked back at the board, the numbers started crumbling. Then I couldn't see them at all, but I knew they were still there somewhere. Even though the light was shining right into the room, it started to seem dimmer and dimmer.

Miss Johnson saw me and asked if I was all right. I said I was, but I could hardly hear her voice. I began to shake inside. I wondered if I were shaking like Alan does. The exact same thing had sometimes happened at the convent and at classes at Westchester. Once, at the hospital, the letters of the words on the blackboard crumbled like a stale piece of bread or a jigsaw puzzle. I was scared. I told Dr. Phillips about it and he explained it was a phobia. He said that if I ignored it, it would go away.

I tried to ignore what was happening in Miss Johnson's classroom at Cherry Lawn that day, but I could hardly see. The whole room looked dark, and I was so scared. Miss Johnson's head looked like it wasn't even connected to her body. Everything in front of my eyes was collapsing and crumbling the way it had before. I remembered the tubs and the isolation room, and my heart started to pound. Maybe

I was just afraid to grow up, I thought. That's what Dr. Phillips said my problem was; maybe he was right.

Suddenly I must have screamed out, right in the classroom: "I do want to grow up!" Everybody must have heard me. I think I must have been really loud because I heard myself in my own ears. Right away I told Miss Johnson I was sorry.

Later they told me that I stood up and walked up to the board and banged my fists against it over and over again. I don't remember, but they told me that Miss Johnson said that if I didn't stop, she'd have to call the school nurse. I must have shouted, "Call the nurse! Call the nurse! Put it on the report! Send me to isolation! Call the nurse!"

One of the kids started screaming: "She's crazy! She's crazy! Call the nurse!"

The nurse—this older woman—came in wearing a white smock over a flower-print dress. It's funny, I can remember every little detail of those flowers. They were blue with pink and white centers. The next thing I remember is waking up in the infirmary and realizing that now they surely wouldn't want to keep me at Cherry Lawn anymore.

The nurse at Cherry Lawn added this to the description of Rickie's sudden collapse.

Miss Johnson sent one of the students to fetch me. When I got to the room, Rickie was . . . catatonic, at least I think that's the right term. She was standing in front of the class, each eye rolling around as if it had no relation to the other, shaking her head as if to say no, and holding her hands stiffly out in front of her. She was trembling all over.

She resisted me all the way back to the infirmary, where I gave her two Valium. She fell soundly asleep in about half an hour and slept for nearly two hours. When she woke up I asked her if she remembered what happened.

She said she did but she didn't want to talk about it. She said she was sorry. But Rickie looked pretty dazed and confused to me. I told her I'd have to call the headmaster and that he'd have to call you. She kept saying, "Please, don't call them, please don't call them, they'll be so disappointed . . . Please, I'll try harder." It made me want to cry.

The headmaster was firm in his refusal to allow Rickie a second chance, suggesting several other schools that offered more intensive psychiatric supervision. He even mentioned in passing that perhaps she should go back into a hospital for a while.

I was determined to avoid another hospitalization. My secretary Bernice, middle-aged and never married, had more or less adopted me like a long-lost nephew since my divorce. She loved all my children, and agreed to stay in my apartment with us for a week or so while I looked into other options.

Rickie seemed depressed at times, but that was understandable. I called a number of schools and several halfway houses and set up a series of interviews for us. With Bernice there, I felt comfortable leaving Rickie to go to work. One evening I met several friends for dinner. We were sitting together in a small seafood restaurant a few blocks from my apartment, finishing the main course, when the headwaiter hurried over and informed me I was wanted on the telephone. It was Bernice, who told me to come home immediately.

As I entered the front hall, I heard Bernice shouting: "Stop it! Stop it! Rickie, you must stop it!"

I ran to Rickie's room.

Bernice was kneeling on the floor, perspiring profusely, her arms surrounding Rickie's slight frame. Twisting and turning, fighting the woman's grip, Rickie thrust her head

viciously against the floor again and again. Bernice was
dulling the impact of the blows with her palm.

"Stop it! Rickie. Please!" I screamed in panic. I helped
Bernice hold her head to break the force of its movement.
Slowly, Rickie's convulsive movements began to subside.
Soon, she lay quietly on the floor, motionless, her eyes
closed.

"You watch her," I instructed Bernice. "I'm going to
call her mother."

Hillary was shaken. "What do you expect me to do?"
She sounded frightened, angry. "I don't know what to do.
Call a doctor! Put her back in a hospital!"

I called an ambulance and rode with her to Gracie Square
Hospital, a small proprietary hospital on the East Side not
far from New York Hospital, where I knew that Rickie could
be admitted at once.

The next morning, in desperation, I called Dr. Kobin,
who came to see Rickie within hours. Afterwards he met
with us. "This kind of thing happens, under the strain of
leaving the familiarity and protection of the hospital, of trying to adapt to a new environment," he said sadly. "Perhaps you should contact Westchester."

"They won't take her back," I told him.

"Not that we'd ever put her back there anyway," Hillary
added. "Besides, I have some ideas of my own."

34

What had been intended to be a brief stay at Gracie Square extended to a period of nearly nine months. At Hillary's request, Rickie was placed under the care of a psychologist, a family therapist who believed that Rickie's problems lay within the context of a disturbed familial constellation. If the balance within such a structure could be somehow shifted, Rickie's recovery would then be possible.

I had serious reservations about a long stay at the hospital. A six-story, modern, white-brick building resembling a motel, Gracie Square was served largely by private practitioners who admitted their patients and managed their care. But I did not feel that long-term psychiatric patients could be properly attended by doctors who devoted relatively little professional time to inpatient service and thus were unable to coordinate effectively the activities of the many staff members involved with each patient. Certainly Gracie Square had few of Westchester's occupational and recreational therapy staff or facilities. And the idea that a family therapist alone could accomplish what three years at Westchester had not, struck me as preposterous, though I regretted it had not been part of Rickie's regimen there. Nonetheless, lacking any other options, and considering Hillary's conviction that it might work, I agreed to cooperate.

Every week, she and I would go to Gracie Square for joint sessions with Rickie and the therapist in the sterile atmosphere of her tidy hospital room. I remember sitting on the

157

bed, Rickie squeezed tightly between Hillary and me; following the therapist's instructions, all three of us held on tightly to each other for five or ten minutes at a time. Afterwards we would discuss what we had felt. Although I didn't really like the woman and honestly felt that her efforts did little to ameliorate Rickie's basic problems, looking back, I must admit that the therapy may have helped restore and warm the interaction among the three of us that had been so rudely disrupted over the years. These sessions stopped after a few months, when Rickie was given an injection of a tranquilizer and the needle produced a serious abscess on her buttock. As a consequence, she developed thrombophlebitis and spent much of the ensuing months bedridden.

When I was at Gracie Square, even though I still believed in God, I sometimes felt my faith slipping. Everything was slipping. One time, I wrote this poem:

CONFUSION

Mad words, lay them down
God damnit why can't I understand
It's all so simple, yet so terribly hard
I really don't know what I'm talking about
What's to understand
What's so hard
I don't know god damnit
Only God knows
The idiot, why won't he tell me
Even just part of it
But Who's really the idiot?
Oh, hell
I know
Damnit
It's me.

At Gracie Square I made friends with a wonderful black man named Thelonius Monk, who I later found out was a famous pianist. After I became bedridden, he'd pull up a chair to visit me, and we'd talk and talk and talk some more. I had to lie on my stomach because of the abscess, and I couldn't walk. Mr. Monk was great. Sometimes he'd bring me snacks and get me to eat. I was very thin at the time, too thin, everybody said. Then, too, being inactive so long, on top of the abscess, I ended up with thrombophlebitis, blood clots in my legs. That was very dangerous.

At Gracie Square we could see Rickie regularly and often, and before she developed thrombophlebitis, she was allowed out to visit us from time to time. This was a compelling reason for us to keep her there, though I still felt little confidence in her therapy.

It was during her stay at Gracie Square that a curious finding was made. I had requested a consultation by a neurologist, who ordered an electroencephalogram and compared it to one done years before, when she'd had the kidney infection and had fallen out of bed.

"Both EEG reports are definitely abnormal, with convulsive discharges occurring over the occipital/visual areas of the brain," he wrote to me. "These indicate cerebral dysfunction, the etiology [the medical term for cause or origin] of which remains obscure. Although I have little faith in treating a youngster with aberrant behavior and abnormal EEG without clinical seizures, I think a trial of anticonvulsant therapy is probably indicated."

Over the phone he reiterated that the findings did not reflect any particular diagnostic pattern, certainly not epilepsy. He did recommend an anticonvulsant, Dilantin, ordinarily used to control seizure activity and purported by some to possess antidepressant effects, even though superficially its influence on brain function appeared to be the very opposite of electric shock treatments. Since so little was known about how either therapy worked, it seemed worth the try. Rickie was given the drug for a short while, but when no improvement was discernible, it was terminated.

One evening that June, Rickie became inexplicably agitated. In the terrible scene that ensued, she injured the leg that had been afflicted with thrombophlebitis and was again forced to stay in bed. Shortly thereafter, the family therapist announced that she felt there was nothing more that she could do for Rickie.

Hillary, who had selected family therapy on the recommendation of friends and had placed so much hope in it, was utterly dejected and felt totally at sea. Haunted by the memory of Rickie thrashing about on the floor of my apartment, I felt that we should seek a consultation with one of psychiatry's noted authorities in the biological treatment of schizophrenia, a Dr. Karl Kasner. I had never met him, but he was greatly admired by colleagues I respected. He came to see Rickie the day after I phoned him.

Kasner called me right after his visit. "Your daughter is still rather heavily sedated," he reported. "I'd rather defer any recommendations until I've had the opportunity to see her a few times. I have spoken with Dr. Stuart and Dr. Phillips. I believe you realize there is a serious risk she might injure herself seriously, even if by mistake. Fortunately, that hasn't happened yet."

Several days later, Kasner had made up his mind. We gathered in a small waiting room off the main lobby at Gracie Square. Tall, silver-haired, with deep-set eyes and a low-slung jaw, Kasner wore an elegant dark blue suit. A strong British accent largely overcame traces of a more native Central European one. We declined his suggestion to sit down. "I believe Rickie should be . . . lobotomized," he announced, looking directly at us.

Hillary and I were horrified.

"She has a history of obsessive pain. Emotional pain, to

be sure, but it is pain nonetheless. Lobotomy may relieve this, and reduce the risk that one of these days she may injure herself seriously, irreparably . . . or kill herself." He seemed genuinely concerned.

Paying no heed to our reactions, he went on: "There are new methods of lobotomy, greatly advanced. Only a small section of brain tissue is affected. By cutting the connections, we may be able to reduce her emotional pain and modify, perhaps even eliminate, the feelings that lead to such self-destructive behavior. I have brought along several reports of work done in England along these lines. You will see patients such as your daughter described." He handed me several reprints from medical journals.

"Out of the question!" Hillary said instantly.

I'd seen several lobotomized patients in the course of my psychiatric experience. They walked the hospital wards with vacant eyes, shuffling, smiling inappropriately, speaking in slurred monotones, spending their days sitting and staring into empty space. I could never tell how much of what I saw was the basic illness for which the patients had been lobotomized and how much was due to the procedure itself.

I stood there appalled, looking straight at Kasner but not seeing him, his reprints in my hand. What in God's name am I doing here? I asked myself, about to engage this man in a serious discussion about cutting the nerves in my daughter's brain. Tell me, Doctor, what are the odds of success? She may be a zombie the rest of her life, but at least she'll be manageable. Yes, of course, that is an achievement. And you say only a small section of brain tissue will be affected? Exactly how much? Well, that's really not a lot. What a relief! After all, you're the doctor, right?

"Thank you very much, Doctor," I said hoarsely, handing the articles back to him. "I don't really need to read these. We're not going to lobotomize Rickie. Her mother and I will find some other way. . . ."

"We've all been under a terrible strain, Dr. Kasner,"

Hillary said. ''Thank you for your time. You'll have to excuse us now.''

Without so much as a good-bye, Hillary and I left the
room, an abruptness I later regarded as regrettably rude
because, in spite of his dreadful recommendation, Dr.
Kasner had struck me as a thoughtful, compassionate man
in his own way. I let Hillary off at her apartment, taking a
rain check on her offer that I come upstairs to talk, promising to phone later.

Working my way toward New York Hospital, through the
narrow side streets, I parked at a twenty-minute meter and
walked half a block to the tiny red-brick church I had attended years before as a medical student. Except for one
elderly woman kneeling quietly in a front pew, the church
was empty. I turned left and knelt before a low row of flick-
ering candles, wanting to light one, but I could find none
unlit. Over my right shoulder, in the distance, shone the
small red votive lamp that was meant to signal God's presence. I looked straight ahead and silently read the invoca-
tion prayer to St. Jude. ''Through your intercession, St.
Jude, may God grant to me, if it is His will, the impossible.''

This apostle of Jesus had become my last link to all the
mystery that had once been at the center of my life. I closed
my eyes and reached out with my soul to touch it for an
instant once more.

35

Convinced that Rickie should be reevaluated at another well-respected private psychiatric hospital, Hillary and I arranged for her to be transferred to the Sheppard and Enoch Pratt Hospital in Baltimore, Maryland. The hospital facilities were not unlike those at Westchester, and I held the staff in high regard; in fact, several years before, I had turned down an offer to work there when my good friend, the noted psychoanalyst Lawrence Kubie, was clinical director.

The doctors' initial reports were quite optimistic. She started school, and on one occasion was permitted out with a group of patients to lunch and a film. After two months, however, as Hillary was heading for a train to Baltimore, Rickie's psychiatrist called to inform her that, without any obvious provocation, Rickie had become suddenly disturbed. In a fit of inexplicable anger, she had thrown a glass vase against the wall of her room and smashed it, injuring her hand. He went on to tell Hillary that he had presented Rickie's case at grand rounds, to a consensus that they could promise little more than had already been accomplished at Westchester—more diagnostic debates and a prolonged, costly hospital stay, with little certainty of ultimate recovery. He echoed Dr. Stuart's opinion that Rickie might better be cared for in a state facility, noting that it would be wise to husband dwindling financial resources for Rickie's eventual discharge and rehabilitation. By now Rickie's care had indeed cost a great deal of money—well over a hundred thousand dollars, in spite of insurance and professional courtesies extended to me as a physician—and we could ill afford to continue on this course indefinitely. He repeated this opinion in a call to me. When I asked about her diagnosis, he revealed the same confusion I had encountered in the past. "Somewhere on the continuum between schizophrenia and mood disorder," he said hesitantly. "The best we could come up with was schizoaffective. There's no hard evidence of schizophrenia, but as you know, that doesn't mean she isn't."

Rickie was taken by ambulance from Baltimore to Central Islip State Hospital, halfway out on Long Island, where the gently rolling land gives way to sandy soil and desolate scrub. Driving to the Hamptons, Hillary and I had passed it a hundred times, barely noticing the gigantic silhouette arched against the horizon. It had never held any meaning for us in the past, except, perhaps, as a chilling place where other people—people whom we'd never meet—went to grow old and be forgotten.

Hillary and I were asked to be at Central Islip the day after her arrival. As we drove directly through the main gates, the scene was utterly demoralizing: huge colorless stone buildings with tiny windows, many barred, surrounded by dry, brown lawns and dead trees that must have been waiting forever to be cut down. Here and there peeling, rusty iron benches sat between lampposts topped with shattered glass.

We were ushered into the office of a senior staff psychiatrist, Dr. Heinz Holzer, who would personally be looking after Rickie. Contrasting vividly with the exterior of the building, the warmth and richness of the room were overwhelming, with photos everywhere, a marvelous Victorian desk topped with tasteful brass accessories, and several comfortable maroon leather chairs. It struck me as uniquely suited to this elderly, gray-haired man, whose round, lined face, and wide nostrils complemented sensitivity revealed by deep eyes and thin, sensitive lips.

"It must be very difficult for you both," Dr. Holzer said kindly. "Schizophrenia is a long battle. But it is my hope Rickie will not have to be here too long."

"How can you say that, with her history?" Hillary wondered. "We really don't need any more empty reassurances."

"My dear lady, I know you feel your daughter has had excellent care—"

"I'm not sure of that at all," Hillary retorted.

"Be that as it may," Holzer continued implacably, "we have found that many patients who have not been helped in the—shall we call it the private system—can actually do quite well here. There are various forms of illness, as you know, Doctor. From what I understand, your daughter still has a great deal of feeling, emotion, determination. A patient like that, put face to face with the bizarre, burned-out, apathetic kinds of patients we have here in abundance, is not infrequently shocked back to health by the face of true madness."

Hillary looked stunned.

"Sometimes they simply decide to get better." He smiled warmly. "And, of course, there is nothing here to invite the dependency that so many patients develop in the more . . . conducive atmosphere of places such as the one in which she has spent, how long . . .? Over three years?" Holzer spoke slowly, haltingly, with a thick German accent.

I felt something special about this man—kindness, depth, competence—as if he had been transported here from some long past time and place. "Where are you from, Dr. Holzer?" I asked.

"Switzerland. I studied with Bleuler. Eugen, the father, not the son. I came to the States in 1939, and Central Islip was the only place I could obtain work. Oh, of course, there have been many offers since then, to go into practice or join medical school faculties. But this is my life. I understand these patients. If I were not here, perhaps they would have no one.''

Hillary was obviously moved.

"Of course," he went on, "you must understand that schizophrenic patients rarely recover entirely. I'm sure you've been told that before. The new drugs, they control symptoms. Patients improve. They can lead modest lives. But then, is life so wonderful for any of us?" Holzer walked to the window of his office and looked out at the grounds, where three patients could be seen wandering about aimlessly.

"It is really too bad we do not have the special towns here, as they do in Europe, where patients like these, and perhaps a Rickie, could work, care for themselves, live in dignity. But then, it is very American to think in black and white terms: sick or well. Hence the struggle to be cured, cured totally, rather than to learn how to live with one's disability. What results is a sense of utter failure when success is not perfect." He turned back toward us.

"What will they do for Rickie here?" Hillary asked.

"Let her settle in. I promise you, I shall give her as much attention as I can. Of course, we're in no position to carry out what you would consider serious psychotherapy, but I imagine Rickie's had plenty of that anyway. Most patients have before they come here."

"And drugs?" I asked.

"If we feel they're indicated."

"Rickie's allergic to the phenothiazines," I pointed out.

"I'll definitely make a note of that."

"She seemed to be doing so much better," Hillary observed sadly.

"Until this episode?" Holzer replied. "Do not be deceived. I would not be surprised if Rickie had been suffering with symptoms all during this time, hiding them as best she could."

I asked him the question that had been plaguing me from the moment I'd learned of Rickie's self-destructive behavior. He wasn't the first person I'd asked, but I'd never really been given a clear answer, nor had I found one in the medical literature. "You know there have been episodes of . . . hurting herself . . ."

He nodded.

"I've personally never had a patient with such a problem under my own care. What does that do for the prognosis?"

Dr. Holzer chose his words carefully. "Self-injury is not a common thing, but it is not as uncommon as some would like to believe. It can be baffling, and hard to manage. Professionals who've had little experience with it tend to assume that it's a sign of psychosis or some such thing. That's really not so. I have seen it in neurotics, especially those with compulsions or compulsive traits . . . perfectionistic, driven, always expecting a lot of themselves, unable to deal with failure. Women more than men, particularly women with low self-esteem, may inflict injury on themselves out of desperation, in an attempt to hold on to some measure of control over their environments, to manipulate. Manipulation isn't inherently negative; it's bad when it's done in a sick way or for destructive purposes."

"You've obviously had some experience with this kind of patient," I observed.

"I wrote a paper on it years ago," Dr. Holzer explained, "one of the few I've had time to write. A case report on a woman who had taken massive doses of a thyroid hormone that she had obtained illicitly, and so fooled her doctors that they surgically removed her thyroid gland."

"What would motivate someone to do something like that?" Hillary wondered, obviously taken aback.

"In her case, a mixture of self-punishment and an urge to die. In a number of cases, self-injury is a substitute for suicide. On the one hand, the patient has an urge to kill herself; on the other, he or she wants to live. So she kills a part of herself, so to speak.''

"Can you stop it?'' Hillary begged.

"It's difficult. The patient has to use all the willpower possible in the beginning, while we doctors have to do everything we can to relieve the inner pain she is trying to deal with. I can tell you what one should not do. Unfortunately for Rickie, a long stay in hospital more often than not makes the problem worse, not better. And everyone involved—doctors, nurses, everyone—has to be guided in their reactions to these patients so as not to make the condition worse. I don't have to tell you that patients who injure themselves can be trying beyond belief. The people dealing with them have a hard time not getting terrified themselves, or frustrated, enraged, even punitive, in response.'' He paused, placing his bronzed palms on the Victorian desk.

"You asked me about prognosis. The answer is, I really cannot say. It's partly up to Rickie.''

"What about the other patients here, Dr. Holzer?'' Hillary asked. "And the staff and facilities? This is the first time Rickie's been in a place like this.'' She was obviously trying not to offend this man, whom we were both rapidly coming to respect.

"I shall be frank. It isn't pleasant here. We don't have enough staff. Some of the patients are, to say the least, in very bad condition; some have been here for many years. I shall put Rickie in one of the newer units. If she likes to paint, do crafts—that we can provide her with, but that's about all. Some patients do volunteer work with the geriatric patients. Some garden. We grow our own vegetables, and some flowers.'' Holzer suddenly looked pensive. "But I would not wish her to be here long. She is a young, attractive young lady . . . it is not always safe.''

"Oh, my God.'' Her mother winced.

"You can visit whenever you wish during regular visiting hours. If she is able, you can even take her out. There is a

Howard Johnson just down the road. The food here, as you might presume, is not exactly the best, and the patients always enjoy a little outing.''

"No restrictions on visiting?" I asked.

"Naturally, if a patient is very disturbed, but only for short periods of time. . . . Encouraging families to come, that is generally our big problem. Many of these patients are forgotten entirely. Some are well enough to leave but have nowhere to go. People have learned to live without them.''

His parting words haunted us as we drove back to the city. The idea of learning to live without Rickie, forgetting her, was inconceivable to either of us.

I received a letter from Rickie a few days later. She must have written it the day after arriving at Central Islip.

Dear Daddy,

I hope you don't mind my spelling mistakes. Miss Henry isn't here anymore to correct them.

The nurse on this ward is Miss Biondi. She seems nice, but she's the only one here and is always busy. The patients are really different. One lady said I looked like I came from money. She also warned me not to go by myself on the grounds or in the halls because I might get raped or killed. Don't worry. I'll be careful.

I also met this girl called Ella. She's thirty. Ella's

*been here more than five years, on and off. Her father
was a drinker and left her when she was three. Her
mother lives with a man who beats her up and hates
Ella. Her little sister's on drugs. She has an aunt who
lives in Queens who used to visit her but doesn't anymore. She wanted to know how I got Dr. Holzer as my
doctor. She called it special treatment. I told her that
maybe it was because you were a psychiatrist, and she
couldn't understand why you put me in a place like this.
I do. Don't feel bad.*

*Ella wanted to know what was wrong with me. She
said I didn't look sick. So I told her I made a lot of
things up.*

*Then there's this other lady who all she does is stand
with her back against the wall and every couple of minutes she screams. The things she says are pretty bad
language, but I'm not shocked. I've heard it all before.*

*Miss Biondi thinks I might like to work with the old
women on the old people's unit. That might be a good
idea. I asked her about school, and she said they didn't
have the money. I don't care. I'm afraid to go back to
school now anyway. I told her that the nurses at
Westchester considered me one of the most difficult patients. She said they didn't know what difficult was.*

*I didn't sleep at all last night. I was thinking. I asked
myself, have I been making believe all along? The patients here made me think about it. Did I really ever
think I was a horse and all that stuff, or did I only make
it up? Could it be that I'm not really sick—that I'm only
pretending, even to myself?*

*Then I thought, what if I was raped or murdered in
one of the tunnels? What if I started yelling all the time,
like that woman in the ward? I saw Dr. Holzer last
night and he told me I would be all right. Funny, he
reminded me a lot of Grandpa. I wanted to believe him.
But what if he was wrong, like the other doctors? He*

told me I might be schizophrenic or I might not, just like that, not like the others who never gave me any real answers at all. He said I could lead a life somewhere, one that counted, even if I didn't get all better. I didn't know what he was talking about, but I did feel better. He told me that being sick like this was nothing to be embarrassed about. He said it's not my fault, and not anyone's fault. It's just an illness like any other, and just because a lot of people don't understand it, doesn't make it any different from having the flu.

The other doctors told me that too, and Miss Henry, but then they'd start asking me to talk, about guilt and how mad I felt, and about you and Mommy, and I couldn't believe them. Somehow, the way Dr. Holzer said it, I could really believe it.

No one has really been able to do anything for me, Daddy. I'm sorry, but not even you. I remember, in the third grade, I was running in a race at the convent and I was way behind and a feeling rushed through me and made me run faster and faster, and I won. I had that feeling for the first time in a long time, last night. Maybe I have to do it for myself. Show them all, I thought. Show them, Rickie.

I said my prayers last night before I went to sleep. I always do. I pray for you, and Mommy, and everyone. You know, when the wake-up bell went off this morning, I felt like I was alive. I felt the bell was ringing so loudly it could be heard all over the world.

Please, come see me soon.

Love,
Your daughter Rickie

P.S. Soon!

═ 37 ═

St. John of the Cross, the mystic, originated the concept of "the dark night of the soul." I had always assumed that such an experience would be a terrifying journey, filled with anguish. It never occurred to me that for someone like me, for whom purpose and life and faith had meant so much, it would possess the additional ingredient of ennui—perhaps the most painful of all.

By now I felt like a veteran, no longer the green recruit who had fallen apart when Rickie had first become ill and Hillary and I were divorced. I began to understand why seasoned soldiers had a better survival rate in prisoner-of-war camps than the younger troops who, although they may have begun the ordeal in much better physical condition, really had no idea what it was to face enemy fire, much less spend years exposed to a captor's hate. In a way, I envied those people whose tragedies could be attributed to villains. Rickie's scenario had evolved without villains, only people whose lives had intertwined like characters in a Greek tragedy, all caught in the same quicksand of ignorance and false assumptions.

With all the efforts having apparently failed, and Rickie now lodged in a state hospital, I felt the time had come for a major change in my professional life, and perhaps in my personal life as well. I felt I had to get away from institutional psychiatry, at least for a while. Although Bill Morris tried to dissuade me, I resigned as director of the metabolic research unit at Payne Whitney and stopped teaching, although I maintained my faculty and hospital appointments on an adjunct basis. No longer did I make rounds with residents. The then chairman of the department at Cornell, Bill Lhamon, undoubtedly apprised of the situation with Rickie, accepted my decision with the peculiar blandness which some consider the psychiatrist's trademark. My friend Dick Kohl was more supportive, if not enthusiastic; he probably hoped that my flight from hospital activities would lead me toward the social scene that he found so fulfilling. Most of the residents with whom I had been working—knowing nothing, of course, about Rickie—assumed that I was about to leave New York City altogether. Why else, as several mentioned, would anyone forfeit a position of such responsibility and prestige?

I found a new office in the east Fifties where I would continue to see my private patients. At least that part of my work was proceeding well; I could choose my patients, and there were no youngsters among them to remind me of Rickie. I also found a duplex apartment with three bedrooms a block from the new office. I promptly went to a hardware store to buy a set of small, oval signs of white china, each of which bore one of my children's names, and nailed Rickie's and Mary's on one door, Johnny's and Matt's on another.

I knew what I was running away from. What was I running to? I wasn't quite sure.

When I was in college, one of my ambitions had been to write. I began to work on a novel, but unhappy with its direction, I put it aside. Then I decided to begin work on a book about the subject which I had come to know most intimately, in my clinical work, in my research, in my own life. Depression.

=== 38 ===

I leaned back in my yellow wing-back chair, folded my hands together above my head, and stretched as far as I could. It had been a tiring day, brutally hot for June. The digital clock next to the chair where my patients usually sat read 6:10. In five minutes I'd begin my last session of the day. Bernice had already left, so when the telephone rang, I reached out to answer it myself. It was Joyce, who'd arranged for a baby-sitter and had gone to my place that evening to fix dinner for the two of us. "Be here by eight," she ordered. "Oh, and you have a surprise waiting for you."

"A surprise?"

"A visitor."

"Who?"

"Rickie."

I was astonished.

"She left the hospital," Joyce said softly. I assumed Rickie must have been listening. "She got a ride into the city and came by just a little after I arrived, about half an hour ago. We've been talking."

"Is she all right?" I asked nervously.

"She's fine. Just be on time."

As soon as I walked off the elevator, Rickie opened the apartment door, wearing a pair of blue jeans and a plaid cotton shirt. She smiled broadly. "I was watching for you out the window. You're not angry with me, are you, Daddy?"

"Of course I'm not angry, Rickie. It's just that . . . What happened?"

"I had to get out of that place for a while."

"How did you?"

"Well, I ran away from the hospital and walked to the train station," she explained, beaming. "I conned a nice man into giving me some money for the train. I made up a story that I had lost my money and couldn't find my way home. He gave me twenty dollars, and I took his name and address and told him I'd pay it back. Then I made it all the way here and rang the bell. Isn't it wonderful?" Rickie looked totally pleased with herself.

"It is, Rickie." I laughed in spite of myself. "Hey, let's go in the living room." Rickie sat on the couch and I collapsed into a pillowed easy chair alongside.

"Daddy, I loved meeting Joyce. She's so nice. We've been talking about all sorts of things, mostly you."

Joyce called amusedly from the kitchen. "Did I hear my name mentioned?" I often teased her about her remarkable hearing. "Rickie's staying for dinner," she announced, as if Rickie's appearance had been the most natural thing in the world.

"You'll have to go back, Rickie," I reminded her reluctantly.

"I know that, Daddy," Rickie replied, "but please, let me enjoy being here for a little while. Then I'll go back, if you want me to."

She seemed so normal, I thought, groping for words. "It's not what I want, Rickie. It's just that—"

"We'll talk about it after dinner," Joyce interrupted.

Later Joyce and I sat on the couch in the living room while Rickie stood in front of the window. "This is a great apartment, Daddy. A view of the river and the bridge! I really like the built-in bookcases. I love walnut. And an upstairs and downstairs, just like a real house. I love it! Joyce showed

me around upstairs earlier. I saw my name on the little—
what do you call it?''

''Uh, a door marker, Rickie.'' I hesitated, unsure of the
correct term.

''The one that said 'Rickie's room,' and the others,
'Mary's room,' 'John's room,' 'Matthew's room.' '' She
walked slowly across the room, taking everything in, stopping in front of one of the bookcases. ''Those statues—they
must be the ones you told me about, Daddy. They look just
like us!'' she observed with delight.

I hadn't really looked carefully at the Bing and Grundahls
since moving in, and was delighted that Rickie had noticed
them.

''And those paintings.'' She glanced around the living
room. ''Didn't Grandpa have them in his house?'' She was
referring to Joseph Revere's paintings, one of a Brazilian
girl with a basket of fruit on her head, another of an old
monk reading. And then there was the steamer in distress,
flying its flag upside down. Paul Revere's grandson, General
Joseph Revere, had served in the Civil War, and my mother
had lived with his widow in Morristown for a while. Mrs.
Revere left the paintings to my mother before she died, and
now, on the walls of my apartment, they provided another
thread of continuity in my life.

''You have a good memory, Rickie.''

''For some things,'' she boasted happily. ''I can remember everything about Grandma and Grandpa. Seen Grandma
lately?''

''Not for some weeks. She doesn't recognize me, or anyone, you know, but she is well taken care of.''

''I'd like to visit her. I have a real job at the hospital now,
taking care of old people like Grandma.''

''You told me about that when I was out to visit you a
couple of weeks ago. I'm very proud of you.''

She sighed. ''Grandma must get lonely.''

"That's why we have her in a room with other women, so she has company."

"And they don't mind her not remembering anything, and all that?"

"No. As a matter of fact, her two roommates have told me they enjoy having Grandma there. She's sweet and she still has her sense of humor. I guess they like the feeling of taking care of her, and they probably have a good audience."

"That's good." Rickie glowed. "The staff isn't very patient with the women in the geriatric unit . . . how's that for a big word? But I try to be. I think about Grandma and it helps me be patient."

"You're a beautiful young woman, Rickie," Joyce observed.

"Thank you."

"Why did you run away?" I inquired seriously.

"I was lonely. And I wanted to see you." She sounded apologetic.

"That sounds like a good enough reason," Joyce said reassuringly.

I was curious. "So how'd you actually get out?"

"Oh, that was easy. They don't have the same kind of locked wards as other hospitals. I mean they do, but I'm in an open unit, and they don't watch you at all. I don't even think they'll miss me, not until bedtime. They don't keep track of you if you behave. I think they'd like you to leave."

"I'm not so sure about that, Rickie," I said. "In any event, I've already called Dr. Holzer. He knows you're here."

"Was he angry?"

"He didn't like the idea of you running off like this, but he wasn't angry."

"I rather admire your spirit," Joyce admitted. "How long have you been at Islip, Rickie?"

"Gosh, nearly nine months."

It had been a relatively crisis-free nine months, during which I had visited Rickie every two or three weeks, often taking her out for short excursions. Of course, I knew from Dr. Holzer that she still had her black spells, and whenever I inquired as to how long he thought she would have to remain, he professed uncertainty, determined to wait and watch until he felt assured her discharge could be accomplished with a minimal risk of relapse. "We had her on lithium for a while," he did confide. "I think it helped stabilize her, but it had to be stopped because of side effects."

"You'll have to go back, Rickie, for a while anyway. I can drive you out tonight," I offered.

"I'd like to come with you," Joyce chimed in.

"You don't have to. What about your baby-sitter?"

"I'll call and ask Hattie to stay overnight. I really want to go."

"I'd like her to come with us," Rickie said enthusiastically.

On the drive back to Long Island I felt encouraged by Rickie's seemingly genuine cheerfulness. I watched her every move as she bravely walked into the large, dark building, turning ever so briefly to wave again before going inside. The old familiar feeling that I had somehow abandoned Rickie came over me again. I felt enormously reassured when Joyce took my hand and told me she was convinced that anyone with Rickie's determination would make it in the end.

39

Joyce and I were married the following September at the United Nations chapel in a ceremony officiated by the resident minister—a Presbyterian, I believe. A week before the wedding my mother had died quietly in her sleep. The doctor who called to tell me was the same family physician who had informed me of my father's death six years earlier. Dad's death had come as a terrible shock, but after years in the nursing home, my mother's was a not unwelcome release from her suffering. Joyce and I had driven to Red Bank in a heavy downpour, met the priest at the cemetery, and recited a few simple prayers by the graveside.

A few close friends came to our wedding: Bill and Celia Morris, Joyce's parents, her children and mine. John, now fourteen, was best man, growing tall and starting to look less like me and more like John. Matthew, now ten, who had anxiously asked me several times beforehand to promise we'd still see each other just as often, was in good spirits that day; he had evidently taken heart from my assurances. Mary, now a tall, pretty, twelve-year-old, wore a blue lace dress and smiled all through the fifteen-minute service. Afterwards, Joyce's uncle gave a small reception at his apartment. Rickie sent us a Hallmark card from the hospital gift shop, covering it with the traditional symbols of hugs and kisses.

We hadn't been back from our wedding trip three days when Dr. Holzer called to inform me that in his opinion

Rickie was ready to be discharged. He was convinced that she had been incorrectly diagnosed as schizophrenic, at least according to his quite precise criteria for such a diagnosis. She'd never had any delusions or hallucinations, her thought processes were always rational, she'd never been catatonic. Most impressive to him was her tremendous amount of feeling and uncommonly wide mood swings. All in all, Holzer attributed much of Rickie's progress to her own courage and determination.

In preparation for this moment, Hillary had located a couple, Bob and Marie Nolan, who were setting up a halfway house for young girls in New Jersey. During their careers as schoolteachers they had become very aware of the plight of youngsters whose education, along with everything else, had been disrupted as a result of prolonged illness. In spite of limited financial resources, they had decided to create a small community where formerly hospitalized patients such as Rickie could resume their academic work and relearn ordinary social skills, thus improving their chances of successfully reentering everyday life. We had other options, of course, but since the Nolans were located only forty minutes from the city, we chose the one that would enable Rickie to become a more regular part of her family once more.

My memories of the ten months she spent with the Nolans are scattered: driving to visit with her there or to bring her back into the city; the Nolans themselves, a nondescript couple usually dressed in Sears dungarees, shoulder-shrugging, friendly, kind; their equally nondescript shingle house, its hunger for a coat of paint ignored in the press of more important matters; a domesticated raccoon kept as a pet in the backyard; the jumble and disorder of the house where the Nolans and their five girl students lived; their old jalopy; and the trailer camp they all went to in the Catskills near Woodstock in the summer of 1972.

After all she had been through, Rickie understandably felt very grateful to be there.

* * *

*I was glad when I went to the Homestead to be with Bob
and Marie. At my interview I impressed them because one
of the girls had overdosed with a lot of pills and everyone
was naturally very upset, but I knew just what to do. I talked
with her and got her to talk, keeping her awake until the
ambulance came. They were impressed by my resourcefulness.*

*I always liked to help people. Anyway, Bob and Marie
accepted me. I loved being free. I felt I was finally going to
make it.*

*I was in with four other girls whom I genuinely liked.
Every now and then we'd go to the movies. For a while I
worked as a nurse's aide in a nursing home, and believe
me, that was hard work. There was a McDonald's down the
road, and sometimes Mom or Dad and Joyce would visit me
with my brothers and sister and we'd go there for a burger
or Big Mac. It was like being a family again.*

*Bob gave me my first driving lessons and I bought a car,
a little green Renault. Grandpa had put ten dollars into the
bank for each of us grandchildren every Christmas, and I
had three hundred dollars saved up. I wanted to use that
money so I could think of it as a present from him.*

*They had a school there—Bob and Marie were both
teachers—and I was having classes and getting ready for
my high school equivalency test, which they call the GED.
I was nineteen going on twenty, and I knew it was about
time for me to complete high school, but I was pretty scared.
I had trouble learning, just like I had before. The exam was
scheduled for the fall, but as the date grew closer, the more
I studied, the more confused I felt and the more I forgot. I
just couldn't concentrate. The letters would crumble; so
would the numbers. Sometimes everything just disappeared,
and it was easier to close my eyes than to try to deal with
the real world.*

I started to have slipbacks. Even though I didn't really

*want to, some part of me wanted to go back into a hospital
again. I was tempted to do terrible things again, and as
much as I fought the urges, I finally gave in. I remember
stealing a plate from the dining room table and smashing it
on the floor. I cut my hand on a sharp edge as I picked up
the pieces, and that wasn't altogether accidental. I didn't
feel the pain until it was over. When I looked at my hand, I
was terrified, afraid I'd cut it to the bone.*

*A couple of more episodes like that one, and I found my-
self where I must have been trying for—Bergen Pines, the
local mental hospital. I thought I'd feel safer; at least I
wouldn't have to take that test and wind up a failure again.
Then it was the same thing happening again. Doctors were
asking me questions and trying to decide how to treat me.
One of them prescribed Thorazine, and I really got sick.
Then they gave me six more shock treatments. I didn't mind
the shock so much; it made the pain go away for a while.*

*In June they let me go back to the Homestead, just in time
to go with Bob, Marie, and the girls to their summer place
in Roscoe, New York, in the Catskill mountains. What a
wonderful summer! I felt really well. But toward the end of
August I began to feel scared of going back and having to
study for the GED. Just thinking about it made my terrible
pain come back. I didn't know what to do, so I told Marie
about it, and she and Bob spoke with my parents. They all
agreed that something should be done so that I wouldn't
have to go back into a hospital again.*

That's when Dad came up with Gould Farm.

Rickie's relapses had been discouraging, but even the impact of her hospitalization in New Jersey was greatly miti-
gated by the periods before and after, during which she
seemed well, and especially by her reintegration into the
fabric of our family life. Of course, by then Rickie had two
families—three, in a way, given that John, Matthew, and
Mary became part of each, depending on time and circum-

stance. She seemed to adapt remarkably well to what I thought might have been a troublesome situation; in fact, I believed that these circumstances provided her with variety and stimulation, and certainly increased the number of caring people on whom she could rely. Though naturally distant, Hillary and Joyce were cordial and noncritical toward each other. I was especially pleased by the genuine interest Joyce took in Rickie, treating her more like a sister than a stepchild; she seemed to take Rickie's long bout with illness very much in stride, and in a generous, courageous way, never resented it. She stood ready to help, while acknowledging that the responsibility for Rickie's care was Hillary's and mine. Without overlooking Rickie's limitations, Joyce instinctively addressed her as a young woman struggling with all the normal challenges of becoming an adult.

When the Nolans alerted me about Rickie's continuing distress, I felt that she'd have a better chance of avoiding institutionalization in a rehabilitation program that provided more structure and supervision than the Nolans were able to offer. Hillary agreed.

I had known about Gould Farm for years; several of my former patients had done very well there. It was located in western Massachusetts, not far from Pittsfield, and in my opinion, Gould Farm was the closest thing I knew to the kind of European community that Dr. Holzer had described, where patients could shed the demoralizing consequences of hospitalization, engage in productive work, and regain self-respect.

Arranging for Rickie's acceptance there seemed a little like arranging for a youngster to attend college. First the staff at Gould reviewed her history. Then came the admissions interview. Rickie's past history of self-injury scared them a bit, and it was up to her to convince them that she wouldn't continue to be such a risk. After due consideration, Rickie was sent a welcome letter, with copies to me and her mother.

Rickie and I drove alone together to Gould Farm. She seemed in very good spirits, although still remote, saying little. As we passed the large frame farmhouse where the patients lived, and then the barns and silos and fenced-in pastures, her eyes brightened and she told me how much she loved animals.

Just before we got out of the car, she took me by the hand and said: "Thank you, Dad. I was so afraid I'd have to go back to a hospital again. I know I'll love it here. I'll do my best, I promise you I will."

"I know you will, Rickie."

"Oh. One more thing. Please don't ever sell this car," she said, referring to the now five-year-old Mercedes. "At Central Islip and the Nolans, I'd wait and watch for you to come, and when I'd see the red car coming up the road, I'd feel wonderful all over."

"I can't say I'll never have to part with it, Rickie, but I can promise it's still a long way off."

40

Kent Smith, the director at Gould Farm, was a soft-spoken man who exuded a quiet gentleness tempered by years of experience.

"We don't use the word 'patient' here," he told us. "We call them residents. Rickie will work on the farm, like the others. Every youngster has an assignment. We grow much of our own food. A couple of times a week we meet in groups to talk about ourselves, to get to know each other and learn ways to cope with life. We call it social skills training. You can understand how important that is for those who, like Rickie, have been out of the mainstream of life for years. We also have an arrangement with the local public school system so youngsters who want to can finish their education. And although I hope it won't be necessary for Rickie, we have several consulting psychiatrists available; they are called on in emergencies and actually see a few of our residents on a regular basis if more active psychotherapy seems indicated.''

During her first months there, Rickie described herself as being happier than she could remember since the spring of 1965. She loved working with the animals, even though it was physically arduous.

In one of her letters she wrote:

Dear Dad:

I really like it here. I have a good time. I love the animals. I don't love shoveling manure, but even that isn't too bad. Every morning we get up and do chores. The weather doesn't matter. Hot, cold, rain, whatever. A lot of the days I walk down to the barn, shovel the cow dung, feed the cows, take care of any calves that have to get their milk, and then do a general cleanup. It is hard work, especially cleaning up, but it's okay. Sometimes I get to help milk the cows, but we don't do it by hand. We attach the milking machines.

I get a big kick out of the calves. When I stick my hand in their mouths, they suck on it. Boy, their tongues feel like sandpaper! The odor in the barns leaves a lot to be desired, but I've learned to breathe through my mouth instead of my nose.

The one thing I hate is the chicken house. I had to clean it one day, and collect eggs; I got a small case of chicken lice from that experience. My friend Lindy had

*it all over her body. I hated the chickens so much that
they haven't made me go back in there again!*

    *I also like the weaving shop and looms. I've made a
lot of gifts in that shop already.*

    Come see me soon.

*Love,
Rickie*

Rickie had her own room on the third floor of the main
house, with a large window that overlooked a pasture with
white birch trees standing in the far distance. She seemed
to fit in well with the people at the farm.

    *Most of the people had been in a hospital at one time or
another before coming to Gould Farm. I did like them a lot.
Lindy came shortly after I did, and we became best friends
quickly. A nurse, she suffered from diabetes, and shared my
occasional urge to hurt herself. She often abused herself by
eating candy or sometimes an extra piece of bread so she'd
go into insulin shock. I'd be there to pour the orange juice
down her throat when that happened. Lindy was an attention getter, like me, and that meant competition. I didn't
like it! But it seemed that our whole lives had revolved
around being ill. Now that I think about it, that was true
for most of the people at the farm.*

    *Though I had promised never to hurt myself while at Gould
Farm, I wasn't quite sure if I could live up to it, and that
thought gnawed at me quite often. Just as often, though, I
didn't think about it at all. I enjoyed working outdoors in
the summer and indoors in the winter. And the farm itself
was great! There were about forty people in residence. The
main house had a large, wonderful kitchen, a huge dining
room, and a television room. Western Massachusetts' winters get freezing cold. I used to beg to stay inside, but we
had plenty of warm clothes. Everyone had their own room,
and I cherished my privacy. We were all responsible for*

keeping our rooms clean and tidy. They were small rooms, but they were very, very nice.

Kent Smith, the director, had a lovely wife, Nancy. I liked her a lot. Then there was "Miss Eleanor," as she was called, an eighty-two-year-old woman who had lived there from the very beginning, when Mr. Gould had opened his home to others in need. The farmer Tim and his wife Elizabeth were also good friends of mine. When they had their first child, they asked me to be the godmother. I felt truly honored.

I wanted so much to be successful there, like I had as a little girl at the convent winning my très bien. Sometimes I even thought that although I didn't want to spend the rest of my life there like Miss Eleanor, it wouldn't be all that terrible if I had to.

Hillary visited Rickie at Gould Farm faithfully once a month, either driving up with a friend or taking the train. I'd spend the weekend about every six weeks, sometimes alone, usually with Joyce and a varied assortment of children. To this day my memories of those visits—walking about the farm with Rickie as she explained her chores, watching her dive into the swimming pool at our motel, sitting together at an inn in Lenox, surrounded by our family, hearing her laugh as if nothing had ever gone wrong in her life—possess a special feeling of nostalgia.

$=41=$

By the fall of 1973 the pieces of my own life had fallen
solidly in place. The children were growing up. John had
entered Trinity Pawling School in Pawling, New York, for
his third year of high school. Matthew, twelve, had become
fascinated with our movie camera and busied himself with
writing and producing his own versions of a feature film.
Mary, nearly six feet tall at fourteen, was a freshman in the
first coeducational class at Loyola High School in New York
and on her way toward honors work and a varsity basketball
position. Mary hadn't been happy at the convent, and although I could never put my finger directly on the problem,
I suspected a subtle prejudice, born of the reaction of several teachers and students to Rickie's history there and her
abrupt disappearance into Bedlam. There were too many
birthday parties to which Mary had not been invited, and
undeserved comments between the lines on her report cards,
as if there were expectations of the sister of a mental patient.

That was the year Winifred, nicknamed Winnie, was born,
profoundly changing our lives. Mary was especially thrilled
by the start of a lifelong friendship, and I was delighted by
Rickie's obvious joy as well. Happy, bright, animated,
Winnie was the bearer of joy, and after much searching I
finally located a Bing and Grundhal figurine to add to my
collection, a young girl with sandy hair, laughing, arms out-
stretched in welcome.

Sometimes Winnie seemed uncanny. For the first few years of her life she bore an incredible physical resemblance to Rickie as a child. Once, when she was about four and we were alone in my bedroom, she pointed to a photograph of my mother on my dresser. "That's your mother, my grandma?" she asked. I nodded. "I knew her," Winnie said assuredly. "How could you, Winnie? My mother died before you were born," I replied. "Oh, but Daddy, I did know her, before I came here," she insisted. "She sent me to you."

One evening that October, Bill Morris came by alone for dinner. Afterwards Joyce retired upstairs to help Lisa with her homework, giving us a chance to talk.

"I've been trying to formulate my ideas within the framework of a theory," I told Bill, "something that can tie together a lot of loose ends . . . like calcium changing when people are depressed, and depression itself being a natural phenomenon and becoming an illness only when it's not properly managed. I decided to call it the 'resilience hypothesis,' a law of disruption and reintegration. Nature's mandate. People fall apart when confronted with serious stress or change in their lives. Then, if they have what it takes, they put themselves together again in a different way. After their breakdowns, a lot of my patients reach better levels of coping. I've taken this concept much further, viewing the breakdown itself not necessarily as an unfortunate event, but as an inherent part of adapting to change, setting the stage for personal growth. If you don't go through it, that's when you're in trouble."

"You're suggesting we should all get depressed?" Bill quipped. "Ugh! They'll be throwing stones at you on the streets."

"Not necessarily clinically depressed, but some degree of emotional disruption. I think that what makes depressed people who come to us 'sick' isn't the fact they're depressed. It's that they can't contain the extent of their depression, or pull out of it."

"And what makes for the difference?"

"Something I call resilience. It's physical, of course, and psychological as well. If you're flexible, creative—if you believe—you can get through these times and come out of them more than you were before."

"Believe?" Bill asked. "Are you talking about some kind of religious experience?"

"Not necessarily. But the prototype for resilience is right there in the New Testament. Death and resurrection. In our field's preoccupation with Freudian doctrine, we missed it."

Bill picked up a photograph of Rickie from a small antique table and studied her face. She was wearing jeans with a patch on one knee, sitting on a log with a backdrop of autumn birches.

"Rickie's certainly grown into a very pretty young woman," he mused. "Where was this taken?"

"Gould Farm."

"She's been there over a year, hasn't she?"

"Right."

"She's twenty-one years old!" he exclaimed. "I can hardly believe it."

"I have a drawer full of her poems that go back years," I said. "Take a look at this one." I handed him one that I had received only that morning.

PEOPLE AND TIME

Life is Time,
And time is limitless.
A day, even a minute
Can move mountains
A stream can change course,
A flower can bloom.
People can grow in time,

Evolve from the tiny attics of their minds.
Beyond the inner self,
There is fullness.
Sharing a thought,
The gentle words of comfort
Are things to be valued.
People need time
Just as people need people.

Bill sat in silence for a moment. "You have a drawer full of these?"

"She's been sending them to me from the beginning."

"I'm going to stop worrying about Rickie from this minute on." Bill chuckled. "Anyone who can express feelings and ideas that way . . . Right on, that business about people needing time."

"You know, it's seven years since I came to your apartment that night after Hillary and I split. I was a broken man." I groaned, covering my face with my hands and feigning despair.

"Well, you don't look so broken now," he said, glancing around the apartment. "I guess you've learned something these years."

"Something."

"How's Rickie doing?" he asked, placing the photo back on the table.

"She loves it there."

"See her often?"

"Practically once a month. She's been down to New York a couple of times. Last weekend Joyce and the kids and I went up. We had a great time."

"Where do patients like Rickie fit into your concept of disruption and reintegration?" he asked seriously.

"I haven't made the leap beyond stress and depression."

"Why not? You know what Laing said. 'Psychoses are simply a different order of reality, akin to a waking dream.

Calling such patients sick and mad invalidates these experiences as a basic interpersonal maneuver.' He called psychosis a potentially healing experience for a person who has the proper life support during the experience. Personally, I don't think anyone can say how long that might take. Everyone's got to go through it at his own speed.''

Bill leaned forward and went on eagerly. "Of course, Rickie's never been psychotic in the usual sense of the word. But how do we know that Rickie hasn't been trapped right in the middle of a very normal—normal for her, that is— reaction to stress, and can't get through it to the other side? Maybe it's just taking her longer.

"Or maybe," he went on seriously, "all the efforts to help her have only thwarted the process and left her demoralized. How do we know that everyone's attempts to cure her haven't inadvertently frozen her in limbo, smack in the center of a natural state of disruption?''

Bill's remarks made me think of the events of the summer and fall before Rickie's hospitalization at Falkirk: Grandpa's death, the beginning of puberty, losing her très biens at the convent, the trouble that had erupted between Hillary and myself. Suddenly I remembered something else from that time, something that I had never before connected with her illness. I must have looked astonished, because Bill asked me what was wrong.

"She nearly drowned," I blurted. "August. The summer my dad died. In East Hampton, at the Maidstone. Rickie and Christy had gone out into the surf. The two of them found a sandbar, like a little island, and they were jumping around in it, having a great time, when suddenly I could see them waving their hands in the air and screaming, even though it was too far away for me to hear them. I knew that they must have been trapped in a sea puss.

"I rushed into the surf and tried to pull myself through the waves in their direction, but the closer I got, the stronger the whirlpool became. I could hear Rickie calling, 'Daddy!

Daddy!' I was terrified. Back on the beach the lifeguard was still sitting on his tall, white seat, chatting with a couple of girls, seemingly oblivious. The people in the cabanas were absorbed in sipping their afternoon cocktails. I was furious, and panicked.

"Then I saw a bunch of people from the public beach running toward Rickie and Christy. They formed a human chain, arms locked, one after another stretching out into the sea until someone in front reached Rickie then Christy and yanked them out. I watched them pass the girls from one person to the next until they were back on shore. I ran to Rickie and took her in my arms."

"My God," Bill muttered.

"Now I remember her saying something about being afraid she'd die."

"Do you have any idea what coming face to face with death can do to a kid that age?"

"Of course I do, Bill. It would traumatize the normal sense of invincibility all kids enjoy. You're not supposed to realize your own mortality until a lot later on. . . ."

"Like middle age, in this day and age of medical miracles," Bill agreed sardonically.

"I just thought she'd gotten through it okay."

"On top of everything else . . . My God! A real case for your theory."

I was too distressed to reply.

Bill refreshed his crème de menthe on ice, then, adopting a lighter tone, asked: "How's that book of yours coming along?"

"I have a contract with Bantam, and a real, live advance." I was relieved he had changed the topic.

"I envy you."

"What? The book?"

"No. The way you've changed. How much you've been through, how much you've learned. My life just goes along uneventfully, year after year. Yours is packed with . . ." He searched for a word. "Adventure."

The image of Bill behind the wheel of a racing car in Provence flashed into my mind. "Adventure comes in a lot of different packages," I pointed out. "Can you honestly imagine a full life that doesn't involve some kind of adventure?"

42

John, sixteen by now, gave me a set of poems he had written as my Christmas present that year. One of them was to Rickie:

> *i remember east hampton*
> *the maidstone club house*
> *the green golf course*
> *the pool*
> *and your bathing suit*
> *blue with yellow stripes*
> *and the bee that stung your back—*
> *i remember the apartment*
> *where our parents divorced*
> *the corner room, my room*
> *the alligator in the tub*
> *that bit your finger*
> *because you taunted it*
> *throwing things against your door*
> *that connected our parents' room with yours*

when they loved, you knew
when they fought, you knew
we were in the back
furthest away from everything
tucked neatly into small corners
blessed—
our prayers listened to
our dreams acknowledged
our childhood diseases catered
one by one—
and i remember
your long stays away from home
the hushed whispers
the hospitals—
and soon you were forgotten
and another memory lost
but i remember
we would laugh on your birthday
taking each other through the great swamp
finding secret paths into woods
where we played so often
as we had such good times together
and now—
you stand alone
your eyes rolled up into
your illusions
and gone—

=== **43** ===

When I drove Rickie back from her Christmas holiday visit with us later that year, Kent Smith expressly asked me to have a talk. Even though, on the whole, Rickie seemed to be doing well, he told me that the staff was concerned about her hesitancy and occasional outright refusal to leave the farm to go into town, on planned outings, and most of all to school. The only exceptions were her off-campus visits with us or her rare trips into New York, on which she seemed to embark with joy.

"I know we've talked about this before," he went on, "but I feel strongly that the time has come for us to do something about her . . . let's call it phobic attitudes, for lack of a better word. In many ways she's done very well here," he emphasized again, "but we can't let her fears go on indefinitely obstructing her progress. We both realize she won't be staying here forever. We have to figure a way to break through this stalemate."

His quietly stated comments sent a shiver of fear through me. I couldn't tell whether my reaction was an overresponse based on years of sensitization, or a premonition. "What do you have in mind?" I asked.

"I think she should have some sessions with one of our consulting psychiatrists, Dr. Flanders."

"Rickie's already had plenty of psychotherapy. I can't see how more can make a significant difference. In fact, I'm not sure that some of the therapy she had didn't delay her re-

covery in some perverse way. Besides, she's in group therapy here, isn't she?''

"Yes, but I don't believe that's enough. I feel strongly
about this,'' he said firmly.

"You're not giving me much of a choice.''

"It's in Rickie's best interests, I assure you.''

"Well,'' I said hesitantly, "give it a try. But if it makes
things worse instead of better, please, let's catch it in time
and call it off.''

"Of course.''

I looked Ralph Flanders up in the biographical directory
of the American Psychiatric Association. He was in his late
thirties and seemed sufficiently qualified. He telephoned me
the day after his initial consultation visit with Rickie. "I've
reviewed Rickie's history,'' he said with an air of confidence. "The major error in her treatment since she left
Westchester, in my opinion, has been the complete absence
of any planned program of individual psychotherapy. I think
she should be seen regularly for a while.''

"I told Kent Smith that I would go along with it for a
while, but if—''

"I understand your concern,'' he interrupted, "but I don't
think there's a significant risk of creating undue dependency
or stirring up old wounds. We'll be careful, I assure you.''

"How can you be sure that she won't regress?''

"Please. I think you're putting yourself in my shoes. You
must know it's hard to be objective about one's own daughter.''

For a moment I was furious. "Dr. Flanders, I've lived
with that remark from Rickie's psychiatrists for years, and
it hasn't gotten her or me anywhere.''

"I can understand your feeling,'' he said quietly.

"Besides, how do we know there isn't something else
wrong with Rickie?'' I demanded. "Something physical?''

"I do understand where you're coming from, Dr. Flach.

I'm not married myself, but if I had a child as ill as Rickie's been for as long as she has, I'd be grasping at straws too.''

"Grasping at straws!''

"I'm sorry. I didn't mean to offend you.''

I didn't speak with Rickie's psychiatrist again for another three months. He had discouraged such communication, since Rickie was now approaching twenty-two and should, understandably, be regarded as an adult; then too, I was kept up to date on her overall progress through Kent Smith and from Rickie herself. However, at Rickie's request, Dr. Flanders did call me again in late June, about four months after she had begun to see him once weekly in the farm-house's front parlor.

"Things seem to be going along very well,'' he reported. "You know, I'm not so sure she is schizophrenic. She has too much emotion, too much feeling. She reminds me of several young neurotic patients I treated quite successfully during my analytic training. I also agree with you that, to a degree, some of her pathology may have been iatrogenic, picked up by imitating various patients in the hospitals and as a learned strategy for coping—not too healthily, of course, with all the different situations she had to face in them—and reinforced by some pretty brutal things done in the name of treatment.'' He sounded like a true ally, echoing my own misgivings, which had haunted me episodically, certainly ever since Donna's phone call to me about Rickie's pro-longed stay in isolation and my subsequent confrontation with Dr. Wheelock at Westchester so many years before.

"As I see it,'' he went on, "the cure lies in reestablishing in her relationship with me the core of her early childhood traumas and thus resolving them. I don't have to tell you about transference. I already have evidence that this process is taking place. In our last session she expressed feelings of love toward me for the first time. A projection, of course, but I believe a real basis for conflict resolution has been established.''

I felt alarmed. "I don't know that Rickie can handle a transference relationship," I admitted. "If you're wrong about her diagnosis, if she isn't just neurotic, what you've described could set off a downward spiral. Even a normal, suggestible young girl might have trouble with what I assume you're describing."

"You're still thinking of your daughter as if she were an adolescent. Ask Rickie, if you have any doubts. She'll tell you she's feeling a lot better."

Rickie was at Gould Farm and, as far as I knew, doing well, when in September 1974, my book, *The Secret Strength of Depression*, was published. To my surprise and gratification, it was extremely well received, publicly as well as professionally. Several weeks later I received a phone call from a Norman Weissman, a film producer who had happened to hear the first chapter being read on a radio talk show while driving down the Connecticut Turnpike one morning. He bought a copy as soon as he reached the city and read it that night. The next day Norman invited me to lunch, and we hit it off at once.

Several months later I was approached by representatives of a pharmaceutical firm that produced and marketed the antidepressant drug Tofranil. They wondered if I would be interested in creating a teaching film to instruct doctors how better to recognize and manage clinical depression. Since they had no producer in mind, I suggested Norman.

In early March 1975, as the camera and sound crews finished shooting the film's final scene and began to pack up
their gear, Norman and I sat on folding chairs, allowing
ourselves a moment of relaxation after our arduous work. I
remember that Norman's chair seemed much too small for
his enormous frame. He handed me a can of Coke, opened
his own, and proceeded to tell me some of his adventures
as a World War II Navy fighter pilot in the Pacific. He went
on to describe his turbulent days in Hollywood and explained how, in spite of his success, he had chosen to move
to Connecticut, to get away from what he called the "tin-
seltown craziness."

The power and sincerity of his personality created an atmosphere of intimacy, and I decided to tell him about
Rickie. Norman was visibly saddened. "Gould Farm's one
of the finest rehab centers I know of," he reassured me.
"But you really have to go to Gesell in New Haven, Fred,
and see what's going on there."

I knew of the Gesell Institute, as over decades it had won
a reputation as one of the country's outstanding centers for
the study of childhood development. But I had no idea as to
the basis of Norman's suggestion. "Why Gesell?"

Norman smiled. "It might give you some added insight
into Rickie's problems. A neighbor of mine when I lived in
Westchester is a Dr. Melvin Kaplan, and for years I assumed
he just practiced regular optometry—you know, fixed you
up with glasses and that sort of thing. But I learned he had
lost a child; he was broken up by that and took some time
off to study at Gesell, and that's how I heard about their
work. A Dr. Appel's in charge, also what they call a developmental optometrist. They've been studying visual perception in autistic children. By God, they've gotten some pretty
exciting results retraining these youngsters. I've seen it myself. Some day I want to do a documentary on their work.
Bottom line is I think you ought to get Rickie's vision
checked."

"I can't believe that with all the hospitals she's been in, her eyes haven't been checked."

"By ordinary eye doctors, maybe," Norman shot back, sounding exasperated. "These people do special tests. Oh, I can't explain it, I just think you should have it done. It's a simple exam, can't take more than half an hour. You just don't know what might turn up."

"If I can persuade the people taking care of her to arrange for it," I said resignedly.

"Just what do you mean by that?" Norman exclaimed.

I tried to explain how often and how persistently I had been told to stay out of Rickie's treatment.

"No one can do for you what you can do for yourself," he said adamantly. "Isn't it about time you took matters into your own hands and did something about Rickie? You are her father, aren't you?"

45

In April 1975, Rickie told both her mother and me that she did not want us to come to the farm the weekend of her twenty-second birthday. Bewildered, we nonetheless agreed amicably, attributing it to a newfound sense of independence. In early summer, however, Hillary shared her growing concern with me, which sharpened my own.

She had received several letters from Rickie during the previous weeks. Rickie had lost her precise convent handwriting years before, but it had still maintained some resemblance to the careful letters she had been trained to form.

In one of the letters Hillary now showed me, a nearly un-
intelligible scrawl ran unevenly across the page.

The content was even more alarming—intense rage toward Hillary and myself. She blamed us in a way she never
had before. Hillary had called Rickie's psychiatrist. To her
amazement, he seemed pleased, interpreting Rickie's anger
as indicative of progress, the expression of long pent-up
feelings.

I called Kent Smith, who cast further doubt on Rickie's
health, describing her as having grown more withdrawn during the previous month. She was often silent and morose,
and had become negligent toward her work responsibilities.

In the next morning's mail I received a letter.

> *Dear Daddy,*
>   *I'm fine.*
>   *Why are you and Mommy always interfering? If you'd
> stop, maybe I'd get better a lot faster. I'm learning to
> grow up and have grown-up feelings. My doctor is a
> wonderful man. I adore him. I think I'm in love with
> him. He's the only one who's ever understood me. I
> couldn't survive without him.*
>   *Please. Leave me alone. I can take care of myself.
> Don't make me hate you.*
>
>   *Love,*
>   *Rickie*

I was profoundly saddened, feeling that if there was one
thing I hadn't done all these years, it was to interfere. I
called Flanders several times, but two days later he had still
not returned my call.

*Dr. Flanders started at Gould Farm after I had been there
a while. He gave his private therapy sessions in one of the
front offices, and after a while I was one of the people chosen to see him. I loved that man. I guess I had a crush on*

him. To some extent, I almost idolized him. I felt he was a good doctor. But most of all, he cared about me, which was something I felt had been lacking in many of the doctors I had known in the past.

He was in his mid-to-late thirties, with reddish-brown hair and a mustache. Usually he smoked a pipe, which reminded me a little of Dr. Phillips, and he'd fiddle with it during our sessions—which consisted of a lot of game playing on my part.

During our first sessions I told him about my various adventures, my childhood, the loss of my grandpa. I dwelled on Grandpa's death and how I felt afterwards. Dr. Flanders was a good listener, and I had a lot to say, so much that I wrote him on days he didn't come to the farm—sometimes three or four letters a day.

Things went along all right for a while, but then things started to happen. I'd see him and I'd start faking. I'd hyperventilate, and he'd give me Valium or Amytal. I had him wrapped around my finger, and I was completely obsessed. In the notes and letters I wrote to him between sessions, I'd go on and on about hurting myself and about problems I had with my parents. Generally I blew these way out of proportion, sounding so upset that I eventually became genuinely upset. I don't know if he knew when I was playacting, but I don't think so—at least not from what I could tell. Here's an example of one of those letters.

Dear Dr. Flanders:

I am scared to death. I can't pin it down. Had my hair washed. A lot of blank spots today and a lot of confusion and tension. I think I'm handling it okay. Today I felt a lot like needing people, like sitting in someone's lap, like crying for a while. A lot of pain inside. I wish I had parents who could understand me. Don't want to be sick. Wanna be myself, who is I don't know who. Keep on fighting.

feel alone sometimes
scared about tomorrow
sick to my belly
wanna sing sometimes
don't smoke as much
try to eat as much as I can, don't like throwing up
have to go to the bathroom (really hard)
I walked in the rain for the first time in my life—it's
wonderful
feels so good—don't like the thunder (God is angry)
                                                    Rickie

Toward the end of my stay at Gould Farm, all I could think about was how much I wanted to be sick, or even crippled. Lindy had purposely cut her hand on some barbed wire, and I found myself incredibly jealous. I wanted a bandage too, and the attention from Dr. Flanders and the staff.

One night shortly after that, I proceeded to take one of my shoes and bang it down hard on my leg in the calf area again and again. I worked myself into the same trancelike state of mind I had used before to block out the pain. The swelling became considerable, so I stopped and went to sleep. When I woke up in the morning, my leg was sore but not as swollen as I had hoped for, so I banged it some more. Over the next couple of days it became hard to walk on, quite discolored, and very, very swollen.

Well, when I showed it to someone on the staff, they took me to the emergency room of the Pittsfield hospital, probably because I told them of my history of thrombophlebitis. I saw an Indian doctor who saw no cause for concern, telling me to keep my leg up and put warm soaks on it. I was so disappointed. I didn't take care of it like I was supposed to, however, and a few days later it began to hurt terribly. When I was again seen by the doctor, he diagnosed phlebitis and hospitalized me. As he phoned Kent Smith, I felt thrilled.

* * *

Three weeks had gone by, and though Dr. Flanders had still not returned my calls, Kent Smith did telephone. "I don't really know what upset Rickie so much," he admitted, "except perhaps that we had planned for her to change rooms next week, and I know she's become very attached to her room." I could tell from his tone of voice that he was very distressed.

"It was the night before last. She'd just finished her psychotherapy session, and went straight to her room. When she didn't show up for dinner, a couple of the girls went up and they found her lying on her bed, crying. I can't begin to describe the room, and I don't know how we failed to hear the noise. Everything was torn apart, sheets, pillows, clothes, ripped to shreds. She must have had a terrible tantrum. It's a lucky thing she didn't injure herself more seriously, but she did bang her leg, and it looks like the old phlebitis is flaring up. She asked me to keep this from you, but of course with the leg problem, I can't. I asked her to call you, but she doesn't want to speak to you or her mother right now."

I was too shattered to speak.

"Naturally, she can't stay here. We couldn't take the risk, and, of course, we can't manage the medical problem. I'm afraid she'll have to be hospitalized, for a short while anyway. When she recovers, she can certainly come back."

I asked him where he had in mind.

"There's a general hospital in Pittsfield. They have a psychiatric ward there, or maybe they'll take her on the medical floor since the main issue right now is the phlebitis."

"I guess there's not much choice," I admitted sadly. "I hope she can be kept off the psychiatry unit. It could be terribly demoralizing for her to find herself back in one."

"We'll do our best," he promised.

I knew he meant it, but I couldn't help reflecting that Rickie's years had been filled with professionals "doing their

best." What if, as in the past, their "best" proved once
more not to be good enough?

=== 46 ===

*I found myself in the medical unit of the hospital with
orders to stay in bed with my leg propped up. I watched a
lot of television soap operas,* General Hospital, One Life to
Live, *and sometimes kept my bad leg tucked up under me.
Every day it got harder and harder to straighten, as if it
had become locked in that position.*

*I hate to admit it, but I enjoyed being crippled. The nurses
were good, and they gave me a great deal of attention. In
the mornings one of them would come in and help me wash
up, and then she'd braid my hair. I felt like a little kid. At
one point I decided to stop eating. I drank only soda pop
and smoked cigarettes. Being bedridden and getting no exercise, I wasn't too hungry anyway. I had to use a lot of
willpower to avoid eating, but to my delight, I got down to
117 pounds, which for me is really thin. The fact is, I had
been obsessed with weight ever since I first laid my eyes on
an anorexic girl in Westchester.*

*I received sleeping pills, and sometimes Demerol for pain.
Believe me, the pain—physical, not just mental— was real.
I liked the feeling of well-being the Demerol gave me. After
a while they were giving me an injection of Demerol every
four hours, until Dr. Flanders decided I might be addicted
and had to be taken off it. For about three days sweat poured
off me, I shook on and off, and felt terribly nauseous. Some-*

times I had the feeling that ants were crawling all over inside and outside my body. Then the symptoms eased up and my interest in Demerol faded, but I was left very depressed.

Meanwhile, the doctors seemed puzzled. They were putting my leg in a straightening brace for about four hours a day, but otherwise I kept it bent whenever possible. My thin leg began to atrophy, and I had to be transported everywhere in a wheelchair.

Then they started taking me down to physical and occupational therapy. They would put me in the whirlpool and work my arms and legs in an effort to build the muscles. I loved the squishing water and the way it swirled around me. The physical therapists were wonderful too. They were my buddies. I loved going down there and enjoyed the people I met from the outside. I still couldn't walk, but I was having a good time nonetheless.

The other patients in rehab suffered with terrible handicaps. Some had no legs; others were crippled by various diseases. The saddest ones were children who had arthritis, multiple sclerosis, and muscular dystrophy. Some of them would get so frustrated they'd cry, and the therapists would say: "Come on, you can do it. You can do it!" I began to wonder what it would be like to be crippled that way for the rest of my life.

I became friends with a girl there named Kitty. She was about sixteen years old and very quiet, but she smiled at me whenever I saw her. One time I saw her trying to comb her hair. She couldn't hold the comb right, because she had polyneuritis, a nerve disease that had crippled the muscles in her hands so that they were useless. So I combed her hair and made a ponytail in the back. I didn't do too good a job, but a therapist helped us, and then we all laughed and had a cigarette together. In a strange way, I was a bit jealous of Kitty's disease. I even started to imitate her crippled hand, pulling my fingers under into a fist and not using them. Amazingly, after a while they did begin to atrophy! When I

*look back, I see what an actress I was. I was a mimic, a
copycat. When I saw an affliction, I played the role, so there
I was, acting as if I had deformed hands.*

I wrote this:

Dear Dr. Flanders:

*I have lots of thoughts about harming myself, and
have to freeze in one spot until the feeling lessens. So
far I have been stronger than the thoughts. My hair is
still falling out and I am getting sores inside and outside
my mouth. I'm wondering if I might have a vitamin de-
ficiency. Believe it or not, I'm already thinking about
Christmas, though I don't like to and sometimes get
very scared. I don't want to talk about it anymore. I'm
going to ask if I can watch* All My Children *now.*

                              Good-bye, Rickie

*During this time, I was on Percodan for pain and Placidyl
to go to sleep. I'd take both of them together, and about
twenty minutes later I'd start to get this great buzz, like a
huge rush going through me, and then everything would go
black and I'd pass out.*

*One evening I was sitting in the ward's kitchen area with
a bowl of oatmeal after taking my Placidyl and Percodan. I
suddenly passed out, and my face fell into my cereal, and
they had to pull my head out of the bowl so I wouldn't
suffocate in it. Then one night I apparently was trying to get
up out of the bed and into the wheelchair, and I fell. So
they started putting me in a pose at night, which kept me
in bed but also made me feel secure and comfortable. Things
were going pretty well that way, but one day I felt really
bored, so I faked a seizure. I guess I'd lost my touch. The
doctors weren't fooled, so they decided to transfer me over
to Jones II, the psychiatric ward at Pittsfield General.*

*I didn't want to go, but they took me anyway. Of course,
I was in bed, since I hadn't walked in two months, and they*

*put me in a room by myself. No one was in the other bed. I
felt so depressed that I stopped eating altogether. All I took
was orange juice, which induced diarrhea and helped the
weight come off even faster. By then I weighed 112 pounds
and was a bundle of bones.*

*One afternoon after I'd been there a couple of days, I was
lying on my bed. The room was small and dark, and as I
was thinking how much I hated it there, I started feeling this
rage growing inside me. I twisted and pulled at the pose
that held me in the bed. How could I have let myself end up
on a psychiatric ward again? I'd been doing so well at Gould
for so long, and now, here I was back in Bedlam. I was
furious with myself.*

*I was furious with the doctors and nurses too. If there
were only some way to get back at them for leaving me
alone, I thought. They only come by to check me to see if
I'm alive. I wonder what would happen to them if I killed
myself? With that thought, I began to look around the room.
My suitcase lay only a few feet away. I could touch it! I
reached out my hand and began to rifle through the con-
tents. My heart was pounding, my mind speeding so fast I
could hardly keep up with it. I found a pair of knee socks,
tied them together to make a rope, put them around my neck
and started pulling as tightly as I could. I was so mad,
I pulled and pulled. I was so ANGRY, ANGRY, ANGRY
and . . . HOPELESS. There was nowhere to go. I started
wheezing and gasping, feeling as if I were beginning to fade
into this dream place. I didn't pass out, but I could feel
myself turning blue. I didn't think I would actually die, but
I thought I wouldn't care if I did.*

*I heard them coming in, rushing to the side of my bed,
somebody yelling "Oh, Shit!" and pulling the socks away
from my neck. "She's purple!" I pretended I couldn't
breathe. They gathered around the bed, demanding: "Why
did you do such a stupid thing?" I realized that once again
I had done the wrong thing. Now what would happen to me?*

It didn't take long to find out. They brought in leather restraints and they tied my hands and feet, though not without a struggle—I gave them my best. Then I started to worry about what Dr. Flanders would say.

Dr. Flanders was very angry. Red-faced, he puffed rapidly on his pipe. "I won't tolerate this kind of behavior," he pronounced. "I'm sending you to Northhampton State Hospital until you can learn how to behave."

"Please don't send me there," I begged. "I'm sorry! I promise I won't do it again! I promise!"

"They can't handle this kind of thing here, Rickie," he lectured sternly.

"I wouldn't have died. I made enough noise that they heard me! I did!"

"Rickie," he said, "you have to find better ways to get attention. Maybe Northhampton will help you realize that you should take advantage of the opportunities you have in life."

"You can't send me there without my parents' permission!" I protested in desperation.

"I can and I must, for your own sake Rickie. I'll call your family to tell them, of course, but you're past twenty-one now, an adult, and their approval isn't necessary anymore." They transferred me to Northhampton that same day, taking me by ambulance on a stretcher, because I couldn't walk. Even I knew from the scuttlebutt at Gould that the place was reputed to be one of the worst hospitals in the state. I felt terribly betrayed by Dr. Flanders, but I also realized he had no other choice. When they carried me into the closed ward there, I heard people sighing and wheezing in the distance, and one lady sobbing. Then I think I passed out.

When I woke up, I was alone in a dark gray room with a tiny barred window high up on the wall. I felt tight leather straps holding me down to the bed. The smell of urine blended in with cigarette smoke, disinfectants, and dirty

*bodies, made me feel like throwing up. I was in the "watch"
room. An aide sat in the corner crocheting and occasionally
taking a long, deep drag on her cigarette. I wanted one so
badly.*

"You sure slept long enough," she commented cheerfully,
coming over to my bed, "almost two days! Do ya have to
go to the bathroom?" I nodded my head, even though I
could feel that my bed was already soaked. The aide began
to unfasten the restraints and two more aides came in to
help her.

"Okay, get up!" one of the aides ordered. "Come on,
we can't wait all day."

"I can't walk," I said.

"What are you whispering for?" one demanded. "Speak
up!"

"Look how skinny she is," said a tall, heavyset blond
aide. "She's nothing but a skeleton."

"I can't walk," I cried louder.

"Don't give us that shit," the blond aide insisted. They
pulled me out of the bed.

As I tried to stand, I fell and hit my head on the back of
a chair. Lying there crumpled on the floor, I realized that
my monthly period had begun; I was covered with blood.
They hovered around me for what seemed like hours, waiting for me to get up, angry because they thought I was faking. Finally the doctor assigned to me, a tall, dark-skinned
Indian man in a white coat, came in. He bent down to kneel
next to me and asked me why I was on the floor. When I
whispered that I couldn't stand because of my leg, he ordered the aides to bring a wheelchair for me.

That evening they wheeled me along a dimly lit tunnel
to the cafeteria. On each side of the tunnel were dark,
dungeon-type rooms where they had kept people chained up
in the 1800s. It was so creepy. The ceilings were high and
arched, everything was so dark, and it smelled terrible.

Somebody later told me the hospital had been built before the Civil War.

The food was awful, hot dogs that tasted like rubber. The next morning, and every morning, they served powdered eggs and soggy white toast, or chipped beef on toast, or sometimes cold oatmeal. Because I was now down to about 110 pounds, the staff stared during meals, so I had to pretend to eat.

The people in Northhampton seemed really crazy. They were a lot older than me, and they'd been there for a lot of years. The only girl even near my age was a teenager, but she was autistic and never said or did anything. You had to watch out; you always knew you could be attacked anytime, but nobody ever hurt me. Even Central Islip seemed a palace by comparison.

This same nice Indian doctor took care of me. The first time I spoke with him, he looked me straight in the eye and asked: "Why did you try to kill yourself? Did you really want to die?"

"No," I told him, "I didn't want to die. I just did that for attention, and because I was so mad at being transferred to the psychiatric ward! Dr. Flanders punished me by sending me over here. How long do I have to stay?"

The doctor sat back in his chair and laughed. It was one of the few times I had ever seen a doctor smile, much less laugh. He said that maybe Dr. Flanders had done the right thing. He also said that the prank I pulled was very dangerous. That was something I didn't have to be told.

I used to wear painter pants—like jeans with a bib—and later this doctor would grab the back of the pants and try to help me walk across the room. "Okay," he'd say, "let's do some walking!" I felt like a rag doll or a puppet with him holding on to my straps and guiding me around.

After I'd been at Northhampton for a week, I asked my doctor when I'd be able to go back to Pittsfield General. He said he'd have to contact Dr. Flanders to find out. "I have

*spoken with Dr. Flanders recently,'' he informed me a few
hours later. "He is pleased with your progress. Perhaps at
the end of this week . . . but no promises until I talk with
him again.''*

The annual reunion of Cornell Medical School's Class of
1951 was held that spring at the Plaza Hotel in New York.
A day filled with lectures and conferences by Cornell's illustrious faculty, it ended with a cocktail reception and dinner dance in the Grand Ballroom. I hadn't been to one of
these reunions in ten years, and it was only at Bill Morris's
insistence that Joyce and I now attended.

Old friends still represented a part of my life I didn't want
to get too close to—studying long into the night, proudly
wearing my long, white clinic coat with my stethoscope
tucked neatly in the pocket—a time filled with a sense of
importance, of excitement, and of promise. The world had
stretched out in front of me, seemingly within my command, and the immediate connection with God at daily mass
had given me a sense of strength and special destiny.

As we walked into the small reception room reserved for
our get-together, with its dazzling chandelier and a white-
lettered Cornell red banner announcing CLASS OF '51 hanging on one wall, I was surprised to see that the twenty or
so classmates looked much as they always had. Some of
their wives, however, had started to manifest the price of
marriage to a physician: fatigue, pent-up frustration, too

much weight, early gray hair. Some even looked as though they had never been young.

"Fred!" Roger Lochhead grabbed my hand and shook it hard. Roger had lived down the hall for all four years, and he now had a successful cardiology practice in New Jersey. One of our colleagues joined us.

"You're an expert in what, Fred? De-what?" he asked. "De-pression. What's that? I thought that ended in the 1930s. Oh, I'm only kidding. I know what you do. Say, I've never been depressed a day in my life, and here's why!" Unsteadily, he brandished his glass of scotch.

"Looks like he's doing research into the metabolism of Johnnie Walker Red," Roger whispered as the doctor weaved away. As our class secretary, Roger kept careful tabs on the comings and goings of anyone who would answer his periodic questionnaires. "Can't place him," Roger confessed. "I don't think he's one of our class. Whoever he is, I hope he's not a brain surgeon."

Roger poked me in the ribs. "You're looking good, Freddy. Cute wife, you old dog." He eyed Joyce, who was busy talking with Celia. "You know, I always liked Hillary. By God, I'll remember that wedding of yours forever. Best damned party!"

"I thought so myself."

"Well, times change, people change. *C'est la guerre*. Looks like you've done all right. How are your kids?"

"Okay."

"That's good. A lot of people are having real problems with their kids nowadays—drugs and all. Mine are okay too, thank God, but you read the papers, and I can tell you first-hand that out where I live, money and education and all, it's a mess. Good kids, from good homes. A real mess."

"I know."

"And nobody's willing to do anything about it! This one patient of mine kept insisting his kid didn't have a problem. The police picked him up with a bunch of others, the kid was hooked on heroin, and confronted right smack in the face with the evidence, would you believe that the father still wouldn't believe it was true? Sometimes I think someone's poured something into the water supply that makes everyone stupid. If we don't watch out, we're going to have a lost generation in this country." Roger looked up distractedly. "Here's someone I'll bet you don't remember," he wagered, motioning to a tall, distinguished, dark-haired man with wire-rimmed glasses walking in our direction.

"Oscar Kruesi," the man announced with a smile, in the event I had not remembered him. Oscar had been married all during medical school. Living apart from the other students, he had had very little contact with us except during class hours, but I recalled him instantly.

"You're in psychiatry, aren't you?" he asked me. "I've read some of your papers on calcium metabolism. Very interesting. I'm sort of in the same line myself. Of course, my real speciality is internal medicine. I have a practice in Morristown, in Jersey."

"I used to own an old mill in Ralston," I said.

"Sure. I know the place. I didn't know it belonged to you."

"Past tense. I sold it four years ago, when I got married again. Expensive, and when the county decided to widen Route 24—to about twenty feet from my house—I finally let it go."

Roger, offering to refresh our drinks, headed for the bar.

"I'd heard you were divorced," Oscar said, "but I didn't know you'd married again. I hope it's working out okay."

"Better than okay, and it's certainly different. That's my wife over there," I replied, pointing in Joyce's direction. Then, pulling out my wallet, I produced a photo of the family taken the previous Christmas Eve.

"Quite a gang," Oscar chuckled. "Say, who's this?" His finger rested beneath Winnie's face.

"Winnie. Two and a half. Any idea how great it is to have a little girl at my advanced stage in life?"

"Keeps you young, eh?"

"It sure helps." I replaced the snapshot. "Incidentally, Oscar, what's your involvement with psychiatry?" His earlier comment had aroused my curiosity.

"Not actually psychiatry. In fact, you fellows frown on what I'm into."

"What's that?"

"Orthomolecular therapy. I work with Carl Pfeiffer. That is, I don't actually work with him, but he runs a laboratory and research center near Princeton. I'm on his board to do fund-raising, medical input, add an element of respectability, I suppose, although he certainly shouldn't need it."

"I'm sure you know the mere mention of nutritional therapy makes a lot of psychiatrists see red."

"I've watched them become apoplectic about it myself on occasion," Oscar admitted placidly.

"Wasn't there a report by the Canadian Psychiatric Association concluding the findings in that area were pretty shaky?"

"You too, eh?"

"I just don't know enough about it, only that its effectiveness has never been established by control studies and that there seem to be a few colleagues around exploiting the idea for a pretty substantial profit."

"A few bad eggs out there, sure, and we haven't been able to get the kind of government or foundation funding necessary for control studies. The drug boys get it, along with members of the biogenic amine fraternity . . ." Oscar was referring to the fact that investigations into brain chemistry centering on epinephrine, norepinephrine, and serotonin metabolism had been in vogue for years. The politics of science being what it always is, obtaining support for other, less conventional research, was extremely difficult. "But let me tell you," he insisted, "in some cases it works wonders. With your interest in calcium, I'm surprised you haven't looked into it more.''

Roger had returned. ''What are you two talking about?''

''Nutritional therapy in schizophrenia,'' I replied.

''Beyond me,'' he admitted cheerfully. ''I'll just go see Harold Kirsch and his wife. He's down in Virginia, you know, orthopedic surgery.''

I turned back to Oscar. ''Do you think it really does work?''

''As I said, in some cases dramatically. It's not just vitamins, it's a total nutritional play. Pfeiffer analyzes mineral, histamine levels, other factors too, and chooses a regimen according to his lab findings. He thinks copper's a poison, and that most of us don't get enough zinc.''

''As I see it, it's a big leap between changing a patient's diet and curing the serious symptoms of schizophrenia.''

''You still believe in schizophrenia? I thought you were too smart for that.''

''Not really, except as a shorthand among professionals.'' I wanted to say I wasn't sure I believed in a lot of things I once had, but held back.

''In the right hands, maybe,'' Kruesi went on, ''but psychiatric diagnosis is only a potpourri of symptoms that resemble each other. In the wrong hands, it can become a self-fulfilling prophecy of diabolical proportions. You know as well as I do that the term schizophrenia covers a multitude of poorly understood clinical phenomena. Hopefully the day will come when we understand as much about the underlying physiological problems of patients in your field as we do about heart disease or a great many other diseases.''

I nodded enthusiastically. ''You say you've seen patients helped by Pfeiffer's approach? Even those who have been ill . . . for a long time?''

''That's what I said.''

"Even some who have been ill for years, and where everything else has failed?"

By now I had fully recalled Oscar as he had been in school: brilliant, meticulous, careful, conservative. Even then, in his mid-twenties, he had carried himself with an air of confidence that exceeded his years, and he had lost none of it. Such an endorsement for a treatment approach held in such low esteem by colleagues I respected was one I might have summarily disregarded from almost anyone else. But from Oscar . . .

"I have a friend, Oscar, who has a daughter. She's in her early twenties, been quite ill for a number of years now. How does one arrange for Pfeiffer to see a case?"

Oscar smiled. "I assume the patient you're talking about is your daughter?"

I was startled. "How did you know that?"

"When someone as capable a doctor as you starts talking like a layman and asks the kind of questions you've been asking—like whether nutritional therapy works, three times—and then tells me about a 'friend who' or the 'child of a friend who,' what other conclusion can I draw?"

"You're as sharp as ever, Oscar, I must admit. My daughter's name is Rickie." I felt foolish, but relieved.

"Well, if you do decide you want Carl to see Rickie, call him. Use my name, although I'm sure he knows you by reputation. He'll oblige."

Oscar excused himself to rejoin his wife. Bill Morris, drinking Diet Coke, joined me. "What were you two so engrossed about?" he asked.

"I was telling him about Rickie. Oscar's been involved with megavitamin therapy. He thinks I should take Rickie to see Carl Pfeiffer."

"Not a bad idea," Bill said. "Didn't Hillary mention something about that years ago?"

"In passing."

"Of course, you'll have a hard time convincing her doctor

to go along with it,'' Bill pointed out. "If you think I'm
trying to give you some sort of message, you're right.''

He didn't have to spell it out.

=== 48 ===

*I was so excited to be returning to Pittsfield. I got dressed
in my jeans and T-shirt before I slid myself into my wheelchair, so thin I felt like a twelve-year-old. An aide brushed
my hair and made braids for me, while I prayed that the
doctor wouldn't forget to come and sign the transfer papers.*

*When we finally got into the car, I sat between two aides
in the backseat, puffing away on my cigarette and smiling
inside the whole half hour. When we arrived, I was a little
nervous, wondering if the nurses were still angry with me.
When I got to the floor, though, they gave me the same room
right across from the nurses' station. I put my stuffed animals on the pillow and I felt I'd come home. It was so much
nicer here than at Northhampton, cleaner, quieter, and the
staff so much more friendly and helpful.*

*Dr. Flanders had also asked me if I had really wanted to
die when I put the socks around my neck. "I don't think
so," I told him. "But once I started, I felt like I didn't care
if I succeeded.''*

*He seemed to like that answer. He wasn't mad anymore,
which made me so happy. Then he told me that my mother
had called and wanted to come and see me. That was great.*

*I was expecting all this sympathy for being in a wheel-
chair, but Mom was smart. She said she was disappointed*

to see me that way. She told me she wanted to see me walking the next time. My mother really drove it home when she phoned me afterwards. "I don't think you're really trying," she said, obviously frustrated and angry. "You made me feel like you wasted our visit! Why don't you get out of that chair!"

When she finished, I got mad too. I'll show her! I thought, and lifted myself out of my wheelchair and took a few steps. I could do it! My right foot dragged behind me a little bit, but I didn't mind that. I walked up to the nurses' station, dragging my foot behind me, and said: "Hey, everybody look! I'm never going to use that wheelchair again!" They were all plainly excited.

It wasn't long after that that things started changing for me. Everything started going at a faster speed. I felt hyped up. One day when I saw Dr. Flanders, I told him, "Rickie's gone." At first he didn't react, but then he asked: "Where is Rickie?"

"I don't know," I replied. "I feel like little Rickie from a long time ago. I don't know what's happening to me." My mind was racing a hundred miles a minute. I had begun to believe I was a little girl again.

I didn't know that this was the start of a long and timeless time for me, months that seemed years, like being in a strange time machine. I wasn't depressed, more like living in a state of unreality. One of the nurses was pregnant, and when she was about to have her baby, I got pains like labor pains and felt like I was having a baby too. My insides felt ready to explode, and it seemed like it took forever to pass, but when it was gone, I felt so much better. At the same time, I felt like a baby myself, and then a little kid. When other people had visitors, I'd pretend they were there to see me as well. Sometimes I would sit in their laps, and sometimes they brought me stuffed animals and other presents.

I wrote Dr. Flanders often.

Dear Dr. Flanders,

I am very glad to be out of Northhampton, but I am so lonely I can't stand it. I played records, crocheted, and I took a walk. There is no one to talk to except myself, and the truth is, I don't like myself very much. I haven't the faintest idea what to do this weekend. I wish I wasn't me. Why can't I be someone else?

There is still a little girl inside of me. I can feel her. She likes things that are fun. She doesn't like to work, she loves being with people, and she feels a lot of pain. If she were physically disabled, she would be fine. In a way, she has tried to become crippled in some way many times. She loves attention . . . She is very cold most of the time. She likes things like stuffed animals and dolls. Unfortunately, I think she is too smart and it gets in her way. I don't want to die, but I can't really see anything that great about living either. She daydreams a lot, and becomes funny sometimes in her own world. She doesn't want to be me. She wants to stop now, and so do I.

Rickie

Most of the time, I enjoyed being a little girl. The night nurse at Pittsfield—her name was Sally—cozied me into bed every night and always made me feel good. I loved her tucking me in. I remember pillows on each side of me, with the sides of the bed drawn up, all tucked into my pose, secure and happy.

One time I met this older man who had come to visit his daughter. I saw him and yelled "Grandpa!" running full speed toward him with my pigtails flopping, and then hugging him. He became my friend. He'd visit with me whenever he visited his daughter, but he would always remind me: "Remember, I'm not your grandpa, I'm just your friend." Then one day—I recall it was especially sunny—when I was standing alone in my room, I started to cry. "I want my grandpa!'' I wept. ''Grandpa is gone. Grandpa is really gone.'' I felt so much hurt and awful sadness. My head in my hands, I pressed against the corner of my room and sobbed hard and loud. With my eyes closed, I could see Grandpa standing right in front of me, but I knew I had to let him go, to admit he was dead, really dead. I finally did, but I knew somehow that I could still talk to him. For more than nine years I had clung to his death, but now I let it go, and I felt like a great weight had finally been lifted from my soul.

After that I went through all those stages of growing up again, from being a little girl all the way up to age twelve. One day when it was pouring rain I went outside and stood underneath a drainpipe and let the falling water gush over me. I let it run into my clothes and shoes, and it felt so good. I was suddenly feeling things I hadn't felt before, or at least not in many, many years.

In early August 1975, Dr. Flanders asked me if I wanted to go back to Gould Farm. I was ready with my answer. ''No, because I want to live with a family and go to school. I want a chance to live in a home and grow up like everybody else.''

When Sally tucked me in that night, she whispered, ''You're a rascal. I don't know how many people will want to take you into their home.'' She kissed me good night and tied the pose—which now was used mainly to keep me from wandering around the unit in the middle of the night. A week later Dr. Flanders told me that Sally and her husband wanted to take me into their home and that my mother and father had agreed to it. I could hardly believe it. I loved Sally, and couldn't believe she was really going to take care of me and let me grow up in her home!

I had dinner out with Sally and her husband Joe, who drove a bulldozer for a living, and my new ''brother'' Sam. Everything went well, and in two days I packed all my stuff and off we went—into a whole new way of life.

Unfortunately, it didn't last long. I had plans to attend the local high school, but I got scared, as I had so often in the past. I didn't know how to make decisions, how to live in the world or attend school. So a week later I ran away. I kept thinking to myself: I've screwed it up again. I've blown it for sure.

I hitched a ride to the hospital and was dropped off at the main door. But then I figured that to be readmitted, something would have to be wrong with me, so I stood by the road and watched the cars, my pulse pounding hard in my throat. Some of the cars were going too fast. If one of those hit me, I might be seriously injured or even die, and I definitely did not want to die.

Then a noise behind me frightened me. A cab was headed slowly in my direction. I darted out in front of it. The cabby, a woman, beeped her horn and swerved, but I went right up over the hood and bounced back to the ground on my back. I remember the driver standing over me saying, "Oh my God, I've hit a child!" I kept thinking, "I didn't get hurt enough," but they brought me back in to the emergency room on a stretcher.

Sally and her husband came to the hospital to see me, and obviously were very sad and upset. Of course, they didn't want me back, and I couldn't blame them.

I told Dr. Flanders that I wanted to get an apartment of my own and a job, claiming that things hadn't worked out at Sally's because it was too crowded there and that, besides, I hadn't been ready to go back to school. He seemed surprised. At first he said no, but a couple of days later he acquiesced, explaining that he was agreeing only as a way to prevent me from having to be hospitalized again for a long, long time. I spoke to Dad about it on the phone, and he was dead set against it and said he was going to call Dr. Flanders. I guess the doctor didn't pay attention to him, because he arranged for a social worker to help me get a one-bedroom apartment, with a big old tub. I put all my stuff away and cleaned it out. I stocked the refrigerator with four six-packs of Diet Pepsi and some chocolate candy. Then I drank a Pepsi, ate one of the candy bars, and began to cry. I took a hot bath and then called Dr. Flanders, but he wasn't in. I didn't know what to do. I called my dad, and he said he'd drive up the next day to see me. Then I called my mom, who was very upset. I was thinking, Gould Farm didn't want me, Sally and her husband didn't want me, my family didn't want me. That night, haunted by these feelings all night long, I decided that the best thing was to take all the medicine I had in the house. I figured I would never be missed anyway. So I swallowed all the Prolixin and then the Placidyl and I went over to the bed and lay down. As I did so, I wondered what would happen if I really died. My family would care. I wouldn't ever have a chance not to be sick. I decided I didn't want to die.

I decided to walk to the hospital. I had only been walking about five minutes when I must have blacked out. I woke up with a tube in my nose, and there were IVs in my arms and beepers on my chest. I was in intensive care.

Several days later in the hospital, I found out that I had been picked up by a police car. I told Dr. Flanders it was all right to let my parents know I was back in the hospital, but not that I had overdosed. I was still very confused and upset, but I was well enough to ask him that. I wrote a note to myself.

Dear Me: It's August 29, 1975. I just called my father to tell him that it had nothing to do with him that things got messed up. We had a very good talk. He supports me in what I want to do. I didn't tell him what really happened. Dad was really happy to hear from me. I told him a little about how I was feeling. I think he understands. He said he would call me tomorrow night.

My body hurts, especially my stomach. I am lonely. I can't seem to cry again. I was so glad to see Dr. Flanders today. The coffee was good. Boy, am I cold! I feel all broken

*up. I just don't understand why God makes people be born.
I feel like my head is swelling. If we weren't born, we'd
never know it, so then why? Someone wants to stab someone
with a big long sharp knife, maybe gouge out his eyeballs.
Someone gentle says that is wrong; cut off your own hand
instead. I wish I had a pacifier or a bottle with warm hot
chocolate 'cause I don't like milk. The little girl is crying,
she's awfully cold and her favorite doll is dead 'cause she
threw up in its head. She can't reach it 'cause it's at the top
of Mommy and Daddy's closet. They are going to throw it
away. Baby-sitter Jonesy has funny-looking feet. Her toes
are crooked. Mommy made me eat sauerkraut the other day
and I got sick because of it. Boy, do I like to suck my finger.
Where is my blanket? Daddy brought me two teddy bears in
a big, white box. Mommy and Daddy argue. I watched* The
Hunchback of Notre Dame *on TV and it frightened me. I've
got the measles or something, because Mommy made the
room dark. I'm scared of the dark. Was there a reason for
me to be born? Someone wants me to rock; I've got to rock.*

*I keep looking, but everything is far away. Licking my cuts
makes them feel better. My walls are blue. Everything seems
false, pretend. Someone says that I can make my heart stop
if I want to. Maybe I'll shave that person's head. She'd
probably claw me with her fingernails. No, she'd stab my
stomach 'cause it hurts. Someone says to smile and rock.
Play with my fingers; they are fun to bend. Where are people, real live, walking talking people? Could the devil be in
me 'cause I can't find God. Am I evil? I wonder what it
would be like if I was covered with wax. Bugs scare me. It's
awfully cold. The ceiling seems so far away. My heart hurts.
The little girl is lost. She likes to hide in the closet. I'm
afraid of fire.*

*Someone told me I was a witch. I'm leaving. I have to
rock.*

49

As Rickie's condition worsened, Dr. Flanders had made himself much more available, yet the details of Rickie's situation were curiously sparse. When I called this to his attention, he reminded me that she was no longer a minor and that he had to observe the rules of confidentiality. I felt this stance was rather arbitrary and told him so, but to no avail. Rickie herself would call me from time to time, sometimes sounding cheerful, sometimes despondent, telling me in the most general terms that she was being well looked after at Pittsfield General, making light of her sojourn to Northhampton, reassuring me that her physical rehabilitation program was proceeding well and repeatedly discouraging me from visiting. Once, when I was close to insisting that I come see her, she fell sharply silent for a minute, then angrily accused me of lacking confidence in the only psychiatrist that she had come to care for and respect.

It was from Hillary, after her visit to Rickie, that I began for the first time to piece together a truer picture of what had been happening. When Rickie described her automobile accident, she understandably omitted her own involvement, assuring me her injuries were minor. As an experienced clinician, I should have doubted the accuracy of her narrative, but as her father I believed her because I wanted to. Even as the doctor in me voiced serious opposition to her being allowed to find an apartment, Rickie's dad could not help but hope it would all work out for the best.

In one of our conversations, I told Dr. Flanders about Oscar Kruesi and the Brain Bio Center, asking him if he didn't think that orthomolecular vitamin therapy should be given a try. He asked for Kruesi's telephone number, but in a subsequent conversation he said that Kruesi had not returned his phone call. I urged him to try again.

"I will." His bland tone clearly implied I was windmill chasing. "I don't want to do anything that might distract from our main focus in therapy."

Pursuing Norman Weissman's suggestion, I asked Dr. Flanders on more than one occasion to have Rickie's vision checked with a developmental optometrist in Pittsfield whose name I had obtained from the Gesell Institute. He consistently met my request with equally polite skepticism, always referring to more pressing matters in his care of Rickie. Finally he dismissed my idea altogether, saying that he had discussed the matter with a local ophthalmologist who found the notion completely absurd.

I began to wake up in the middle of the night. Unable to get right back to sleep, I would wander downstairs for a glass of milk and a second reading of yesterday's newspaper. Norman's admonition kept running through my head: "You are Rickie's father, aren't you?" he had said uncompromisingly.

One such night, Joyce came downstairs in her navy-blue bathrobe and my wool slippers to sit across from me at the dining room table, somewhat disgruntled. "Every time you wake up, I wake up. If you keep this up, you'll have to sleep in another room. Just what's bothering you?"

"I'm Rickie's father."

"I know that. What's on your mind?"

"I'm Rickie's father. I mean, for years now I've let everyone else take care of her and tell us what to do, and look at what a mess things are."

"You know what I think of psychiatry," Joyce said frankly. "I mean, it isn't exactly the most precise science.

Besides, Rickie's twenty-three. She's been sick for ten years, more or less. Sooner or later you may have to accept the idea that Rickie may never be entirely well.''

"I can't believe that. I won't. I never stopped believing, even when I had my worst doubts. Besides, I never had any other options.''

"Do you now?'' she asked.

"Maybe I do.''

I knew unmistakably that the time had come for me to stop letting everyone else make the decisions about Rickie, and make up my own mind. What was the other thing Norman had said? "No one can do for you what you must do for yourself.''

The next morning I spoke with Carl Pfeiffer in Princeton, and afterwards to Mel Kaplan. When I placed a call to Dr. Flanders, surprisingly, I got him directly on the line for the first time. Before I could say anything, he told me—and I discerned genuine grief—that he felt he could no longer look after Rickie. Her case had become too much of a drain on his time and energy and he felt profoundly disappointed in her complete lack of progress. He had arranged for her to be transferred to Poughkeepsie State Hospital, which he considered to be one of the better New York State institutions and where, as an original resident of the state, her right to hospitalization, now being disputed in Massachusetts, could be assured for the rest of her life.

= 50 =

The idea of being separated from Dr. Flanders tore at my insides. As he tried to reassure me not to be frightened of Poughkeepsie State, that it wasn't at all like Northhampton, I wanted to scream it was not where I was going, but being without him that was upsetting me so much. But I couldn't.

At the last moment, I did get emotional and struggled against going, so they gave me Valium. I was half drugged on it during the ambulance ride from Pittsfield to Poughkeepsie, and slept most of the way. When I awoke, I found myself lying on the floor, huddled into a ball in a dark cor9ner. My body was trembling, partly from fear, partly from the good old medications. By now I'd been on so many different ones, I couldn't name them all, and they made me feel like ants were crawling around inside me. I could hear one of the aides walking toward me, bitching. "Mop it again," she ordered a patient. Then she must have seen me. "What are you doing on that floor," she shouted. "Get up! This girl has got to mop!"

It may not be as bad as Northhampton, I thought, but it's bad enough.

I ignored the aide and wandered into the dayroom of the closed ward. The television was blaring. All women again, some pacing, others sitting and staring into space, or lifting their heads to howl. Another zoo. As before, I thought: What am I doing here? I'm not as sick as these people. They're scary. I'll bet a lot of them have been here forever. Some are probably criminals from penitentiaries who'd steal the clothes off your back if they had a chance.

I didn't want to stay in the dayroom, even though it wasn't badly decorated and the furniture was a lot more comfortable than I'd expected, but I didn't know where else to go. I briefly tried the bathrooms, but the toilets were completely open and were filthy and unflushed, making the already foul air stink worse than ever.

All night long the whining, screaming, snoring, and crying never stopped. It was all too familiar. Nor could I sleep on the plastic mattresses. No more than five minutes after I was under the worn blanket, the sheets would slip off, exposing my body to the awful plastic.

In the morning they'd rouse us to sit around forever waiting for breakfast. No showers until later. They always passed out cigarettes, but I had my own and I was allowed to smoke a pack a day.

We were shuffled in and out of the dining room. Between meals I had to sweep the floors and mop the dormitory. When I did clean the dorm, there was only one other patient, who was never taken out of bed. Covered with a canvas and tied down, she never spoke. She had slit her throat open not long before, and I heard that she was very violent toward others, but she didn't scare me. In fact, I walked close to her and said hello, for several days running, but she never once acknowledged my presence. When I had finished, I brought mop and bucket to the washroom, emptied the dirty water, wrung out the mop, and headed back to the dayroom for a cigarette.

There, an older lady sat knitting, a walker beside her. When I asked what she was making, she showed me some crewel work. "It's beautiful," I said.

"You've got a lit cigarette," she commented, looking at me with a smile. "Let me get a light off yours." I obliged.

At least when she talks, she makes sense, I thought. I hoped there might be others, because so far I hadn't been lucky about making any friends outside of talking with the student nurses. As I took back my cigarette, a heavyset girl bounced into the room, headed toward us and introduced herself as Paula. She had lipstick smeared on her face, her skirt was up to the bottom of her underpants, and nothing she wore matched at all. When I asked later on, someone told me she'd had some kind of brain infection as a baby. When I finally got permission to go to the rehabilitation building, I went with Paula. I was excited to find a store that was practically like a regular store, a bowling alley, swimming pool, and a cafeteria.

"You wanna get something to eat?" Paula asked, leading the way into the cafeteria without waiting for my reply.

"Sure, it smells good." I had an allowance from my dad that worked out to about ten dollars a week, and candy, food, and cigarettes were a lot cheaper in those days. I ordered some french fries and sat down with Paula, who was hurriedly stuffing her sandwich into her mouth. When she had finished, I offered her some fries. She grabbed a handful and gobbled them down, reaching for more. "Leave me some!" I yelled. "I didn't mean you should eat them all." Paula got up and stomped out of the cafeteria. "You get mad too easy!" I called into the air. "I can't even talk to you." After she left, I ate the rest of my fries. Then I went to the store and bought three chocolate bars, some potato chips, and some red licorice—one of the mainstays of my diet at Poughkeepsie.

One night after I'd been in the hospital for about a week, I was sitting in the dormitory putting on my red-striped pajamas when I heard this screaming. "I'm burning. I'm on fire!" In the dayroom one of the girls, Mary, was standing there as flames licked up the sleeves of her nightie. The aide squirted a fire extinguisher on her and put out the fire, but Mary kept screaming and screaming. The nurse in charge put cold dressing on Mary's burns and asked her how it happened. Mary didn't say a word.

One of the other patients spoke up. "I saw her do it. She tried to set the wastepaper basket on fire and it caught on her sleeve."

The nurse asked Mary if that was true. Was she trying to start a fire in here? Mary looked down and nodded, mumbling that she was sorry.

"You know you'll have to go into seclusion for this," said the nurse. "This is serious."

"I don't want to go!" Mary started to scream. "Don't make me go."

The nurse called for help, and some male aides arrived and carried Mary out, still yelling and cursing. I watched, terrified, reflecting that we all could have been on fire if she'd gotten the wastebasket to burn. I went back to bed and thrashed around trying to find a comfortable position. The medication still made my body feel like it had ants crawling around inside.

The next day at lunch I watched a lady next to me pick up her sandwich, crumble it into pieces, and proceed to eat it, slurping her milk and spilling it down the front of her dress. I got up and went back downstairs to the dayroom to try to enjoy my cigarette. It was crowded with patients waiting for their meds. The rule was we had to wait there for medication until we could leave again, which usually took about an hour. That day we waited two hours, until I felt like I couldn't stand it anymore.

As soon as the meds had all been passed out and they unlocked the door, I darted down the stairs and into the main lobby to the pay phones to call my dad. I told him that I'd been moved to an open hall, that I felt better, and that I wanted to get out. "This just can't keep going on," I pleaded. "This has got to end. I want to get well. There must be something else—some other way!"

"Well, Rickie," he said, his voice calm and firm. "I think there just might be something else—something definitely different." He told me about something called visual therapy,

*and also about a place called the Brain Bio Center that used
all these vitamins to help your system get back into balance.
He said he'd call and set up some appointments, and that
he'd tell me more when he came up to see me on Saturday.*

*I told him I was willing to do just about anything to get
well.*

==**51**==

The next weekend, just before Election Day, I drove alone
up the winding and hilly Taconic Parkway to Poughkeepsie.
It took a little over two hours, and I felt exhilarated as I
turned north on Route 9 for the last ten minutes of the journey. As I approached the large stucco administration building, the word "Bastille" leaped to mind.

"I'm here to see my daughter," I said brusquely to the
attendant at the information desk, giving her Rickie's name.

"Ward B. Building Eight, across the common. The old
red-brick building. You can't miss it," she instructed.

I was stopped at the entrance of Building Eight by a nurse
asking for identification. No, she didn't know Rickie. She
told me to try the third floor. As I entered the ward and
headed for the nursing station, I heard Rickie calling me.

She was standing on a sturdy wooden stepladder in the
middle of a long white wall, studying the broad stroke of
yellow paint she had just added to a purple and red one.
"Now I need blue and orange," she muttered to herself.

"What are you doing, Rickie?" I called.

"Making a rainbow!" she cried out excitedly.

"It looks beautiful!"

"Oh, it is. Rainbows bring good luck. Besides, this place has miles of empty walls just crying out to be painted. Bare walls are ugly, don't you agree, Daddy?"

"I never thought about it, Rickie," I admitted cheerfully.

"If I stayed here a long time, I'd probably paint them all. But I won't have to, right?"

"Come on down for a few minutes, Rickie. I want to talk to you."

Clumsily, carefully, rung by rung, she moved down the ladder. Before me stood a smiling, attractive young woman, dressed neatly in blue designer jeans, a bit wan perhaps, but not looking much like a chronic mental patient. "I stood at my window for an hour, watching for you," she said. "But then I gave up and came out here. I think a rainbow cheers the place up, don't you?"

She seemed a far cry from the disturbed girl Dr. Flanders had described to me only a couple of weeks before. My sense of excitement heightened. I was at a loss for words.

She led me to the visitors' lounge. "This isn't visiting time," she explained, "so we have the place all to ourselves." Her mood changed visibly, and suddenly she seemed quite depressed.

"I'm sorry, Daddy, about those awful things I said to you in my letters to you and Mom," she whispered. "I was just mad, that's all. I didn't really mean them."

"You don't have to apologize, Rickie. I understand."

"I didn't seem to handle it very well when Dr. Flanders said he wasn't going to be my doctor anymore. I don't handle things well when things that I love are taken away from me." She lowered her head to avoid my gaze. "Do you always do what the doctors say?" she asked suddenly.

"Funny you should ask that question Rickie. Too often, I'm afraid, but thank God not always. I listened to them when you were in Westchester and when you went to Central Islip, and since. In a way, I listened to Dr. Flanders. I felt

I didn't have any other choice. I didn't believe I could be . . . objective, when it came to you—and I can't. But I trusted them even as others have trusted me. It's not their fault, by and large. It's no one's fault, Rickie. . . . But they failed. We all failed, obviously, or you wouldn't be here now. But you won't be here long, Rickie.''

"I hate places like this, Daddy, but sometimes I feel . . . well, that I've been through about everything anyone could think of. I've been sick a long time. Oh, I'm okay today, but yesterday I wasn't and tomorrow I might fall apart all over again, over nothing. I'm afraid to go outside alone.'' She began to sob, in a tightly contained way.

"I've tried. I've tried so hard, Daddy. There were plenty of times they'd tell me I didn't want to get well, that I was fighting against it. But I did, I always did. Really! I just don't think I have the energy to try anymore. If this is what God has in mind for me, maybe I should just . . . accept it.''

"God doesn't have anything like this in mind for you, Rickie. Remember what I told you on the phone? I have some new ideas, important ones. I've come to take you out!''

"Now?'' she asked, looking up.

"In a couple of weeks, as soon as I have everything in order.''

She began to cry, but her tears were not the kind I had seen her shed so often. She was smiling at the same time. "Where to, Daddy?''

"Another place.''

"I don't want to start all over again. I want to go home.''

"You're going home, Rickie. Not immediately, but eventually. Can you give it another try?''

She said nothing. Then she nodded slowly.

"This isn't easy for me,'' I continued. "It means going against everything I've ever been taught, and I can't promise you it will work.''

"The visual stuff and the vitamin therapy?"

"Dr. Carl Pfeiffer has a halfway house called Earth House near Princeton, New Jersey, where people can live while they're being treated. Maybe I should have done something about this sooner, but you seemed happy at Gould Farm until a few months ago, so I put it aside. Then, too, my colleagues scoffed at Pfeiffer's work. Well, I called Dr. Pfeiffer this week. He's willing to interview you and do some preliminary tests to see if he thinks he can help."

"Do you want me to try?" she repeated.

"Of course I want you to," I urged, "don't you?"

"Yes." Her voice picked up.

"I want to have your eyes checked too," I added. "Okay?"

"Dr. Flanders thought it was silly. But you know, ever since you called, I have the strangest feeling about it. A good feeling, like this could really be it."

"And one more thing, Rickie. Do you . . . still pray? It's all right if you don't, but do you?"

"I've never stopped."

I reached into my coat pocket, pulled out a small colored picture with printing on the back of it, and handed it to her.

"What's this?" she wondered. "It looks like one of the holy pictures the sisters gave us when we made our first communion."

She read the inscription. "St. Jude. Who is St. Jude?"

"A very powerful saint, Rickie."

"Through your intercession," she read, "grant me the impossible." She put the card in her pocket. "I'll keep it forever. When do we start?"

"Week after next. You know, when I told your doctor here, I can't think of his name . . ."

"I can't remember it either," Rickie said. "It's a long foreign-sounding name."

"When I told him what we were going to do, he squeezed

my hand and said that I was being a wonderful father to you.''

''You've always been.''

''I'm not so sure. I've tried.''

She took my hand. ''I'm afraid,'' she confessed softly.

''You're not the only one, Rickie.''

Part Three

52

Just as we shall never forget the date in 1966 when Rickie first was hospitalized, John's ninth birthday, so too we shall never forget the date when Rickie left the Poughkeepsie State Hospital for the final stage in her long and terrifying odyssey. It was Thanksgiving Day, 1975. She was going to visit with us for a while, then go to her mother's for dinner and the night. The next morning we had an appointment with the developmental optometrist, Dr. Kaplan, in Tarrytown, a suburb an hour's drive north of the city. And after lunch we had another appointment with a Dorothy Sawyer in New York City, who had been strongly recommended by Kent Smith; he was convinced that for many psychiatric patients the key to sustained recovery lay in coherent, judicious rehabilitation planning coordinated by a professional trained and experienced in the then-new field of rehabilitation counseling. On Saturday I would drive Rickie to Earth House in New Jersey, the residential program affiliated with Dr. Pfeiffer's Brain Bio Center.

A couple of children were reading comic books in Dr. Melvin Kaplan's waiting room when we arrived. His secretary, who sat behind a counter in a white technician's uniform, confirmed our appointment and promptly filled out a large record card. As I considered the gravity of the examination Rickie was about to undergo, the rack of stylish sunglasses on display seemed particularly incongruous.

Dr. Kaplan appeared in less than five minutes. He was a

241

short man with tousled hair, no more than five feet nine, wearing a maroon sports shirt, tan wool trousers, and, naturally, horn-rimmed glasses. He spoke with a definite New York accent. "Well, so this is Rickie," he greeted her cheerfully. "Come in my examining room, won't you. You too, Doctor." He sat Rickie on an examining chair and asked her to identify rows of letters projected onto the opposite wall. "Her visual acuity is 20/30 in each eye," Kaplan pronounced. He then swung a large black metal optometric device in front of her face; it looked like some creature with a hundred eyes from another planet. A lens covered each eye in turn as he tested her vision.

My usual scientific skepticism about Kaplan's outlandish notion that Rickie's vision might be an important element in her illness was dispelled by my eagerness, even desperation, for some sort of miracle.

"Gross nystagmoid movements," he muttered. He shined a light through the lens into Rickie's eyes, and abruptly she jerked back in the chair as far as she could, wincing. For an instant she seemed seized by terror.

I jumped to my feet, alarmed. "What is it?"

Kaplan placed his hand on Rickie's arm to reassure her. "Don't be afraid. It's only a test." Then, addressing me, he explained. "It's called an objective test. When you shine a small light in a normal patient's eye to see the retinal action, you should get a nice directional movement from the retina. But in Rickie's case I got a scissor motion. Amazing!" Removing the machine, he asked her to read the letters again. "My God! Her acuity's dropped to 20/200. That's legally blind. She's totally compressed her visual system."

"Did you say blind?" I asked, bewildered.

"She has shut off, literally suppressed her vision. That's what I mean by blind."

"How can that be?" I wondered. "Rickie reads and walks around; at times she's even driven a car. How can she be blind?"

"Functionally," Kaplan replied, as he moved the instrument aside and briskly put a pair of wire-frame glasses in place. He promptly asked her to read the chart again, and observed that Rickie's visual acuity had returned to normal. "Unpredictably, especially when she's stressed, she shuts down her whole visual system," he described. "That can last minutes, hours, even days, during which time she's really not seeing at all. The rest of the time she's getting by, but only by a great expenditure of energy."

At the time I barely grasped the implications.

"It's like computer software," Kaplan went on. "Nothing's wrong with the machinery, but the programming is defective and the messages that are supposed to travel from the eye to the brain don't get there the way they should." He turned to Rickie. "When you look at anything, Rickie, how long does the image stay?"

She hesitated, puzzled.

"Does it stay or does it disappear, vanish?"

"It stays. I mean, I can make it stay."

"What do you mean, make it stay?"

"Well . . ." She paused, considering. "If I look at you for a minute or so, you start to disappear. But if I get my willpower going, I can keep you in sight for a long time."

"And what happens to the rest of the things in this room? The lamp, the walls, the eyeglass stand over there?"

"At first I see them, and you. Then, as I concentrate harder on seeing you, they get dimmer and dimmer, until I can't see them at all."

Dr. Kaplan seemed excited. "You see! You see!" He waved his hand. "Rickie can't sustain a visual image for more than a minute without beginning to shut down everything else. She has to muster all her energy to keep seeing. I'd assume that she's been struggling with this since she was three years old, perhaps even earlier."

"Isn't that the way everybody sees?" Rickie asked.

"My God, Rickie!" I exclaimed. "You mean you thought that was normal?"

"Isn't it?"

"No, Rickie, it isn't," Kaplan went on to explain, "and a routine eye exam wouldn't reveal your problem. Optometrists and ophthalmologists usually only ask that first question—'What is it?'—and fixing you up so you can focus on 'it' more clearly. What they're not examining is how long it takes you to find what you're trying to see." Kaplan smiled. "But wait, there's more." He took us into an adjacent room, which looked more like a storeroom than a laboratory.

"You see that piece of wood over there?" he asked Rickie, pointing to a plank about eight feet long, a foot and a half wide, and a few inches off the floor.

"Yes."

"Stand on it."

She quietly obliged.

"Now," Kaplan directed, "walk along the plank to the other end."

Rickie took one step, then another. On her third her foot missed the board and landed with a thud on the floor. Her arms waved around wildly as she struggled to keep from losing control altogether and falling down.

"I'm not sure I could do that," I spoke up.

"Yes, you could," Kaplan assured me. "Now, Rickie, try it again."

Rickie resumed her position on the board, but again missed her footing and slipped off by the third step. She blushed slightly. "What's the matter with me?"

"Not to worry, Rickie," Kaplan said kindly, putting his hand on her shoulder. "You have a balance problem, and we can fix it. Now, I have a surprise for you. I want you to do two things. First put on these prisms." He handed her the pair of glasses he had used in the examining room. "And hold these beads in your hand, tightly now."

Rickie obeyed, then moved from one end of the plank to the other with the grace of a dancer.

"You see," Kaplan tried to explain, "Rickie has no instinctive idea of where her body is in space. She can't coordinate her visual input with the messages she's receiving from her body. The prisms expand her sense of space, so she can command it better. The beads give her a sense of security—like holding onto a banister when you're going downstairs. They enable her to regain her natural sense of gravity."

"Gravity?"

"If we didn't have some kind of antigravity control mechanism, we wouldn't be able to stand up. We'd spend all our lives lying down. You see the difference?"

"I couldn't help but see it," I conceded. "But why wouldn't something like this have been detected a long time ago?"

"No one thought to look for it," Kaplan pointed out simply. "Of course, in my opinion, that's inexcusable. Even in your medical literature there are many reports of visual-motor difficulties in children who later, as teenagers or adults, become psychiatrically disabled. But as far as I know, no one has followed up on those leads. Too simple, perhaps, or too threatening to popular theory."

Rickie was walking along the board again.

"Rickie was always accident prone. Could this have had anything to do with that?" I wondered.

"If you can't see one foot in front of the other and figure out how far things are from you and from each other, I'd think you'd be very accident prone, wouldn't you?"

"What *are* those glasses you keep putting on her?" I asked.

"These are called directive yoked prisms, base down. But they're not ordinary prisms. Don't confuse them with the prisms vision specialists routinely use. They're quite different. They look like ordinary glasses, but they actually expand the space she perceives and help restore depth perception . . . you could say they work like a wide-angle lens on a camera.'' He held his hands in front of his eyes, palms on his temples, fingers meeting about three inches in front of his nose. Then he slowly moved the fingers of each hand away from each other, as if opening a fan. ''What the lenses do,'' he explained, ''is create divergence of vision, not by directly affecting the eyes themselves, but rather by inducing an illusion that the space around the objects you are looking at is enlarged.''

I repeated his gesture. ''You must be redirecting light,'' I observed excitedly, ''shifting more onto the peripheral part of the retina.''

''You do know something about the eyes.'' Kaplan chuckled.

I laughed. ''I won the ophthalmology prize in medical school, God knows why! Tell me, is this a condition you run into often?''

''Optometrists have compiled a terminology to describe it, classifications such as overconvergence and the like, but their concepts and language really don't do justice to what's happening here. Frankly, it's cutting-edge stuff that we're just beginning to understand.''

Rickie hopped off the board, a wide grin on her face.

''She's seeing—the way you and I see—for the first time,'' Kaplan pointed out, taking her hand. ''When someone's been living in a visual prison and you suddenly enable them to expand the space around them, it can be an amazing experience.''

''The prisms seem to have quite an effect.'' Despite the evidence before me, skepticism persisted.

''Precisely,'' Kaplan responded, sensing my doubt. ''It's hard to explain; even my colleagues are confused about my work with prisms. You have to understand Rickie's visual system. When she looks at things far away from her, it is as if she were looking into empty space. Then, when she closes in to look at things closer to her, she overdoes it, tunnels in, and gets locked in that tunnel. Imagine looking at the world through a tunnel all the time, jumping from field to field like bits and pieces of an old motion picture, a frame at a time, trying to figure out what was going on and working laboriously to pick up and integrate the slightest piece of information, all without the benefit of depth perception. With the prisms, her visual scope is abruptly broadened and she can see peripherally as well. Without peripheral vision, we can hardly function, yet that's something she'd lost as a result of stress. We only have so much energy to spend, and people who are vulnerable, like Rickie, close down their vision to conserve energy when they're under too much pressure. Unfortunately, that leaves them more helpless than ever.''

''I still don't understand,'' I admitted, unaware that even Dr. Kaplan's understanding was itself still in an early stage of development.

''Context. That's the key,'' Kaplan posited. ''When you look out into space, you have to see things in relation to each other and to yourself. Every time you look at something, you're automatically asking yourself not only what it is, but where is it, and where am I. If your eyes don't function effectively, you have to fall back on a number of unhealthy strategies for the answers. Maybe you have to walk along the street looking down at the pavement. Or maybe, when you're reading, you can't be distracted by things around you, and when you get up from your chair you bump into the first thing in your path. Or you may not be able to answer those basic questions at all.

''All right, Rickie. That's fine,'' Kaplan said, giving her shoulder an encouraging squeeze.

''You've been taking this all in, haven't you?''

She nodded.

''Any questions?''

"No. I'm trying to pay attention to what you're doing and saying."

"When you have as much trouble seeing as you do, young lady, you become a very good listener, I'll bet."

She nodded again, a rueful smile across her face.

"We have a few more tests, and then we can talk some more."

Back in his office again, he inquired: "Are you familiar with the work of Piaget?"

"Certainly." Piaget, the Swiss psychologist, had evolved a theory of early childhood learning, a step-by-step process whereby infants and children learned not only to come to terms with themselves and their environment, but how to develop a *capacity* to integrate new knowledge and new ways of coping throughout life.

"Anything that interferes with that cycle can have serious complications," Kaplan affirmed. "If I knew nothing else at all about Rickie, from this examination alone, I could reveal things about her personality and her life that might amaze you. It's no surprise to me that she has been so crippled."

"For instance?" I asked.

"Since you've already told me that Rickie's had severe psychiatric problems, what I'm going to say may not sound very convincing. But I'd hazard a guess she was always shy as a child and had difficulty making friends, because the world outside her seemed to encroach on her limited space and frighten her. She probably was afraid of the night, of going to sleep. Clumsy. Accidents playing sports, running. Trouble in school. In fact, I'd think any effort to get her to work in school, except perhaps in the earliest grades, would provoke panic. Rickie's led most of her life in a state not unlike sensory deprivation."

Rickie was engrossed in what Kaplan was saying. "That's true," she eagerly confirmed. "Every time I tried to go to school, I'd panic and fall apart."

Remembering Rickie's being placed in isolation for weeks, I was furious. If Kaplan's postulations were accurate and she were already suffering from a profound lack of external stimulation, such treatment must have intensified her helplessness and terror. I recalled how frightened she had been of the darkness as a small child, and the time she fell running and bruised her face. "In your opinion, how would something like this have begun?" I asked.

"Inherited perhaps," he said. "Or the result of stress of some kind, mental or physiological."

I mentioned the operation she'd undergone at six months for the tumor on her forehead. I also recalled the unusual activity in the occipital/visual area of the electroencephalogram that had been done years before at Gracie Square Hospital. Could there be a connection?

"Maybe," Kaplan acknowledged. "A Dr. Gray Walters wrote a book called *The Living Brain* in which he had some interesting information about visual problems and abnormal occipital EEG readings. You might want to look it up."

I suddenly remembered an incident when Rickie was three. We were vacationing in Lake Placid, and she and I were standing in front of a large window that overlooked the forest when Rickie began trembling, apparently afraid. I asked her what was wrong. "The trees are coming to the house," she had cried. "They're all coming in here."

"That could have been the beginning of it," Kaplan mused. "Space collapsing, the loss of depth perception."

"Why then?" I wondered.

"I don't know why then," he replied, shrugging his shoulders.

"Can anything be done to correct this permanently?"

"You've already seen immediate benefits," Kaplan pointed out, "and if Rickie will cooperate, we can try for more significant and lasting changes."

"What would that involve?"

"I'll give her a pair of these prisms to wear all the time

for the next few months. Eventually her own brain will learn how to take over and do the rest on its own. I assume you're familiar with Stratton's famous experiments which showed that wearing a pair of glasses that turned everything upside down for several days left the subjects with an upside-down perception lasting for days after the glasses were removed. The brain obviously had adapted to the new information, holding on to it well after the distorting influence of the prisms had been removed.''

It sounded familiar.

''Well, it's the same principle.''

''That's all there is to it? A pair of glasses?'' I was still incredulous.

''By no means. Rickie's problem is too deeply embedded. She'll have to be extensively retrained too. We have to help her learn how to use spatial cues to stabilize her visual systems. We must give her more visual flexibility. If possible, I'd like to see her once a week for at least six months, maybe even a year. And she'll have to do exercises faithfully every day on her own.''

''That might be hard,'' I said. ''Rickie will be staying at a rehabilitation center near Princeton. I don't know whether they'll let her come or how she would get all the way here.''

''I *have* to do it,'' Rickie insisted excitedly. ''I know it'll work!''

''If someone at the center were willing to supervise her training exercises, I could show them what to do,'' Kaplan offered.

''I don't know how open they would be to your ideas,'' I admitted. Then I said firmly: ''I'll see that they do.''

''Small enough effort for the possible rewards, eh?''

I still could not entirely dispel nagging doubts. ''Has any of this been exposed to scientific scrutiny?'' Kaplan appeared puzzled. ''I mean, have any of these ideas and treatments you've described been put to the test in controlled

studies?'' I'd read Sinclair Lewis's *Arrowsmith* twice as a
teenager and, during my many years immersed in research,
had never forgotten his old professor's admonition to subject
his theories to rigorously controlled investigation. I also
knew only too well that few practitioners really grasped the
critical importance of such efforts to separate wheat from
chaff, consequently spending much of their lives bewildered
by the refusal of their colleagues to accept anecdotal data
as valid. Choosing not to press my point, I took a more
practical stance. ''Have you ever treated this condition in a
patient like Rickie?''

''Frankly, I've treated plenty of visual disabilities before, but never in a psychiatric patient like Rickie.'' He
smiled. ''There always has to be a first time, right?''

Considering Rickie's long struggle and her enthusiasm,
that was good enough for me.

53

Dorothy Sawyer's office was at Thirty-ninth and Lexington. Finding a place to park a block away, I remarked on
the good omen.

''Do I look silly in the glasses Dr. Kaplan loaned me?''
Rickie asked as we walked toward the Tuscany Towers.

''Those horn-rims make you look very intelligent.''

She seemed reassured.

Dorothy Sawyer's consulting room was part of her professional apartment. We pushed the button on her intercom.
She buzzed us in. We found ourselves standing in a quiet,

small room, comfortably furnished with several overstuffed chairs and a long couch covered in light blue wool plaid. A nineteen-inch television set in one corner was one of several clues to the fact the area was used as a waiting room for clients in the daytime and otherwise served as Dorothy's living room. Before we could sit down, a heavyset gray-haired woman with a friendly smile entered from another door and held out her hand.

"I'm Dorothy," she greeted us warmly. "This must be Rickie. I'm so glad to meet you, Rickie."

I was instantly moved by the genuineness of her manner.

"If you'll have a seat, I'm just finishing up with a client. I'll be with you shortly."

A young woman, attractively dressed in a brown business suit, came out of Dorothy's office a few minutes later, smiled at us, picked up a briefcase sitting by an umbrella stand and left.

Dorothy returned. "I'd like to speak with Rickie alone," she said authoritatively. "Then I'll talk with both of you together."

After nearly forty-five minutes and four issues of *The New Yorker*, I joined them in an office that also bore the trappings of a home. A small room full of flowers, it held a half-finished sweater with knitting needles perched on a side table, and against the wall, an antique writing desk piled with papers. Although the windows were closed, we could hear the irregular screech of Lexington Avenue buses and honking horns far below.

"Well," Dorothy began, "Rickie is a very delightful young woman. We've had a good chat, haven't we, Rickie?"

Rickie nodded.

"She's been through an awful lot, poor dear. But you know, I think she's managed it all very well indeed." Dorothy spoke in a soft, distinctive voice, midwestern I guessed, emanating a powerful supportiveness. "Of course, that's all behind us now," she said.

I liked the way she said "us."

"Time to begin building a new life. She told me you're taking her to Earth House Friday. I think that's wonderful. I know Ronnie LaRoche. She organized Earth House, as you probably know, Dr. Flach, and she's the program director. Ronnie's a very special person. She works closely with Dr. Pfeiffer, and I'm certainly familiar with his work as well. I've had several clients there who've done very well."

"Dorothy was asking me whether anyone ever did vocational testing on me, Daddy? Did they?" Rickie inquired eagerly.

"I don't know," I admitted. "I don't think so."

"I don't remember anyone talking with me about what sort of work I might like to do someday. I guess they were too busy trying to get me well," she added.

"I'm a rehabilitation counselor," Dorothy said patiently. "In case you aren't familiar with the field, Doctor—I don't mind, as it's a new field in mental health and there aren't many of us yet—I'd like to explain. Psychiatrists like you like to get at the root of people's problems and help them solve them. You do a wonderful job. But where we come in is when a client has to deal with the real world: find a job, get a place to live, make friends, discover strengths and talents to use in getting better and staying better. You could say we put a lot of emphasis on positive thinking, and we do. A medical paper recently concluded that people who cope well with their lives tend to have a slightly prejudiced point of view about themselves, in their favor, of course. They're optimists without carrying it to an extreme. Are you an optimist, Rickie?"

"What's an optimist?"

"Someone who dreams, and believes that she can achieve her dreams, who thinks the world is not such a terrible place and that she can find some measure of happiness in it."

"I'm afrad Rickie hasn't had much to feel optimistic about over the past years," I admitted regretfully.

"Oh, but Daddy, if what Dorothy described is right, then I really am an optimist," Rickie broke in, sounding genuinely excited. "I've always had dreams of what I wanted to do, the kind of person I wanted to become. Even at my worst moments, I always knew that somehow, somewhere, I would reach those dreams." Her eyes revealed a spark of animation I'd seldom seen.

"That's a very good foundation to build on," Dorothy encouraged, reaching out her hand to Rickie's.

Sometime before, I had come to the conclusion that any truly effective psychotherapist must possess a gift of healing, undoubtedly enriched and directed by training and experience, but nonetheless a sine qua non. Without it, all the education in the world produced at best a mediocre, by-the-book professional. I was convinced that Dorothy Sawyer had the gift of healing.

"Let me explain how I work," Dorothy offered. "I don't set up regular, by-the-clock sessions. Of course, I do make appointments, but I work on a small retainer, and while a client is with me, she—in this case Rickie—can use as much or as little of my time as is necessary. I'll want to see you at least once a week in the beginning, as soon as you have settled in at Earth House. If it's desirable, I'll come down there for a while to see you. I want you to feel free to telephone me any time you want, no matter what the hour or day. We have a lot of work to do together."

As we stood to leave, Dorothy looked straight at Rickie. "I have a great deal of confidence in you, young lady. I know you're going to be just fine."

Back in the car, I struggled vainly to get my seat belt safely inserted in its clasp. Rickie reached over and deftly took care of it.

"I've never met anyone like Dorothy," she said admiringly. "She's really interested in me, not just symptoms and how I feel, but me as a person, who I am, what I want, what I can be.''

"To be honest, I'm not sure I have either, and I'm impressed.''

"Do you think this will take the pain away?'' she asked hopefully.

I took her by the hand and squeezed it tightly.

=== 54 ===

Finding Earth House was no easy matter. What should have been an hour's trip took twice that, as we kept crossing tiny bridges that spanned the Delaware-Raritan Canal, searching for a white farmhouse and red barn along a road lined with white clapboard farmhouses. Finally, in desperation, we pulled into a driveway to ask directions, only to discover that we had chosen the right place. Another good omen, I pointed out to Rickie.

A pretty woman whom I guessed to be in her middle thirties, with auburn hair and wearing a light brown corduroy jacket, came out of the barn and walked toward us. It was Ronnie LaRoche. Later, when I discovered that she was the niece of Rosalind Russell, the popular motion-picture actress of the 1940s, I could see that she had inherited some of her aunt's striking beauty and presence.

She took Rickie's hand and walked toward the main building.

"Do you have any animals here?'' Rickie asked.

"Dogs and cats.''

"I was thinking of cows and horses."

"This isn't a farm," Ronnie said. "That's right, you did live on a real farm for a while, didn't you, Rickie?"

"Yes, and I loved it. It was hard work, but I really loved it."

"Well, you're going to have to work hard here too," Ronnie said, "but not farm work."

"Doing what?" Rickie asked apprehensively.

"You'll see."

By now we had reached the front door of the rambling main house. Ronnie let us in and led us through a large living room crowded with mismatched easy chairs and tables that looked as though they'd been acquired at rummage sales over the years. We passed a young man in his twenties, who sat reading in front of a stone fireplace, feet warmed by smoldering embers, and a young woman carefully completing a jigsaw puzzle. In Ronnie's makeshift office, papers strewn about attested to a busy schedule. A hardware-store calendar with enormous black numbers hung too high on one wall, over a yellow metal desk and three yellow filing cabinets. "I'd like to show Rickie around the place, Dr. Flach, and have a few words with her privately," Ronnie said commandingly.

I told her I'd wait.

"It's going to take a couple of hours," she noted. "Perhaps you'd rather go for lunch? I'd like Rickie to have lunch with us." She directed me to a restaurant called Charlie's, farther down Canal Road toward Princeton. I cheerfully obliged. She struck me as the kind of person who could easily persuade you to do whatever she wanted, and do it happily.

Ever since I had picked Rickie up in Poughkeepsie, I had been riding high, elated by the prospect that this entirely new approach might finally produce the recovery we had prayed for all these years. Halfway through my club sandwich and coffee, however, my good spirits evaporated as the events of the past few days assumed a completely different hue. Kaplan's examination suddenly seemed bizarre, his chatter about systems closing down and opening up and controlling space a form of hastily-edited science fiction. The idea that a diet could ameliorate Rickie's intractable illness struck me as preposterous. Dorothy Sawyer and Ronnie LaRoche were warm, well-meaning, and undoubtedly intelligent women, but Rickie had been under the care of an endless line of professionals no less dedicated to her recovery, many of whom had credentials to spare. What could Earth House or Pfeiffer or Kaplan do for Rickie that hadn't already been done? In a few months, I figured, I could expect the usual phone call telling me that Rickie would have to be hospitalized once more.

I was still depressed when I reached Earth House. But as I entered the building and saw Rickie talking cheerfully with several other youngsters in the living room, I found my optimism—that was the word Dorothy had used—returning.

"I think this place is great!" Rickie exclaimed, jumping from her chair and running over. "Ronnie said that if my blood levels are what they think they are, I can come and stay here, if I promise not to hurt myself. I'd have my own room too." She was trembling with excitement.

"Rickie will have her blood and urine analyses done tomorrow," Ronnie announced in a businesslike manner. "When we get the results, we'll start her on the right diet."

"What else goes on here?" I inquired.

"Our program is designed to teach our students what they need to know to function in the world," she explained in a husky, direct voice. "Our patients are students because they're learning how to recover—and how to live again. They're learning about their illness, its biochemistry and its history. They also practice the skills of daily living. They eat well and learn about good nutrition and vitamins, and they exercise daily.

"I don't know whether you know it or not, Dr. Flach, but I'm a recovered schizophrenic myself." I was startled

by her admission and slightly humbled by her frankness and
courage. "Many psychiatrists have said that that's an im-
possibility, since I'm functioning now. But Carl Pfeiffer addressed my nutritional imbalances, and now I'm in a position
to help others with what I know and have been through. I
do hope Rickie qualifies. If she comes here, I think she can
learn what she needs to recover."

"When will I meet with Dr. Pfeiffer?" I asked.

"In about a week," Ronnie replied, "as soon as the tests
are done."

55

My appointment with Dr. Pfeiffer was set for the second
Monday in December. Finding the Brain Bio Center was
considerably easier than Earth House; it was located at an
intersection on Route 206, in a two-story brick building
shared with a Goodyear Tire outlet.

From the tidy waiting area I was led past several spick-
and-span laboratories to Dr. Pfeiffer's office by a young
woman in her mid-twenties. "You work here?" I asked idly
as we walked.

"Part of the time," she said. "I live at Earth House."

Pfeiffer stood in front of his tinted-glass office door waiting for us.

"It's a pleasure to meet you," I said.

"It's a pleasure to meet a pioneer in calcium research,"
Dr. Pfeiffer said, taking me by surprise. "I call you that in
my book, you know," he added, pointing to a copy of *Men-*

tal and Elemental Nutrients perched prominently amid hundreds of volumes that filled the bookcases extending to cover an entire wall. Through another wall, entirely glass, I could see two technicians hovering over test-tube racks. "You were one of the first to demonstrate a connection between calcium and psychiatric illness. You should be proud of that. Oh, but do sit down, and please, call me Carl." Pfeiffer was a man in his late sixties, but his ruddy complexion, sparkling eyes, and quick movements revealed intensity and enthusiasm, the mind and spirit of someone half his age.

"I'm not just involved in giving patients a magic diet," he said frankly. "When we talked originally, I told you that Earth House couldn't agree to keep Rickie unless her blood and urine findings were consistent with what we believe we can treat . . . and I'm glad to say they are."

I felt a chill, the kind I could only recall having experienced a few times in a lifetime, like when the voice came onto the loudspeaker system at the naval base announcing that the Japanese had officially surrendered and the war was finally over.

I'd read through Pfeiffer's textbook before coming, although I had evidently missed the paragraph in which I was mentioned. The human mind is curiously fragile; until this meeting I had never made the obvious connection between Pfeiffer's work and the calcium research that had absorbed me for years. Though I had rigorously controlled the dietary intake of my subjects to ensure the accuracy of laboratory examinations, and had even attempted to relieve depression by systematically administering calcium intravenously, the idea of inducing improvement via nutrition had simply not occurred to me.

Pfeiffer postulated that there were at least three different types of schizophrenias, perhaps more. In fact, he regarded the term itself as a poor label for what he felt represented a variety of physical illnesses. One group had abnormally high blood levels of histamine, an amino acid intimately involved in brain function; a second had abnormally low levels of histamine; and a third showed pyroluria, the excretion of high amounts of an abnormal metabolite of purine metabolism. He called this the "mauve" factor, naming it after the purple color of the chemically treated urine.

"Clinically, Rickie is a low histamine type," he informed me. "She has all the features: obsessions, confused thoughts rushing pell-mell through her mind, lack of self-control, strangely altered perceptions of herself and her environment." He glanced through his notes. "She has a history of left upper-quadrant abdominal pain," he went on.

I was puzzled by this observation. She had indeed complained of abdominal pains on and off since childhood, but they seemed irrelevant, except as nonspecific manifestations of stress, or as a bid for attention.

"She also had difficulty sleeping," he went on, "and apparently had a great deal of such trouble as a small child. Well, it may surprise you, but those two symptoms—unexplained abdominal pains and persistent insomnia—are characteristic of what I call pyroluria. It's a metabolic disorder. Patients who've been sick a long time and who suffer pyroluria seem to have more insight into themselves and more feelings left than the chronically burned out, apathetic cases. They can do quite well with proper treatment.

"Rickie's laboratory results confirmed my initial impression," he continued almost gleefully. "Her blood histamine level is definitely low. Her copper is a little high. And her pyroluria is forty! It shouldn't be above ten." The enthusiasm in his voice was contagious. He described the regimen that he intended to establish for Rickie. Had I not been somewhat prepared, I might have viewed it as a potpourri off the counter of a health food store.

To raise her histamine level, Rickie would take 3000 milligrams of vitamin C, 800 mg. of niacin, and 4 mg. of folic acid daily, supplemented with injections of 1000 mg. of vitamin B-12 twice a week. To reduce her pyroluria, she would take 1500 mg. of vitamin B-6 and 60 mg. of zinc each day.

"It takes several months to get results," Pfeiffer stated, "and sometimes the second month is particularly difficult. The patients can get pretty upset, probably due to the extensive physiological changes going on. But after that you can begin to see real improvement."

"I hope so," I said quietly.

He reached out and placed his large hand firmly on my shoulder. "I know this wasn't an easy decision for you," he said compassionately. "My work is not exactly held in high regard by many of your colleagues, not officially, at any rate. But Rickie's not the first relative of a physician I've been asked to see, and I'm sure she won't be the last. They usually come to me when everything else has failed. Even then, they're skeptical, as you must be." He smiled wryly. "A friend of yours—I don't believe it appropriate to mention his name, but I'm sure he'll tell you about it once he learns that Rickie's here—brought his son to me some years back. A hopeless case, so everyone believed."

I had no idea whom he had in mind.

"Well, his son was one of our outstanding patients. He graduated from law school this year."

"Then . . . there really is hope for Rickie."

"Hope? There's always hope," Pfeiffer pronounced. "Hope is the catalyst that keeps this whole damned universe from coming apart at the seams. However, first things first. Let me show you around the laboratories and you can tell me about your own research."

"I've not been doing research for a few years."

"My, my, what a loss," he muttered as he picked up a test tube filled with pastel liquid. "Mauve," he observed.

=== 56 ===

Despite the fact that I'd spent most of my life waiting, this time around I was terribly nervous. So much seemed to depend on my getting into Earth House. My dad told me to keep praying to St. Jude, and I did. For ten whole days I stayed at my mother's house. Dorothy Sawyer had arranged for me to have companions, licensed practical nurses around the clock, so that my mom wouldn't be nervous about having me there. I kept myself busy. I took walks, I painted, I knitted. I was quiet and pretty withdrawn, but inside I believed this was really the answer for me. I don't know how I knew, but I did. And when I was told I had been accepted, I thanked St. Jude and made a promise that I would try my very best to succeed.

I remember Dad took me out to Earth House in his old maroon Mercedes. Ronnie came out to greet me and show me to my room. I was terribly excited, and afraid too.

"You can arrange and decorate it any way you like," she told me as she opened the door to the most beautiful room I'd seen in a long time. A queen-size mattress lay in one corner, and the roof sloped to one side, with two low windows at the lowest point. There was a bookshelf, a couple of pictures on the wall, and a huge closet. A bathroom that I would share with Ronnie was right next door, and I could even lock it! That in itself was thrilling.

Ronnie told me I could have some time by myself to unpack and put my things in the closet. She said lunch would be ready at noon, so she'd see me there. When she left, she closed the door behind her. I just sat there and looked around me. "I'm really here," I said out loud. "I'm really going to get well."

I started to put my things away, stopping several times to look out the window. When I'd finished, I went downstairs to see what to do next, feeling like I was finally at home.

57

Once a week a staff aide drove Rickie to Tarrytown for visual training with Dr. Kaplan, where a variety of tasks, described as feed-forward and feed-back situations, had been designed to reorganize her management of visual space. For example, because she had serious problems judging location and distance, certain exercises employed instruments that simulated archery; she'd aim at a target, see where she would have hit, then try to correct for her error the next time around. Also, since Rickie's brain couldn't process too much visual stimulation effectively and would simply shut down, she had to learn to adapt gradually to progressive increments in visual input. She was also taught to grasp her physical location in relationship to what surrounded her, and to trust that awareness.

At Earth House someone was assigned to see that Rickie faithfully wore her prisms and did her exercises—following a moving ball in space, tracing a "lazy eight" on a blackboard, attacking a checkerboard tacked to a wall with a pointer, one eye at a time and then with both eyes at once.

Considering the staff's dedication to nutritional therapy and social skills rehabilitation, I could only admire their commitment to visual training which was beyond the scope of their understanding. It was a heartening contrast to professional attitudes I had encountered so often.

Pfeiffer had predicted that it would take at least four months on the nutritional program to produce any real results. True to his warning, for a couple of weeks she was more depressed, silent, and withdrawn; her histamine level was reported to be slightly better at that point but her copper level was strikingly elevated and her pyroluria had barely changed. By the fourth month of treatment, however, she seemed to be considerably better. Ronnie confirmed my impression. "She is better. Her copper's down. So is her pyroluria, to a level of seven."

Kaplan appeared no less enthusiastic. "She's using her eyes together," he told me on the telephone sometime in April. "She's gone from using one eye at a time to being binocular, and she's regained depth perception. I think it's time for her to drive herself up to see me. In a couple of months I wouldn't be surprised if she can do without the prisms except in times of special stress." This was encouraging, to say the least.

I was no less impressed by the tremendous efforts to retrain Rickie in social skills she would require to function in the world. Ronnie was truly a pioneer in psychiatric rehabilitation, employing strategies that have since become standard procedure at the best of today's treatment centers, though I didn't appreciate that at the time. But it was Rickie herself who really began to convince me that what she was experiencing was substantially different.

My days at Earth House were the most wonderful ones since childhood. I learned to do yoga and a few simple dance steps. Jane, the housemother, gave me ballet lessons every morning. Cliff, one of the staff members, who was built like a lumberjack, got me to do my house chores and crafts; he had a strong voice and a gentle way about him. When he said, "Go clean your room now," I wanted to. I was eating well for the first time since Gould Farm, and faithfully taking the vitamins Dr. Pfeiffer prescribed.

I still had lots of symptoms, though. Sometimes, in the middle of a conversation, I would shake all over, as if I were freezing cold. Ronnie explained that the shaking came from the exertion of communicating—and that with time I wouldn't shake anymore or roll my eyes or my tongue, which still happened sometimes.

I also hated being touched, but slowly I became used to it, and even began to like a hug from Ronnie, or to give one now and then. She'd often say, "You did such a good job! Can I give you a hug?" I had known from the first time I saw Ronnie that she was one of the few people who really understood how I felt. She had so much empathy. She knew how I suffered, and I just looked at her and I knew that there was my answer.

A longstanding habit was to go over what I wanted to say in my head before saying it out loud, to make sure it came out right. As a consequence, I didn't say much, and when I did, it was in a very soft voice. Ronnie helped me to get my voice out there with my thoughts. She told me that the brain has so many thoughts that sometimes it feels as if you're tuned into fifteen radio stations, or that you're not in the real world. That was true. What we were working on was getting tuned in and getting right down to earth.

After about two weeks at Earth House I was sitting in my room looking out my window and realized I was feeling better. I was able to look out of myself and see other people for the first time since I couldn't remember when. I noticed a change inside of me too. I still had urges to hurt myself at times, but they were growing much, much weaker. It was as if I had a lot more room to move around in, not just outside myself, but inside my head as well. My thoughts weren't so loud anymore, not so insistent. Plus, Ronnie had made it clear that if I hurt myself one time, I'd be out!

Also, I was getting attention for good behavior instead of bad. Unlike elsewhere, the focus at Earth House was not on why I had been sick but on how to get better and stay better! I was being taught how to take care of myself, how to cook meals and do all sorts of things on my own. I was learning how to take care of my body, how to put on makeup and how to dress.

I was also deeply involved in my daily eye exercises. After I'd been going up to Dr. Kaplan's for about three months, I renewed my driver's license and started driving myself to Tarrytown for the appointments. One time in early spring nobody in his office recognized me—not his nurse or receptionist. When I told them, "It's me, Rickie!" they called Dr. Kaplan out and he couldn't believe his eyes. He said, "You look beautiful! You look like a tall, gorgeous model. This is amazing!"

I was also learning how to smile. When you're in an institution, you don't realize it, but you get a vacant, blank look just like everyone else in there—and you rarely smile. It was hard to learn how.

David Smith, our yoga teacher, was the one who taught me. In his early thirties, David looked twenty-two. He was an adventurer who swam huge distances, climbed mountains, and accomplished unbelievable athletic feats. At Earth House he taught us yoga and took us on exercise trails to look at nature.

Anyway, David sat me down in front of a mirror and made me smile. He would make me assume different smiles and practice them during the day. It wasn't easy. I felt like it was fake because it didn't come naturally at all, and I didn't like to look in the mirror. You could hardly see yourself in the hospital ones because they were aluminum or some material that you couldn't break, so that was ten years without looking at myself in a mirror.

Ronnie worked with me on videotape so that I could see and hear myself. We'd have conversations on camera, and when I watched the tape afterwards, I saw how much better I looked when I smiled, and what I looked like to other people. When I had to make my first dentist appointment, we practiced it on videotape. We also practiced a lot of other things to show me how to be a determined person doing things for myself.

In the spring David Smith took all of us out on an "Earth Adventure" to the Delaware Valley, where we were to camp and hike for three days in the wilderness. We were going to paddle canoes and climb steep trails. The theory was that if we could conquer our fear in unknown situations out in nature, we could overcome problems in the everyday world.

I felt sick to my stomach on the bus ride to the Delaware Valley, and I trembled all over when I was climbing up the first mountain trail. It was very steep. My fear grew until it paralyzed me and I just stopped.

Ronnie was up above me, shouting that I could do it. She told me to put my right hand up, grab a small tree, and pull. She said it was okay to be afraid, but to remember that I was the one in control.

David Smith called out that we all should imagine that we were in India and that the peacocks were screaming a warning that a tiger was near. To be safe we had to get up to the ridge as soon as possible. From the ridge we could get a clear view of the land and see if the tiger was close. He made a loud noise that was supposed to sound like a peacock giving us a warning.

I began climbing again. When I got to the top of the ridge I laid down flat on the ground before I sat up to look around. Ronnie came over and hugged me.

David Smith looked out over the ridge. He yelled that the tiger had retreated and we were all safe!

When we were finished with our three-day trip, I knew something important had happened to me. I'd overcome a *lot of fear and anxiety in the course of it, and I'd been a real success. David told me that now I should know I could do anything I set my mind to do.*

=== 58 ===

Ronnie spoke to me a lot about getting well. I'd become aware of how self-centered I'd been for so many years, just thinking and worrying about myself. Now I knew I had a chance to give something of myself to others. I wanted people to know and like me as a well person, not to just feel sorry or be nice to me because I was sick.

Dr. Kaplan, Dr. Pfeiffer, the staff and students at Earth House, and especially Ronnie, were all making such a big difference in my life. So was Dorothy Sawyer, whom I visited every couple of weeks to talk about the kind of life and work I wanted to pursue on my own. I was getting better and better. That summer I bought my own car—a beat-up old Nova—and I was beginning to feel really grown-up.

Then, about six months after I'd arrived at Earth House, the time came to talk to me about graduating. "The nutritional regimen has done its job, Rickie," Ronnie told me, "and we've done ours."

I didn't want to leave at all! I kept telling her I wasn't ready, that I didn't have enough skills to make it in the world.

"Graduation doesn't mean you'll be perfect, Rickie," she reassured me, "only that you are recovered enough to take the next step." She reminded me of how far I'd come al-

ready, but that in order to keep growing, I would need to take on new challenges.

The plan was for me to rent a room from a woman named Betty Jenney, the treasurer of Brain Bio and an old friend of Dr. Pfeiffer's. It was a good situation, and I knew she was doing a special favor for me, but the thought of leaving Earth House totally panicked me.

The morning I was supposed to leave I got up early and walked outside to say good-bye to the house and the animals and the trees. By the time I was supposed to go, I was falling apart with fear. Ronnie literally had to drag me out to my car, put me in, and shut the door. "You're going to be fine!" she exhorted. "You can do it!" She also reminded me that I would be coming to Earth House for dinner on Wednesday and that I could call or see them anytime I wanted to.

And so I left Earth House and moved in with Betty. A kind person, Betty had a comfortable house. The spacious living room had two picture windows offering a beautiful view of the huge backyard. My room was small, but nice and cozy. The television room was right next to my room, and her bedroom was across the hall. We were going to split the cost of the groceries and share the housework and lawn work. She told me that I had to smoke outside because she had a bronchial condition and was allergic to smoke.

I paid my share, enjoyed the housework, and especially enjoyed working outside, riding the lawn mower. I also enjoyed washing the cars or just lying in the sun.

For a while I did volunteer janitorial work at Brain Bio. But then one day when I was going into a seafood store in the shopping center to get a cold drink, I noticed a sign taped on the window: Part-time Help Needed. I asked a woman behind the counter, who smiled, said her name was Sue, and went to fetch her husband Jerry from the back.

They gave me the job. I worked from ten A.M. to two P.M. every day, cooking and serving fish sandwiches, and work-

ing the cash register. By the end of the first week I was working the fryers as well as making sandwiches. It got really busy during lunch every day and the pressure was intense for about an hour, with sometimes as many as twenty people standing at the counter. Keeping track of the orders was a big challenge, but I tried not to get flustered. At first I was shocked at how well I did and that the people there liked me so much. They didn't know about my history; they just liked me for what I was. I found myself talking more and more with Sue. I told her more about Brain Bio, and eventually I told her my real background—not living in Massachusetts on a farm, as I had told her originally. I told her she could tell Jerry but no one else, because if other people didn't understand, they might be frightened. I was glad I'd told her the truth, but I knew by now that certain people just wouldn't understand.

At the end of the summer I got two weeks off and set off on a vacation by myself. Renting a tent, I borrowed a cooler, a lantern, and other necessities. Betty helped me chart out a route on an AAA map that would take me to Bar Harbor, Maine, and then back through Massachusetts. I set out early one Saturday morning, my car packed with food, clothes, vitamins, and camping gear. I drove four hours at a stretch until I saw signs for Acadia National Park, where I was directed down the road to a small campsite that turned out to be great! I pitched my tent near some trees, locked my stuff in the car, and found the nearest beach. The water was too cold to swim in, but that didn't matter.

That night I lay in my tent and felt so happy. Exhausted but proud, I snuggled into my sleeping bag and fell asleep. The next morning I woke up to sunshine streaming into my tent. I spent most of the day on the beach. I thanked God for letting me be well and having the opportunity to see such beauty! As I was picking up sand dollars from the beach, I realized that I didn't feel lonely, nor did I feel any pain.

Every day was better than the one before. I met a couple

of girls from Florida who were also camping, and we went hiking and sightseeing together. When it was time to leave, I headed for Pittsfield. I hadn't been in the area since an ambulance had taken me off to Poughkeepsie nearly a year before, and I wanted the people who had known me then to see the difference. I'd gained weight and had a really nice figure, I didn't shake all the time, I smiled and talked easily, and all in all I'd gained so much poise.

I definitely wanted to see Dr. Flanders, and once I was settled in my motel room, I called to ask if he'd like to get together for lunch. He said he couldn't, but asked me to meet him at Gould Farm. I was so excited about seeing him, I made sure I looked my best, all tanned and feeling great. He was surprised and genuinely happy to see me. I told him about the many things I had been doing at Earth House and since, but he didn't comment at all about the vitamins and the visual therapy. I guess it was hard for him to understand. Our visit ended all too soon for me, but when we said good-bye, I felt content and very proud of myself.

That night I met Sally and Joe at a bar in town; I was glad to see Sally but also very nervous, and was relieved when the evening ended. The next day I had lunch with Pam, one of the nurses from Jones II, and I got together with Kitty, the girl with polyneuritis whom I'd met in physical therapy. She was walking with braces, a big step for her. I had also wanted to see Kent Smith and his wife, but they were away on vacation.

When I pulled back into Betty's driveway in Princeton, I was still exhilarated. I felt as if I'd had another Earth Adventure—this one on my own steam. And just like the first one, it had been a success—and I had met the challenge.

On Thanksgiving Day, 1976, our family celebrated my first-year anniversary of being out of the hospital. Everyone was there—Mommy, Daddy, John, Mary, Matt, Joyce, Lisa, Laura, Winnie, and me. My mother gave me a beautiful silver tear, saying that I had shed so many, and she had *too, that this tear was a symbol of all those shed over the years. I was deeply touched.*

I'd been thinking about a full-time job for a while, possibly nursing school, but Dorothy suggested it was too soon for that. In early December I was still working at the seafood shop when Betty told me that the front-desk receptionist at Brain Bio would be leaving before Christmas. I said, "Please let me try! I think I can do it." They decided to hire me!

Sue and Jerry wished me well and told me to come in often to see them. She said she was very proud of me.

In the beginning the job was really hard. I had to answer the phones, take care of patients as they came in, notify the doctors of their arrival, and handle the billing. Sometimes when the phone was ringing and people were waiting and everybody was wanting something at the same time, I'd feel so much pressure that my head would start to shake or I'd tremble all over. I knew it was time to get up and walk around. Ronnie told me that once I got more used to the job, the shaking episodes would pass very quickly since they were just a sign of nervousness, and that eventually they'd probably go away altogether. And as my confidence grew, and as I drew more and more compliments about my courtesy and what a good job I was doing, the shaking did vanish, just as she had predicted.

59

Even though Betty was generous, now that I had a full-time job, I was ready to be on my own. Dad came out one Saturday to help me find a place. We were driving around when we saw an apartment complex called Princeton Meadows being built in Plainsboro, only a short distance from Princeton. We went over and walked through a model. I loved it, and the woman showing us around said I could pick out any unit I wanted and choose the color of the rug. I thought the first apartment was great, and Dad agreed, so I left a deposit that very same day.

Since I wasn't moving in for a few weeks, I had time to pack my things and think about what I was doing. I was going to have a place I could actually call my home and mine alone, where I could do what I wanted and be responsible for myself. Sometimes it seemed like a dream. As for furniture, mine came through an unfortunate incident, the death of my mother's sister, who had had an apartment full of beautiful furniture from my grandmother, and now it was passed on to me.

At the time I wrote in my diary:

Tonight will I dream again of the past? The locked doors and trapped mind? Planning escape each time with anticipated fear? So much is going on. I want to move into my own apartment, but I am afraid. I have no real friends, no people to go places and do things with. I'm

*hoping to make some in the near future somehow. Lone-
liness frightens me, and I try not to feel alone. I don't
know what to go into as a career. . . .*

*It would be comfortable to be sick and to be taken
care of, especially now, but it is not what I want. I am
going to conquer these bad periods and make good with
what I do have. Monday I'm going to see a person at
the Action Volunteer Center and see about doing something for someone else at least once a week. Tuesday
night I go to typing class. I've just got to have the patience to wait, because everything wonderful does not
happen all at once. I guess I'm now learning what real
life is like. I must overcome my fear and take the challenge. I know I'll be proud of myself. Meanwhile, I've
got to try to sleep again. . . .*

Betty helped me with my last-minute packing. She gave
me a new set of aluminum pots and pans, and money for a
television set. When the movers arrived Saturday morning,
Betty and I got in our cars and followed the moving van
over to Princeton Meadows. It must have been ten degrees,
and the new apartment was freezing cold. Everything smelled
so new, and it seemed a little creepy and lonely after Betty
left, but I slept well that night, and the next day I started to
unpack and put my things away.

After that first weekend I went back to work. It only took
me a half hour each way, and I was doing my job well, but
I had stopped taking my vitamins and I wasn't eating very
well. And I was having a terrible time sleeping. So I went
to see a psychiatrist—I can't recall how I got his name—
and told him about my insomnia. I think I was embarrassed
to tell Ronnie or anyone else about my problem, and I knew
that a doctor could give me sleeping pills. When they didn't
work, I bought a bottle of vodka—I'd never really drunk that
much—just to take a small dose along with the pills, which
I'd heard would work well. But the combination induced

*mood swings, even into the next day, and I began to go
downhill fast.*

As the weeks passed I became more and more withdrawn.
One Saturday in late January I woke up shivering. The electricity had gone off in my apartment and I was freezing. It
was still dark out, and when I tried all the lights, they didn't
work. I called the office, and they told me that the cable
was broken but that it would be fixed soon. I piled on some
sweaters and blankets and had a drink to warm me up a bit.
Confused, I couldn't seem to tell whether it was day or night,
nor whether I had taken my sleeping pills. Ronnie told me
later that when she hadn't been able to reach me by phone,
she'd come to my apartment. Comatose, I was stretched out
in the middle of my floor with all my stuffed animals around
me, and I had taken all of my sleeping pills.

I have no memory of any of that, only of being awfully
cold, and of the terrible darkness. When I regained consciousness and saw that I was in a hospital room, I was so
upset that I started screaming and ripped out my IVs. Hours
later I woke up to find myself tied down to a bed. I had been
transferred to Princeton House, the psychiatric division of
the Princeton Medical Center. I couldn't believe how awful
it felt. I was trying to wiggle my hands and feet out of the
leather straps when a male aide came in. "You're not going
anywhere," he gloated, and re-bound my hands more firmly.
Once I was unable to move, he started running his fingers
up the inside of my thighs and asking me how I liked that. I
started screaming at him, and kept screaming even after
he'd backed out of the room. I was scared to death, and sick
from the phenothiazine shots. I told a nurse about him, but
she didn't believe me.

During my few days in Princeton House I was in terrible
shape. Under stress, my vision had gone berserk; I couldn't
see a thing, and felt my eyes rolling up in my head. I knew
I had lost my depth perception, and felt as if I were in a
long, flat, narrow box. When Ronnie came in, she was hor-

*rified and outraged. She said she had talked to my father,
who was just as furious, and that she was taking me to
Carrier Clinic, where they would let me have my vitamins.
Ronnie got me dressed then and there, and literally stole me
away from Princeton House.*

*At Carrier I sat on the edge of my bed, rocking back and
forth, sinking deeper and deeper into myself. The tension
was awful. I started to tear the sheet into little strips and
tie them together, two by two. When a nurse walked in to
check on me and saw what I was doing, she ran out and
came back with some male aides, who tried to grab me. I
fought, but the more I struggled, the further I slipped away
from reality. They carried me down the hall back to the
seclusion room and closed the door. They'd taken away most
of my clothes and left me in some kind of hospital outfit. I
rolled and rocked, feeling as though I were in a time warp,
propelled back years to Westchester. I even began to bang
my head on the floor, knowing I'd lost control. I was frightened, but I couldn't stop. Then the door swung open and a
herd of people rushed in, holding me down while I got an
injection.*

*Much later I woke up and remembered where I was. I
sensed a nurse in the room with me and I was determined
to break through to reality again. I reached out and touched
her arm. I would behave, and could she please walk me to
the bathroom? She did, but when I asked her for my glasses,
she said she was sorry but they had me on suicide watch
and couldn't take any chances.*

60

Rickie had called from Plainsboro the night the heat went off, and I could hear her voice trembling with cold and fear. I told her to call Ronnie and that if she couldn't reach her, to drive to the emergency room at the Princeton Medical Center, where she could be seen by a physician, as my chief concern was pneumonia. I told her I'd come down first thing in the morning.

But before I could leave, Ronnie called with the news of Rickie's admission to the hospital and transfer to the psychiatric ward. Although I was quite agitated, the knowledge that Ronnie was on the scene was profoundly reassuring. We agreed that I'd wait for her assessment of the situation and plan accordingly. Later in the afternoon she reported that Rickie was in very poor shape but that she'd arranged for immediate admission to Carrier, where one of the psychiatrists who was sympathetic to the Earth House program could look after her. She said something about the Princeton House staff not wanting to release Rickie to her, but that she nonetheless intended to whisk her out of there. I was sure Ronnie would have done just that no matter what I said, but I remember saying: "I'm with you all the way, Ronnie. Go for it!" or some such encouragement.

She telephoned me again after Rickie was safely secured at Carrier. "I know this must be demoralizing for Rickie . . . and you," she said sympathetically, "but I have absolute faith in Rickie. So should you."

Two days later I drove to Belle Mead. Having been to Carrier several times over the years, I had no trouble finding the visitors' parking lot fronting the long, single-story modern brick building that housed the patients. It was like many small, private psychiatric hospitals, competently staffed, but I had every reason to assume that the doctors there would be skeptical of Rickie's rehabilitation efforts and revert to the stock-in-trade procedures that had consistently failed her in the past. I was courteously directed to Rickie's unit. As I was let in the locked door, I was horrified by what I saw.

Hunched over like an old woman with osteoporosis, head bowed, arms and hands shaking incessantly, Rickie shuffled clumsily toward me in a blue-striped institutional bathrobe and a pair of paper slippers. I hugged her.

Tears came to her eyes and she said how sorry she was to have failed again.

"Where are your glasses, Rickie?"

"In the nurses' station."

"Why aren't you wearing them?"

"They won't let me have them."

I stalked over to the window that separated the staff from the patients and knocked gently but firmly on the glass. A young, freckled, red-haired nurse smiled pleasantly and went back to her notes. When I rapped again, she came to the door.

"Rickie has a pair of glasses," I explained. "She needs them to get around."

"I can't authorize that without a written order from the doctor," she said helplessly.

"Okay, okay. Where's the doctor?"

"Rickie's doctor isn't in the hospital at the present time."

"Who's covering him?"

"Well, no one, really. He's especially assigned to Rickie, you see." Observing my frustration, she offered: "I can get one of the house doctors."

"Please do. Thank you."

Within five minutes a young man about thirty, in white pants and a short white coat from which a stethoscope protruded, came onto the unit. After briefly speaking with the nurse, he approached Rickie and me. "Can I help you?" he asked, peering blankly.

I told him about the special glasses from Kaplan and wondered what might account for the shaking and whether she was on any medication.

"Stellazine," he replied unemotionally. "That couldn't account for this much trembling. It looks hysterical to me."

"Rickie's allergic to phenothiazines," I pointed out. "Isn't that in her chart?"

"I'll look," he muttered defensively.

"And while you're at it, bring me her glasses." I didn't say, "Would you consider bringing the glasses?" I didn't ask whether he had any objections.

He brought them at once. "Nothing in her chart about phenothiazines."

"Well, put it in."

I carefully put the glasses on Rickie, having a little bit of trouble getting the frames positioned correctly over her ears. Rickie abruptly straightened up and looked squarely at us both. "Wow!" she commented. "What a difference."

"What do you make of that?" I asked the doctor.

"What do I make of it? I told you. Hysteria."

"You really think that's the response of an hysteric to suggestion?"

For a moment he didn't answer. Then he demanded: "Are you on the staff here? Are you a doctor?"

"No, I'm not on the staff here," I informed him, "but I do happen to be a doctor, a psychiatrist, no less. I'm Rickie's father."

"Well, I guess she can keep the glasses, at least until her own doctor comes back," he conceded, still unimpressed and obviously wanting no further confrontation.

"See that she does," I said, smiling.

Rickie stayed at Carrier for another week. Following her discharge, she was met by a friend of Ronnie's who had driven Rickie's car to the hospital parking lot. Rickie sat behind the wheel, started the engine, and drove confidently back to her home, now properly heated, thinking meanwhile of one of Ronnie's many wise sayings: "One step back, two forward." Ronnie had cautioned her more than once not to expect things to move upward in a straight line. "Even success is a strain," Ronnie had pointed out, "and sometimes when everything seems to be going well, a tiny life tremor can shake you up a lot." Like a power failure, Rickie thought. "You have to look at every setback as one more chance to strengthen your courage and faith in yourself."

===61===

The awful episode had passed, but my mind was still fuzzy, so Ronnie hired a friend of hers to stay with me for the first week, and I began to go to Earth House for day treatment.

It was as if I'd lost all the skills I'd learned over the past year. At first I couldn't remember how to play the piano or a lot of other simple things. But then, like bits and pieces of a jigsaw puzzle being assembled, it all started coming quickly back in a way it never had when I'd fallen apart before. Whether it was the diet, or vision therapy, or what I'd learned those months at Earth House, or all those put together, I felt I could tap my inner strength and resourcefulness in a completely new way.

Within two weeks, I was back working part-time at Brain

Bio. I was so grateful that they had saved my job for me, although, looking back, it was typical. They were the first people I could really count on to be there for me.

I actually felt better about myself than before my trip to Carrier. Up until then feelings of pressure or loss of control had led me to assume my sickness was coming back or still had hold of me. I spoke with Dad, who said I shouldn't look at what had happened as a relapse or a recurrence of my "illness." Falling apart under the stress of being on my own for the first time, and the awful cold, wasn't that unusual. Healthy people are supposed to fall apart from time to time and put it together afterwards better than before, he reassured me. His advice enabled me to see my breakdown as a chance to gain even more confidence. It was also a reminder to stick with my regimen, so after that I took my vitamins faithfully, ate well, and did my visual exercises every day. I also learned that any amount of alcohol was poison for my system, and stopped drinking altogether.

I also started writing poetry again. I'd noticed that my vocabulary was really scanty, no surprise since I'd had so little formal schooling, so I began to practice new words. If Ronnie or anyone used one I didn't understand, I'd ask what it meant and sometimes how to spell it, and nine times out of ten it would become part of my permanent memory bank. I remember once asking David what the word "humiliation" meant. He smiled and said that even if I didn't know what it meant, I had certainly experienced it firsthand. After he'd defined it, I thought of all I'd been through over the years and agreed. Then I asked whether the word "humble" was related. "Not at all," he replied. "Humble is what all great people are." Then he defined that word too.

In the spring of 1977 I started working as a part-time volunteer for the Plainsboro Rescue Squad. I was an emergency medical technician—I'd gotten my certification at a first-aid class—and I drove the ambulance and attended victims. I was on call at least one night a week, and I loved it.

I'd carry my beeper, and if I got a call, I'd put a flashing
blue light up on my car and off I'd go.

That was around the time that Chuck Hartman called me
up. Our first meeting at Carrier Clinic, where he was a
psychiatric nursing assistant, had been short and quick. It
was just after I had gotten out of seclusion, and I'd walked
over to him and demanded to know what had happened to
my can of Tab. He'd looked but couldn't find it, and that
was all there was to that incident. Our next meeting had
been more dramatic. He was sitting on a couch in the lounge,
and I'd lost my balance walking by and fallen into his lap.
Since he had a pretty big belly, I looked up at him and
quipped, "Santa Claus?" We both laughed, and I moved
over next to him to talk. We chatted several times after that,
and I enjoyed him, especially his wonderful sense of humor.
He was very funny and a great mimic; he could imitate
Jimmy Stewart and Richard Nixon and lots of other famous
people. And he was kind.

When he called me that first time, he wanted to know how
I was doing. Then he stopped by one evening and read some
of my poetry. He really liked it.

Our first date, in April of '77, was on an airplane! A
friend of his who also worked at Carrier had a plane and
wanted to take us for a flight. We had to jump-start the
plane's motor with a car at Mercer Airport, but then we flew
over New York City and up over Connecticut. It was wonderful. I even got to work the controls for a little bit. We
landed at Westchester County Airport for a snack, but
couldn't get the plane started again. Chuck's friend figured
it wouldn't be safe to fly back that night because it was too
late to have the battery checked by mechanics, so we ended
up getting rooms at the local Ramada Inn, and the next
morning Chuck and I came back down to Princeton on the
train. It was an unusual first date, to say the least, but it
couldn't have turned out better if we'd planned it.

I had started dating a little bit when I was still at Betty's

*house. I'd met a lot of nice men, but no one that I felt truly
comfortable with. With Chuck, I could be me. He accepted
me just as I was—and he had seen the worst!*

As Chuck remembers:

I got interested in Rickie when I saw that she wasn't
really the psychiatric horror story she seemed to be on
admission to Carrier. As her history was initially described to us, she had been through just about everything you could come up with, and they had no hope
for her. But of course, for years and years they hadn't
helped her. Not only were they not getting to the crux
of the problem, I suppose you could say they *were* the
crux of the problem.

I liked Rickie, and was attracted to her, but reading
her poetry really knocked me out. I thought, nobody
crazy writes poetry like this! Of course, I didn't know
that some pretty great poets were crazy, but as I got to
know Rickie better and better, I knew she sure wasn't.

Rickie appreciated the fact that I could accept her
totally for everything she was and had been through.
And I appreciated Rickie because she was completely
natural. She didn't put on any airs and wasn't superfi-
cial in any way. She was authentic and truthful. After
those terrible experiences, she seemed better off to me
than a lot of people I knew who haven't gone through
anything difficult at all. What's always amazed me is
that Rickie carried no bitterness. When it was over, she
just wanted to catch up on what she had missed.

I thought, here's a basically healthy person who was
unintentionally harmed by the medical profession trying to cure her, for the most part due to ignorance and
closed-mindedness! If that had happened to me, I'd be
so angry, but she reminded me that those doctors didn't
know any better. She said that if you hold on to anger,

you don't accomplish anything. I don't think I've ever met anyone so forgiving, before or since.

As I remember, Chuck and I went out until August, but then we broke up for a while. I wanted more time to myself and I wanted to date some other men, especially since I was starting to make a lot more friends in the Princeton Meadows complex, through my job at Brain Bio, and with the fire department. Popular for the first time in my life, I started dating quite a bit, but I didn't meet anyone with Chuck's compassion and humor.

Chuck seemed to understand that I needed to date other people and make up for some lost experience. But he said he'd decided, "Hey, I'm not going to let you get away!"

After a few months of only talking on the phone, Chuck and I had a Halloween date. We didn't really dress up, but we both wore funny masks to the Princeton Meadows club for a party. After that we began to see a lot of each other again. He'd changed jobs too, and was now employed by a computer information service doing some kind of top-secret government work.

I went to New York to spend Christmas Eve with Dad, Joyce, and the other children. Christmas Eve at Dad's and Christmas Day at Mom's had become a family tradition. Born when I was at Gould Farm, my half-sister Winnie was four now, but until I got to Earth House I'd been too out of it to pay real attention to her. I'd been glad my dad had another little girl since I'd let him down by being so sick, but from the time she was two until she was nearly six, she was the spitting image of me. Really, comparing snapshots of her and me at the same age, you couldn't tell who was who! Once I was better, she quickly came to hold a very special place in my heart.

Right after New Year's Day, Chuck called and insisted that he come over to my place because he had something very important to tell me. About half an hour later the door bell rang, and standing right there in the living room, he asked me to marry him. I'd been thinking of marriage and having a family, but I'd never thought that he—or anybody—would really want to marry me, especially knowing about my background. I knew he was in love with me though, and also that I loved him. I walked over to the nearest chair and plopped myself down in it, stunned. After a few moments I looked him right in the eyes and said yes. Later I thought that if he hadn't proposed to me, I might have mustered up the courage to propose to him. Anyway, I was thrilled. We decided on June 17, 1978, which gave us six months to prepare.

Dad expressed misgivings, feeling it might be too soon, but on the other hand he could see that the structure and loving companionship could prove an important asset in continuing to rebuild my life. He left the choice to me. Chuck was twenty-eight, and had lost his own father when he was nineteen, so it was no surprise that he took a special liking to Dad, and it seemed to be mutual. Mom's reservations were stronger; she worried that since I'd only been well for a relatively short time, I might change a lot in years to come and the then-special bond between Chuck and me might not endure. Ronnie and Dorothy thought marriage would be good for me.

Although Mom, Dad, and I talked about the plans together, I was the one who really put it all in place. I got a beautiful wedding dress and organized a reception at a restaurant with about fifty people. Dean Earnest Gordon, the chaplain for Princeton University whom I'd met through Ronnie, married us at the college chapel. All of my family and Chuck's family were there, along with our friends. My sister Mary was my maid of honor and Chuck's brother Donald was his best man. Winnie was our flower girl. Everyone thought I'd done a wonderful job of setting the wedding up, and I had. It was one of the best days of my life!

Getting married and having someone right there to love

who loved me seemed almost too good to be true, but there it was.

TODAY I WAS FILLED

Today I was filled
with the wonder of all worlds
the sea and its loving arms
that reached out
and swept me in
to the calm
such joy I cannot feel
when I walk amongst the cluttered
and puzzled world we live in.
I separate myself from
the mobs
and speak quietly to the sea
whom I have missed for so long
We have been apart
and now it holds me close
riding high on
crests
of foamy lather
I try to catch the sun
and hold this precious moment
Now I'm back at home
I sit here all alone
yet inside
there is
the warm
and pleasant thought
that today I was filled.

Two other dreams also came true that summer. I studied for my high school equivalency examination. Chuck helped

*me, and in the fall I passed! Now that I had my GED I could
start to take some college courses.*

*And, thanks to the help of a hypnotist that Chuck had
found, we both stopped smoking. That was something I'd
wanted to do ever since going to Earth House. We lived in
my apartment at Princeton Meadows. I got a job as a cus-
tomer relations representative at a nearby fragrance firm,
and with both of us working, we were financially in good
shape. We also kept very active because they had swimming
and tennis where we lived, and that helped me keep my mind
off cigarettes. I have to say the first year of marriage was a
pretty smooth transition compared to the experiences of some
friends I've met since.*

*A year and a half after we were married, I got pregnant
with Brian.*

62

I reached down to shift the aging Mercedes into neutral
as I waited for the light to turn green. Across the road to
the right I caught sight of a small white sign perched atop
a fieldstone wall. It read, Church of Saint Jude. When the
light changed, I moved slowly up the drive to the pastor's
house. Turning off the ignition, I swung out of the car and
stood momentarily in silence, looking up at the gray January sky.

A mild flush of excitement ran through me as I rang the
door bell. In a determined voice I asked the elderly housekeeper who answered if I could see Father Donovan.

"Father's having his lunch," she replied. "What did you say your name is?"

I repeated it. "I only want a few minutes of his time to arrange a baptism."

"Father doesn't like to be interrupted when he's eating." She seemed afraid to announce a caller, surprised that anyone would challenge her pastor's privacy.

"I don't have much time," I pressed. "Do you mind?"

The old woman looked at me quizzically, but obliged.

"I'll be down when I'm finished." The priest's voice issued from the speaker in a metallic crackle.

A large Seth Thomas clock hung on the bare white wall, its black hands indicating one-thirty. I threw my sheepskin coat over a wooden bench and sat down. One-forty. I began to feel restless. Ten of two. I was getting annoyed. "How much longer will he be?" The housekeeper, who kept disappearing and reappearing on seemingly pointless errands didn't know. I was just about to leave when a tall, balding man in a long black cassock entered the hall and walked toward me, smiling stiffly.

I held my tongue and simply explained, "I'd like to arrange for a baptism."

The priest ushered me into a small, sparsely furnished office and without a word waved to me to sit down. He opened his desk drawer and took out a sheaf of papers, rustling through them without once glancing up at me. "This is . . ." the priest asked haltingly, "your child?"

"My grandchild."

"Are the parents members of our parish?"

"No." Anticipating the priest's next question, I went on: "My daughter and her husband live in New Jersey, near Princeton. However, this is the most convenient place for the family, that is, especially for the baby's great-grandmother, who is in her eighties."

The priest coughed.

"Rickie has a special feeling for St. Jude. We all do," I added.

"I see. Of course, you'll have to get permission from her own pastor."

"If we can."

"I assume your daughter is Catholic."

"Yes."

"Her name?"

"Rickie. Frederica Hartman."

"The father's name?"

"Charles Hartman."

"Also Catholic?"

"No. Protestant. Lutheran, I think."

"Where were the couple married?"

"The chapel at Princeton University."

Father Donovan covered his mouth and coughed dryly again. "A priest was present, of course."

"No. They were married by someone who had taken a very special interest in Rickie, a Presbyterian minister."

Father Donovan put down his pen and for the first time looked directly at me. "This does present us with a problem, doesn't it, Doctor?" he asked rhetorically. "They're not married, you realize," he somberly pronounced.

"I consider them married in the eyes of God!" I snapped.

"Not in the eyes of the Church," he retorted.

"Father, I'm here to arrange for the baptism of my grandchild, not to engage in a theological dispute."

"Well," the priest elaborated, "before I could possibly agree to carry out this service, I'll have to speak with them."

"About what?" I asked defensively.

"About the fact they are living in sin . . . That if they are to take their parental responsibilities seriously and truly understand the meaning of baptism, they must consider being married under the proper auspices."

I stood up and reached for my coat. "If you feel that's

necessary, we'll have to arrange to have the baby baptized somewhere else!''

"As you wish," the priest replied, unruffled.

"Rickie's been through too much in her life to have to be subjected to any more unnecessary suffering or embarrassment!''

He caught my phrase.

"Too much? What do you mean suffered too much?''

"Years in and out of mental institutions, struggling to survive. Now she's well, all that's behind her. I don't want her to be humiliated by being told she's not married . . . Nor by anything else, for that matter!''

Father Donovan pushed his calendar out in front of him, a trace of compassion crossing his lined face. "What date did you say you had in mind?''

"January seventh, Rickie's grandfather's birthday. He meant a great deal to her.''

The priest made a notation. "Two o'clock?''

"Fine.''

"Two o'clock, January seventh, 1980," he repeated. "And the baby's name?''

"Brian.''

"A good Irish name at that," Father Donovan muttered. "I need the names of the baby's grandparents too. Your wife's name, Doctor?''

I almost said "Joyce," but caught myself in time. "The grandmother's name is Hillary.''

That evening I telephoned Rickie to describe my encounter with Father Donovan in detail. We both laughed. "I'm convinced that when he learned I was a psychiatrist, he figured he'd better hurry up and conclude the arrangements and get me out of there before I started to practice witchcraft.''

"I'll talk to Chuck," Rickie offered. "If it'll please Father Donovan to marry us first, that's all right with me, and I know Chuck will say okay. Tell him we'll be happy to . . ." she chose her words carefully, "renew our vows in front of him. That'll take care of any problems that might come up, in case we ever want to send Brian to a parochial school."

"You certainly have a lot of common sense, Rickie."

She laughed. "I got it the hard way."

"Is there any other way?"

"Thanks, Dad. Thanks so much . . . for everything."

The weather on the seventh of January was extraordinarily balmy, with bright sun glistening off the melting snow. Father Donovan stood at the baptismal font, Rickie and Chuck in front of him, Rickie holding her baby. Next to her stood Joyce, whom Rickie had asked to be the godmother, then John, who was to be the godfather, then all the other children, and Chuck's mother. Rickie had invited Dr. Pfeiffer, but he was lecturing in California. I stood a few feet back, Hillary and her mother on one side, Bernice on the other.

"Do you reject Satan?" Father Donovan asked.

"I do," Rickie and Chuck answered in unison.

"And all his works?"

"I do."

"And all his empty promises?"

They are empty, I reflected, whoever's making them. In the end, there's only one promise that really counts: that when everything seems hopeless and incoherent, there is still reason to hope, a hidden architecture that gives life meaning. I was surprised by an image that suddenly crossed my mind, a scene from an old black-and-white Spanish movie about Don Quixote. As the nobles rode proudly through La Mancha, hooded monks, walking barefooted in front of them, swung incense and chanted to remind them of their nothingness, and their immortality.

"This is the fountain of life, water made holy by the suffering of Christ, washing all the world. You who are washed in this water have hope of heaven's kingdom . . ."

I wondered what was going through Hillary's mind. Was she remembering a newborn Rickie being brought to her in her hospital room and looking down, for the first time, at the tiny child? Was she wishing that somehow it could all begin again differently, and happen differently, with all the wounds and mistakes and lost chances washed away?

"Brian Christopher Hartman . . . you have become a new creation." As the water poured on his head, Brian Christopher Hartman howled vigorously.

What was Rickie thinking as she held him there? Of another cry, a cry that pierced the corridors through which attendants wheeled her, strapped on stretchers, to rooms where the mad were dipped in tubs and wrapped tightly in cold wet sheets in isolation, where day and night were a continuum of agony and fear? Her cry. Her baptism.

Rickie, beaming, looked down at Brian and rocked him gently. His crying stopped.

"In His goodness," Father Donovan went on, "may He continue to pour out his blessings upon these sons and daughters of His . . . wherever they may be, faithful members of His holy people . . ."

I looked around, first at Rickie and Chuck and the baby, recalling the calm, joy, and certainty with which she had carried the child, and the birth that had afforded me an ultimate confidence in the woman she had become.

"May He send His peace upon all who are gathered here."

In the far corner of the chapel I spotted Bill and Celia Morris. They hadn't been able to come to Rickie's wedding, but were deeply moved by this invitation. They returned my smile.

Rising up behind them stood an enormous replica of St. Jude. Who could possibly have any idea what Jude really looked like? I wondered. Plaster and paint, that's all, but a reminder. Judas had betrayed Jesus, and in the end fallen prey to despair. But Jude Thaddeus had remained steadfast,

to die a martyr, believing firmly in what must have seemed
to others the most hopeless and obscure of causes.

I glanced again quickly, at Bill, Celia, Chuck, Rickie,
everyone, and then back again toward the statue. "Thank
you all, so very much," I whispered softly to myself.

$$===\mathbf{63}===$$

Florida, 1990

*In some ways my life has been less perfect than many
people's, but in other ways it's been more so. I mean that I
have been able to put all my suffering to good use.*

*My life improved even more after I had Brian because it
all came so naturally, and I think my mom and dad were
very pleased. They were worried about depression after the
baby, and about the pressure of raising a child, but I loved
it, and I always got out and met other mothers. Then I loved
having our twins too, Heather and Erica, born in 1983.
Chuck said I looked like a globe when I was carrying them.
All this also brought my family together. They all came to
my wedding and to the baptisms, as well as to all the children's birthday parties. It was so wonderful for all of us.*

*When I look back, sometimes I can't believe all of those
terrible things happened to me. It seems like a bad dream.
For a long time I had nightmares, dreaming that I was
trapped in a hospital. Trying to find a way to escape, I'd
run and run. But for years now I haven't had those dreams.*

*Chuck and I built a good life for ourselves up north. I
was very active, joining the Mothers of Twins Association,
working a few hours a week at Earth House and part-time*

in charge of mailing and filling orders for a local publisher. In 1985 we bought an old house in Bordentown, New Jersey, an historical village south of Trenton on the Delaware River, and worked hard to restore it. But it seemed that no matter how hard Chuck and I worked, things kept getting more and more expensive and we were always short of money. The Princeton area itself was changing, becoming crowded and congested. The air and water were getting more polluted, and I was particularly sensitive to pollution. I also hated the bitter cold and the dark days of winter.

So, as much as I knew I would miss being so close to family and friends, we loaded our things in our Chevy sedan and moved here to Florida, feeling like nervous pioneers, even though millions had preceded us. I loved the sun and having a beach to walk along in solitude, not to mention the more laid-back style of life. Another plus was my return to school for a licensed practical nurse degree; I've almost completed the registered nurse requirements.

I miss my family, but they do come down. I fly up to New York at least a couple times a year, and we keep in touch by telephone. In the summers I now work as a consultant at Earth House, talking with students, guiding them—coaching them, you might say, to reenter the world, and showing them how to be proud of themselves in a special way.

When Ronnie died in 1987 after a year's struggle with cancer, I felt full of grief. But I had learned how to deal with it, and even though her dying has left an empty place in my heart, I know that she is still here somewhere, with me. I also know what I want my life to be. I want to take up where she left off, and to use the gifts that—with her help—I've learned to use to help others find their way out of the darkness.

When an Earth House student asks me if I truly understand them, I remember how important Ronnie's revelation was to me. When I tell them I was there once myself, they look at me, sometimes astonished, and ask if there's really hope. And I tell them that as long as they try, there's always hope.

I tell them to hold on to their dreams, like the poet Langston Hughes wrote in a poem I read years ago, when I was still in one of the hospitals, and which I chose for the epigraph.

It's dreams that give us something to strive for, I tell the students. Never let them go.

Negative thinking is tempting to a lot of people; maybe that's why so many have such a poor attitude toward mental illness and people with problems. Or maybe they're scared of what they don't understand, or afraid of their own feelings of sadness. There's a fine line between giving up, or persevering and dealing with each problem as it comes, using your intuition and imagination to deal with life. I can still feel like giving up from time to time, or so frustrated I can't see straight, just like everyone else. The difference between me then and me now is that I've learned how to let those negative feelings go and to pursue solutions when none are right at hand.

Even though I don't consider myself handicapped, I still am. Dad says everyone is, that it's important for people to figure out what their particular handicap may be and to live with it or overcome it. When I'm under a lot of stress, whether because of car payments or a nasty virus, my vision can go on me just like that. I simply can't see. It's like sitting in a little box and looking out a tiny peephole. I shut my eyes, or go to sleep for a little while, or put on my special glasses, and it passes. I'm not frightened anymore, because I know what it is and that it will go away.

I used to be haunted by the feeling of having been branded. For a long time after Earth House I'd step out into a public space—a parking lot, for instance—and fear that people could tell I'd been in mental hospitals because I was walking strangely or wasn't smiling. I don't feel that way anymore.

Until very recently I was still reluctant to tell people my

whole story. I also used to worry a lot about what people would think if they saw the scars on my arms or found out my terrible dark secret. For many years I even had a fake story for social situations in which the questions about my past came up, but it made me anxious.

If I'd had Hodgkin's disease or poliomyelitis or kidney disease and had been in and out of hospitals all those years, I'd feel free. People wouldn't bat an eyelash, just say, how wonderful that you lived!

When people do find out, they often can't believe it. Somehow they expect anyone who's been through so much to be a basket case forever, or shuffle around, or maybe live in a railroad station or be in and out of hospitals for the rest of their lives. That's just not the case, and if everyone got even the kind of treatment that's potentially available right now, one that didn't just try to take symptoms away but that would give them hope, dignity, the skills to live and work in the world, the cure rate (as the doctors call it) would be a lot higher. Dad told me that in 1989 the American Psychiatric Association's theme for its annual meeting was "stigma," and that's a step in the right direction. I know that many approaches to treatment, like family therapy, that were not routine when I began my journey, are commonplace today. I also realize that certain elements that I consider vital to my recovery—such as rehabilitation, visual perceptual retraining, and nutritional therapy—are still in their infancy, and that thousands of people are denied access to them either because of closed-mindedness or because the different professions engaged in treating the mentally ill have yet to learn to respect each other and to share their knowledge and ideas.

Maybe I never did have a mental illness in the textbook sense of the word. Maybe I was just misdiagnosed because nobody considered my visual problems and biochemical imbalances early on. I've been told some psychiatrists would reclassify my condition today as a post-traumatic stress dis-

order, while others would insist on calling it depression. It's even possible that I learned how to be sick by being in hospitals for so long during a very vulnerable, formative period. What really matters, it seems to me, is the relevance of my experience to any person or family confronted with illness, regardless of diagnosis, for it contains one simple message: there's always hope.

I know that I will stay well. Watching a spider at work one day, I went over and took the web down. Well, he spun another web. I took it down three times and he spun three more, at which point I let him alone. I've promised myself that just like the spider, I'll never give up. I've started my journey through life, and I figure it will take a lifetime of sharing and caring and loving to experience it all.

Epilogue

Now thirty-eight years old, Rickie is a vital, competent, resourceful woman, with a unique blend of common sense and wisdom, and a singular capacity for empathy. She has not seen a psychiatrist professionally since her discharge from the Carrier Clinic in 1976.

During the terrible years of her illness, and those since her recovery, I've had a great deal of time to think about what happened and its impact on all of us, yet I still have no certain answers.

I myself have probably become a better person and surely a more effective psychiatrist. Perhaps surprisingly, I have lost none of my respect for my profession. I know many wonderful, skilled, caring psychiatrists, and still regard being a psychiatrist as a vocation in the old-fashioned sense of the word—a calling, a meaningful opportunity to fulfill one's inherent talents in a cause well worth undertaking.

A dear friend of mine gave me a birthday card last year, with a quotation attributed to John Lennon: "Life is what happens to you while you're busy making other plans." Believe me, if I could go back in time and stop Rickie's tragic experience from ever taking place, I would do so instantly, and forgo the wisdom I've gained.

At night I sometimes drift off into vague sorts of half dreams, half memories. A scene from Thornton Wilder's *Our Town* comes back to me, in which Emily is given the chance to choose one day to be alive again, and she picks her birthday. I know exactly what I'd pick—some uneventful day in the early 1960s, before Grandpa died and Grandma went to the nursing home, when the children were little, and I'd go to their rooms at night and ask if they were still awake and kiss them good night. I'd go in Rickie's room and tuck her in and laughingly hug Bear and hand him back to her so she could close her eyes and go to sleep, holding him, smiling.

I believe Hillary and I succeeded in protecting Rickie's siblings from the potentially adverse consequences of her odyssey. Each of them has shown integrity, a remarkable passion for life, and a dedication to achievement that must have been partially shaped by those events. Rickie's brother John, now thirty-two, earned his Ph.D. in psychology; his doctoral thesis dealt with the interaction between styles of visual perception and the creative process. He and his wife have moved to Palm Springs, California. Mary, thirty-one, is married too, and a financial data manager. At twenty-nine, Matthew is the family entrepreneur. Perhaps the hardest thing to realize is that Winnie is nearly eighteen and will start college in the fall.

Rickie's mother has created a full life for herself, knowing, in her heart, that her intense dedication to Rickie through all the dark years constituted a major element in her daughter's ultimate recovery.

When I talk about Rickie's story, colleagues inevitably give a wide variety of responses. Most express a genuine sympathy, along with ill-concealed gratitude for having been spared the firsthand experience.

It does bother me that certain ones, possibly out of embarrassment, prefer not to talk about Rickie. Last year, for example, I had occasion to confer with a psychiatrist about a patient who had moved to his city. We spoke for half an hour and we were just about finished when I asked him a few chatty questions about his background and training. I was completely taken aback when he hesitantly informed me that he had been assigned to Rickie's care for a short while during one of her many hospital stays. What astounded me was that he had made no mention of this connection throughout our conversation; what dismayed me was that I was the one to ask whether he wanted to know what had become of Rickie.

Some of those who know Rickie are convinced she could never have been schizophrenic; otherwise, how could she have made such a full recovery? I am inclined to agree with their conclusion, but not for their reasons. It is a fact that a significant number of patients with a schizophrenic diagnosis do achieve lasting improvement. Manfred Bleuler has observed that many such patients do recover to lead meaningful, productive lives, contrary to popular opinion and professional bias. As a matter of fact, studies have shown that the prognosis for psychiatric patients in general depends far more on their ability to work, study, relate to other people, assume a meaningful place for themselves in society, and regain self-esteem, than on any of the symptoms of their condition or the diagnostic categories into which they have been placed.

I have come to the conclusion that Rickie may not have

been mentally ill at all. This is not a parent's wishful thought, it is a belief I have come to apply to many people who consult mental health professionals, and even to some who have been hospitalized for psychiatric care. I call this new definition of mental health and illness, which has gradually evolved over twenty-five years, the resilience hypothesis.

According to the resilience hypothesis, falling apart emotionally is a normal life experience to which we are all subject, whenever meaningful change or profound stressful events occur. Nature mandates it. These periods of chaos shake us free of obsolete assumptions, identities, and environmental conditions that block growth; they promote new adaptational strategies necessary to mastering life's next phase successfully. A healthy person can enter such a period of disruption, tolerate its pain, learn, and emerge with a new integration. Illness ensues when one cannot bear the uncertainty, or put the pieces of himself and his life together again to form a new coherence.

In 1966 Rickie was certainly subject to overwhelming stress in a very short time. On the verge of adolescence, she nearly drowned, she lost a grandfather to whom she was enormously attached, she was profoundly humiliated at school, and her parents' marriage was in trouble.

She should have been greatly disturbed. She was.

Unfortunately, her distress was immediately interpreted as illness. She was hospitalized, following the recommendation of a psychiatrist her family trusted; her psychiatrist father, to whom this was common procedure in those days, agreed to it. From that point on the power of psychiatric diagnosis, particularly that of schizophrenia, took over, stamping her with a destiny that would span a decade filled with futile efforts by the best of professionals to cure her of a condition they barely understood.

No doubt Rickie learned a great deal about how to be "sick" in hospitals, just as any suggestible teenager learns how to behave from peers in high school. As any adolescent would, she sought attention, tested the limits of authority, and struggled with her own feelings of uncertainty. The goals may have been the same, but the rules of the game were grotesquely different. So too were the consequences of failure.

I do not know firsthand what transpired in Rickie's psychotherapy sessions. However, traditional psychotherapy as it was then practiced might well have added to her burden. She probably sat in a room with a bland, humorless therapist who rarely spoke, leaped at every opportunity to analyze problems over and over again, and interpreted experience within the context of some narrowly reductionistic pet theory. I doubt that the restoration of morale, the core of successful psychotherapy according to noted psychiatrist Jerome Frank, was often considered a primary objective. Ironically, Rickie experienced her most important emotional release—sobbing for hours over the death of her grandfather—alone, in her room at the Pittsfield hospital. At any rate, I'm sure she was never reassured that she had a right to break down, nor that her distress was not a sign of illness, per se, because few psychiatrists thought that way in those days. Nor did I.

Although she predictably reacted poorly to major tranquilizers, such as phenothiazines, she was repeatedly given these drugs in nearly every new treatment setting. I'll never know whether she was given an adequate trial of antidepressant therapy. Her transient improvement following electric convulsive treatments remains a mystery, arguing somewhat for the presence of what psychiatrists call depression.

The question that everyone kept asking was, "What makes Rickie sick?" What we should have been asking is, "Why is she not getting better?" The amazing thing is not that treatment failed, but that Rickie survived for years under such harrowing and demoralizing conditions. The answer must lie in the nature of her individual resilience.

According to my hypothesis, resilience has three components: personality, environment, and biochemical makeup. For all her youth, Rickie certainly possessed a great deal of personal resilience, especially resourcefulness, creativity, a keen sense of humor, open-mindedness to new ideas, and religious faith.

As for environment, the hospitals where she spent so many years could hardly be regarded as fostering resilience, but Rickie was never without the love and support of her family, even when she was not allowed to see them for months on end. There is now solid proof of the rather obvious fact that patients who have families and friends who care do better than those who do not. Numerous staff members—doctors, nurses, recreational and occupational therapists—along with fellow patients and very special professionals like Kent Smith, Melvin Kaplan, Dorothy Sawyer, Carl Pfeiffer, and, of course, Ronnie LaRoche—provided her with friendship, understanding, and guidance.

In Rickie's case, the evidence clearly points to a lack of sufficient biological resilience. In my opinion, the effect of nutritional therapy on psychiatric patients has never been put to the full test. Studies that disclaim its effectiveness are replete with methodologic weaknesses, and Rickie's own experiences are ambiguous. It remains unclear whether the regimen established by Carl Pfeiffer reversed an underlying physiological disturbance or simply corrected nutritional deficiencies resulting from inadequate institutional diets. However, the timing of Rickie's recovery certainly implies a contribution to her cure.

That Rickie was functionally blind is indisputable. She had probably been visually disabled since the age of three, and it is conceivable that until that disability had been corrected, no form of treatment would have produced lasting results. Reviewing her history—her proneness to accident, her head injuries, her episodes of distress with strong visual components, the way in which she retreated into illness whenever confronted with demands of a visual nature such as school studies—it is astonishing that no one made the connection earlier. In part, this enormous delay can be attributed to professional myopia, the ignorance of developments in other fields, and a general resistance to innovation, attitudes that unfortunately persist in force today. Colleagues still smile incredulously at the thought that orthomolecular therapy or visual perceptual training could have contributed in any way to her recovery.

In the years since Rickie's first visit to Dr. Kaplan, however, he and I have collaborated to explore the nature of visual information processing among psychiatric patients. Our search for a medical center where we could carry out careful double-blind experiments was long and arduous, but thanks to Dr. Alfred Freedman, chairman of the Department of Psychiatry at New York Medical College in Valhalla, New York, and its director of research, Dr. Herbert Bengelsdorf, we were finally able to do so. Our investigations have shown conclusively that there is indeed a dramatically high incidence of serious perceptual dysfunction—a syndrome, in fact—among psychiatric patients, especially those whose recoveries are slow and incomplete and who have a hard time studying, holding jobs, or coping with ordinary life stresses. Most importantly, through a variety of techniques, their visual information-processing ability can be restored and rehabilitation greatly enhanced.

But yet another dimension to Rickie's story exists: coincidence. A series of lucky accidents and encounters. What if I hadn't gone to the alumni reunion and had my doubts about nutritional therapy dispelled by Oscar Kruesi? What if I hadn't met Norman Weissman, who directed me to Dr. Kaplan? What if Ronnie LaRoche hadn't created Earth House and been there for Rickie when she needed her?

Coincidence, or something more?

Carl Jung has written about the importance of seemingly

happenstance events in our lives. He called it synchronicity, implying that there is a logic and a destiny to such events, a hidden blueprint that derives from our own particular natures, or the force of the world around us, or perhaps from a supernatural power beyond human understanding. To the extent that our conscious choices move in harmony with this design, our lives find fulfillment. If this is so, there exists the possibility that the suffering and the joy, the defeats and the final victory, were all part of a highly personal yet supremely cosmic pattern that remains, and may always remain, a mystery.

Albert Einstein, a deeply religious man and one of history's greatest scientific minds, was committed to the idea that the more knowledge we acquire, the more mysterious becomes the nature of the universe.

The noted anthropologist Joseph Campbell defined the hero as someone who leaves home and goes abroad to face terrible tragedies and obstacles. Conquering them, he returns home with a wisdom and vision that can be shared with those who were left behind. By this definition, Rickie is clearly a heroine.

But if so, what is her story's archetypal truth? It can only be that of death and resurrection, through faith, and hope, and love.

The issue of whether Jesus was the son of God may not be settled in the minds of many, but it is has certainly not been convincingly disproved. And assuming, for the moment, that He may have been, then we must also assume that He could have avoided His crucifixion with a quick wave of His hand. It was a destiny He freely chose; without it, of course, there could have been no resurrection.

When Rickie was ten she asked why I thought Jesus had died on the cross. I asked her if she had any ideas as to why. "All people die," she replied. "Maybe He was showing us not to be afraid of death."

For me, the message of the cross has extraordinary relevance to our everyday lives. We are born. We die. And with courage and faith, we are reborn. This cycle recurs periodically throughout all our lives in the most natural of ways. Success, by whatever measure, is not simply a matter of making it; it is a matter of doing, failing, doing again. It is the triumph of hope.

Can we influence reality through prayer?

I believe so. A couple of years ago I attended an alumni dinner at St. Peter's College, the small Jesuit school from which I graduated in 1947, and was seated next to the new rector, whom I'd never met. I spoke of Rickie. Startled, he mentioned her maternal grandmother by name and asked me if Rickie could be her granddaughter. "You know," he revealed, "eighteen years ago, when I was the pastor of her church, her grandmother came to me and asked me to pray for Rickie. I have remembered her in my prayers every morning since."

Life is filled with miracles—not the dramatic kind, walking on water and changing water into wine, but the ordinary sort, interwoven in the fabric of human existence. They can happen if we believe them possible. What happened to Rickie, and to all of us whose lives she touched, can be thought of as a commonplace, beautiful, inexplicable miracle.

But even miracles require very special people to make them happen. Some months before her untimely death, I sat at Earth House with Ronnie LaRoche and Rickie, discussing Rickie's recovery. When I asked Rickie what had been so unique about her experience at Earth House, she remarked: "So much. Ronnie for one. When Ronnie told me she had overcome an illness like mine, I felt real hope. No one ever told me that before about themselves. At Earth House I learned a lot I needed to live in the world outside."

She looked at Ronnie. "Your spirit . . . and your caring . . ."

Ronnie smiled, "Certainly not everyone makes it here," she said. "Those that do, have what Rickie had, and still has: a very special power, the will to be well."